Major Doctrines of
Communist China

Major Doctrines of Communist China

Edited by

John Wilson Lewis

CORNELL UNIVERSITY

New York

W · W · NORTON & COMPANY · INC ·

To My Mother

Contents

Preface

WHEN THIS COLLECTION of Chinese Communist writings was first conceived, few such compilations of primary materials were available for the general reader. That situation changed rather markedly in the past year. What distinguishes this volume is its attempt to combine official Party documents with statements by ordinary Chinese and to sample the vast source material on specific categories of doctrine. These selections include some of the most significant statements by Mao Tse-tung, Liu Shao-ch'i, Chou En-lai, Teng Hsiao-p'ing, and Lu Ting-yi as well as Central Committee directives, articles by lower-level Party members, and the Party and state constitutions.

Many of the selections were originally used in my courses and seminars on Chinese government and politics at Cornell University. I am deeply indebted to my students over the past two years for their criticism and suggestions concerning these selections. I am particularly grateful to Paul F. Harper for his research assistance and to Mary Antoinette Findlen for assistance in the preparation of the manuscript. My wife, Jacquelyn Lewis, helped at many stages and contributed an invaluable spirit of interest and encouragement during the compilation and editing of the book.

Although the translations from newspapers and journals have in most cases been checked and made to correspond with the original Chinese, I have followed the translations where available provided by the U. S. Consulate General in Hong Kong, whose kind cooperation is gratefully acknowledged. By adapting the selections from available English translations, this volume demonstrates that a substantial body of materials may be tapped without command of the Chinese language. Some selections have been taken from Peking Foreign Languages Press editions and have been modified slightly to give some consistency to punctuation and spelling. I am, of course, responsible for any errors or distortions caused by modification and selection, for all conclusions presented in the discussions, and for the accuracy of all unofficial translations, including the translations of the U. S. Consulate General in Hong Kong.

Finally, I acknowledge the permission of the Cornell University Press to reprint a table from my book *Leadership in Communist China*.

JOHN WILSON LEWIS

Ithaca, New York

Introduction

ALTHOUGH specialists on China face a staggering quantity of published materials written by the Chinese Communists, well-read Americans generally are unaware of these materials and "eyewitness" reporters seem to perpetuate the idea that the Chinese People's Republic represents some kind of mystery about which only they have relevant insights. This book, therefore, seeks to resolve the paradox of superabundant information and widespread ignorance by presenting a broad survey of significant statements that the Chinese Communists have made about themselves and their objectives over the past four decades.

The pervasive nature of politics in mainland China fully justifies a political focus for a volume on Chinese Communist doctrine. Communist political writings cut across the full spectrum of Chinese life, ranging in content from esoteric dogma to details of daily chores of rice farming. Unfortunately, the general assumption that Party documents simply conceal and distort true conditions in China has hitherto led to their dismissal as improper sources for research and teaching. Although many Communist statements are idealized versions of events and social conditions in China, it is in such statements that Party leaders regularly communicate the ideas and policies which obedient cadres—the Chinese leaders at all levels of Party, government, and social organizations—are expected to apply to a wide inventory of routine tasks. Moreover, since 1949, the ideal patterns fashioned by Communist doctrine have rigorously structured Chinese realities, as Party leaders have devoted unusual attention to the attainment of idealistic dreams formed in the earlier years of life-and-death revolutionary struggle.

On most domestic and international questions, the Communists leave no doubt about their general positions. They do not mince words on topics that range from calculated manipulations of the Chinese people to eradication of their opponents, although they frequently have deleted vital details from published reports destined for export. In the main their statements and reports have been prepared for internal consumption. The selections presented in this book comprise typical rationalizations and policy pronouncements issued by the Peking government and the Party organs, and from such statements and reports as represented here has come the steady stream of textbooks for Chinese schoolchildren, study handbooks for Party cadres, and lesson guides for peasants and workers.

Judgments concerning the nature of the Chinese people cannot, however, be made with any degree of reliability when based on Communist sources. Party statements provide a sensitive index to policy directions and degrees of success, and they establish ranges of policy alternatives and priorities. But what these statements say, implicitly or explicitly, about the Chinese personality must be considered in this light: Party doctrine is based on Communist conceptions of human nature in general rather than on specific attributes of the Chinese people. Students of Communist China at times have unwittingly concluded from Marxist dogma that the Chinese may be as easily manipulated as doctrine implies and thus that the Chinese are peculiarly susceptible to totalitarian social engineering. But Chinese differ markedly from one another and have met Party demands with a complex set of responses. Some Communist programs have received widespread support and others have been stoutly resisted. While traditional Chinese institutions and practices have changed radically under the rule of Mao Tse-tung, the leader of the Chinese Communist Party, many changes—particularly those at the village level—fly in the face of Mao's best calculations. Indeed general social change was well underway long before the Communists attained power in 1949. Furthermore, no one who has ever known Chinese as individuals and friends—known their incredible diversity of intellectual and artistic tastes, customs, dialects, garments, foods, and living styles—can blend them easily into a mass. The subtle and the obtrusive defy amalgamation, leaving us with ambiguous emotions and understanding and only such "Chinese" characteristics as straight black hair and the fairly common use of chopsticks. Yet we generalize from data on a few villages, even when we know that the number of villages in China probably exceeds a million and a quarter. We interview a few dozen refugees and make sweeping statements about 700 million Chinese whom we have never seen. Many Chinese have never heard of Chiang Kai-shek, although presumably most have learned to recognize the picture of Mao Tse-tung and possibly one or two others. A nation famous for learning leads the world in the number of illiterates, many of whom have not yet read a single word written by a Communist leader. Because of such great diversity, the Chinese Communist leadership has adopted policies that may be implemented with extraordinary flexibility. Because of the same diversity, the reader should be extremely cautious of easy generalizations and simple analyses based on his first encounter with Communist doctrine.

The essential tone of Chinese Communist writings stems from the Party's preoccupation with mistakes and deficiencies. Spurred by a doctrine that stresses errors and tensions, Communist writers deliberately arouse dissatisfactions and provoke criticism and self-criticism. They search out mistakes, yet match blistering denunciations of individuals with unlimited faith in the Party's "infallible wisdom." Thus the Party elite does not usually permit popular dissatisfaction with the Party to surface in the press. In the 1957 climax of the "hundred-flowers" campaign, the Central Committee of the Communist Party encouraged the airing of an extraordinary range of opinions, and many incautious non-Communist spokesmen accepted the invitation to extend free discussion to the role and policies of the Party. Since these non-Communists and the organizations that denounced the Party paid dearly for their candor during the so-called "antirightist" suppression, similar expressions of dissatisfaction cannot be expected to reappear in the Party-directed press.

In the framework of one-sided struggle, Party writers stress that no action or policy ever quite succeeds. Keep alert, the Party tells its subordinate cadres and members. The "contradiction" behind today's apparent success, it goes on to say, is incipient smugness that may spell disaster, because such a hidden attitude strengthens the "enemy" whose general skill makes him wily and dangerous even though his internal "contradictions" make him weak and vulnerable, a veritable "paper tiger." Since the Chinese Communists emphatically believe that the world operates according to their perception of it, in their view they alone comprehend "real problems" and can provide meaningful, relevant solutions. Chinese officials are encouraged by this alleged clairvoyance to act with unquestioned certainty after decisions have been reached and from their aura of infallibility comes a unique command presence maintained during crisis and victory alike. This authoritative pose has awed and cowed potential opponents of the Communist regime, but successive leadership failures have disillusioned increasing numbers of Chinese and caused them to question official propaganda and to compare words with deeds. The three years of economic disaster following 1959 severely damaged the credibility of leadership boasts and struck at the heart of the claim of infallibility. Communist control may remain firm, but the shift in popular attitudes toward that control is a change of fundamental importance. Thus real contradictions have replaced contrived ones in the policy problems faced by Communist Party leaders.

Although in theory the Chinese Communists welcome tensions and seek to capitalize on the jangled nerves of others, the nature of the struggle and the actual dimensions of the post-1959 crisis surpassed even their expectations. Mao Tse-tung in 1947 predicted a long-range "continuous revolution," but he did not foresee how fundamentally the character of the struggle *against* the Japanese or the Nationalists differed from the struggle *for* a new state and society. He has learned the lesson taught to many other political leaders that coalitions can easily disintegrate after the victory over a common opponent. Mobilizing the Chinese peasants against the Japanese proved far easier than mobilizing them first into collectives and then into communes. Genuine popular enthusiasm has turned to passive avoidance. For the Chinese youth, Marxist ideology appears less relevant than scientific technique. For the peasantry, rice could be shared with strange Party cadres during wartime emergency but when those strangers attempted to control the peasants and their villages they were far less welcome. This loss of support has struck the Party on many levels, resulting in particular in peasant opposition to being forced into communes and the antagonism of youth and intellectuals to political training and control. These highly publicized developments should not, however, mask either the sources of continuing Communist strength or the acute problem that the Party thus far has been unable to solve: the problem of transmitting to a new generation of Party members the older revolutionary goals and spirit. Selections in this book were chosen in part to convey the scope of the current Party dilemma without distorting the general picture of sustained control and doctrinal consistency.

The typical response of the Chinese Communist Party leadership to crisis has been to reemphasize the fundamental doctrine formulated between 1927 and 1949. Reduced to a single sentence, doctrine states that the Party elite must guide the fate of the Chinese nation so that "the people" can fulfill their rightful destiny and each Chinese can maximize his inner creative potential. Doctrine implies that only individuals—not the Party or its senior elite—can fail and that all individuals must willingly and gratefully support the just, correct Party. It suggests that the Party has an effective method and style of leadership operation for every conceivable problem, that this leadership alone can interpret the world and human nature correctly, and that only the Party leaders can fully grasp and act on these correct interpretations. The republication with elaborate fanfare on August 1, 1962, of Liu Shao-ch'i's *How to Be a Good Communist,* written in 1939, fully illustrates the extraordinary preoccupation of the Party with doctrine in this present period.

Although the Party leaders have confidently reasserted the core of their doctrine in response to crises, the problems of training new Party members and restructuring local society in the Chinese countryside have defied the fundamental postulates of doctrine. As a consequence, doctrine eroded during 1962, and signs of this erosion are reflected in the loss of certainty in Party pronouncements and in the preoccupation with controls rather than consensus, with threats rather than persuasion. The doctrine presented in this volume establishes a base line from which coming changes may be evaluated and new policies assessed. This is a guidebook to Communist aspirations, and the reader may expect any future departures from these aspirations to signal advances and retreats, new areas of optimism or disillusionment.

The language of Marxism permeates each selection, and this language requires a special note of caution. The Chinese Communists print various statements in an attempt to maximize the Party's advantages in domestic and international struggles. Every statement has a specific audience in mind and an educational lesson to be pressed. Ideological purpose outweighs clarity and style, and the texture of Chinese Communist writings often ap-

pears rough because of the Party's tendency to use familiar terms
—*democracy, people,* and *feudalism* are examples—in strikingly
different senses and contexts and with wholly different referents.
For example, Communist writers follow Mao Tse-tung's definition
of *democracy* and stipulate that democracy constitutes the means
by which the elite effects the guided participation of the working
class and peasant population. *People* is used to denote the four
classes joined in the united front and characterizes those who are
willing to abide by the Party leadership. Thus "popular will"
may be safely invoked because any who would oppose the Party
disqualify themselves automatically as members of the people.
Moreover, since only the workers and peasants come within the
scope of democracy, the two other classes of the people (the national bourgeoisie and the petty bourgeoisie) fall into a transitional group strictly controlled by the rules of "democratic dictatorship" and not by the rules of democracy. A Chinese may
choose to resist the Party dictatorship, but he thereby loses all his
rights as one of the *people* and becomes liable for the full ven-
geance of the people against the "enemy." *Feudalism,* the third
example, has been used loosely to discredit selective aspects of the
traditional land-tenure system and relevant social habits and be-
liefs. Although China's rural organization never was characterized
by the social and political obligations and the economic structure
found in European feudalism, the Chinese have found it convenient to discount these "trivial differences" in order to place
China squarely within the Marxist pattern of social development
—from slave to feudal, to capitalist, and to proletarian society.

In addition to such variant definitions of specific concepts,
Chinese writers make important use of certain aspects of publication and the sequence of concepts. On which page of which newspaper an article appears, how many journals carry the same
article, who is the author and what is the occasion for the article,
and, in particular, where the article stands in the long chain of
articles on the same subject have a significance that neither this
volume nor any other translated survey of Chinese writings can
easily convey. As to the sequence of concepts, the Chinese Communists combine theory and practice in such a way that articles
on "theory" first exhort changes in an individual's actions and
later serve notice on erroneous thinking exposed in the course
of "practice." After the Communist leadership perceives that a
minimum of involvement and commitment has developed, it

attempts to manipulate thought directly. What is important for the reader to understand is the interplay of theory and practice— an interplay that is couched in words that apply equally to areas of operation, organization, and thought. Since articles that deal with these areas cannot be classified easily, selections in one chapter may be equally relevant to the subject matter of another chapter, as is pointed out in the text.

The arrangement of the chapters that follow conforms to the general order of discussion usually followed by Chinese Communist authors or, more accurately, to the weight these writers have given key topics. Mao Tse-tung has consistently given priority to the recruitment and training of leading personnel and then to their organization and operation. Hence, Chapters 1 and 2 deal with the development of the Party and its leadership core, and those which follow thereafter examine Party structure and life, Communist principles of operation, and the Party's principal domestic and international strategies and techniques.

More specifically, the chapters attempt to answer these questions: How did the Chinese Communist Party develop after its formation in 1921 and how does the present leadership officially "remember" that development? How did the roles of the Party elite become defined in the revolutionary struggle and who emerged to fill those roles? How did the leadership structures and the provisions for organizational life and training devised in the revolution conform to the requirements for action after 1949? What happened to the code of action formed in the pre-1949 period as it was adapted to the new situation of absolute political authority and to the necessity for effective policies in the key economic and cultural fields? And, what have been the points of stress in the overall system as the revolutionary political code failed to challenge young aspirants to the ranks of the elite and to cope with central economic crises?

The discussion that opens each chapter introduces some of the essential background to the selections contained in the chapter. It is purposely short and should not be taken as an attempt to explain "what the Communists really mean." The Chinese leaders leave no doubt about their "real meaning" and the implications of their value positions for a strategy of human manipulation. The discussion simply keys the selections in the chapter to the broader context of events and related policies.

Chapter 1

The History of the Chinese Communist Party

IN ITS attempt to reconstruct the history of its past, the Chinese Communist Party has stressed the formation of an official memory that will conform to the Party's best image of itself. Once established, this "memory" may then provide the source of praise for present heroes and the justification of policy goals and a lifetime of struggle, while at the same time it constitutes the reservoir of tested knowledge from which Party leaders and their heirs may derive their principles for education and their code of operation.

Reconstruction of history differs from falsification of history. Reconstruction implies selection and interpretation in keeping with the Marxist view that events have intrinsic value and inner "logic" and manifest a certain cohesiveness and consistency in given "periods." Historical periods may thus be judged as essentially "good" or "bad," because, as the first selection in this chapter indicates, the facts that comprise the period are "value-laden." Reconstruction of history also means that the writings of major Communists which appeared before 1949 may be republished with numerous alterations. Frequently an editorial note precedes such a revised document and frankly states that "prior to publication, the author examined the text again, and revised and supplemented it"—but many other items have been excerpted or revised without editorial admission. Revision, new selection, and interpretation may continue, moreover, as the Party's doctrine shifts to current tasks and the leadership passes to new hands.

Official "revised" or reconstructed history is critically relevant to an understanding of Chinese Communist doctrine. In China today, the function of historical writing is to give legitimacy to the Communist seizure of power and to the policies of the Party elite. A similar approach to history can be found in China's imperial past, when for each new dynasty officially employed scholars were preoccupied with historical summation and reinterpretation. The written word commanded respect, and written histories systematically documented the decline of the fallen dynasty and the rise of its successor. And the Communist "dynasty" now follows this pattern of historical summation more faithfully than all but a few of its predecessors.

For the study of doctrine and legitimacy, an accurate and comprehensive history of the Chinese Communist Party is not vital. The selections that follow do, however, outline the major events of Party history as well as the central perspectives of the Chinese Communists on their history. In China, Marxist historians have pressed two themes in their analyses of traditional China: "feudalism" and "imperialism." Chinese "feudalism," as discussed in the Introduction, differs from its European analogue and refers loosely to the patriarchal and landlord-dominated social and economic institutions and to the values and loyalties associated with them. "Imperialism" follows Lenin's analysis of economic intrusion and exploitation by foreign capitalist "monopolies" backed by political, military, and religious supporters. Both themes denigrate the institutions and developments of traditional Chinese society, and by these judgments, the Communists seek to discredit selective aspects of the Chinese tradition and to fit that tradition into the Marxist scheme of societal growth. In general, however, as Chinese Communist policies have moved in the direction of more strident nationalism, a tendency has emerged to tone down the emphasis on "feudalism" and to intensify the assault on "imperialism."

Communist historians divide the years from 1921 to 1949 into four periods: the founding of the Party and the First Revolutionary Civil War (1921–1927); the Second Revolutionary Civil War (1927–1937); the War of Resistance to Japanese Aggression (1937–1945); and the Third Revolutionary Civil War (1945–1949). In the 1921–1927 period, the Communist Party was formally established and held five (out of a current total of eight) Party congresses. Controlled by a coterie of young intellectuals clustered around scholarly Secretary-General Ch'en Tu-hsiu and responsive to the direction of agents sent by the Communist International, the Central Committee of the Party labored against unending internal factionalism and the more popular image of the Kuomintang (Nationalist Party). In the last half of the period, Party members joined in a united front with the Kuomintang in preparation for a joint Northern Expedition from South China to unify the country and eliminate warlordism. After the completion of the first phase of the Northern Expedition, however, Kuomintang leader Chiang Kai-shek, in April 1927, set out to suppress the Communists and in this task was immeasurably aided by events in the Soviet Union. In particular, Stalin at this time attempted to manage Chinese developments to coincide with his power moves against Trotsky. At the critical showdown between Chiang Kai-shek's forces and the Communists in Shanghai, manipulation by Stalin's agents deliberately reinforced Chiang's position and frustrated an effective response by the Communist leadership. The First Revolutionary Civil War thus ended with the abject defeat of the Chinese Communist Party and the rise to power in China of Chiang Kai-shek.

The near-destruction of the central apparatus of the Communist Party relatively favored local Party elements that had operated largely along independent lines and remained apart from Central Committee quarrels. Although Mao Tse-tung, the Party leader in Hunan Province, had risen to a place on the Central Committee, he consistently drew his own lessons of operation from his Hunan—and later Canton—experiences in labor and peasant organizations. The history of the second period (1927–1937) took place largely in "base areas" of southeastern China, particularly in the Kiangsi-Fukien border area that in 1931 became the "Chinese Soviet Republic." The main theme in that history pertains to the rise of Mao as the leader of the Chinese Communist Party, a position that he attained in 1935 during the retreat from South China on the so-called "Long March" to the new "base area" located around the city of Yenan in the northwest.

In the struggle for survival after the 1927 debacle, the small band of Communists under Mao Tse-tung and Chu Teh fought to create a Party that would attract popular support. Although the realization of widespread support did not come until the Japanese invasion and terror struck North China, Mao formulated the principles for obtaining that support before the Long March. He began his quest for an effective Party organization by first revising the standards for Party members and the nature of their organizational life. At the outset he asked: How do we get members who are committed and who will not break in a crisis? Faced with a motley collection of vagabonds, destitute peasants, and bandits among whom were numbered spies and potential turncoats, he focused on discipline and loyalties to the Party of his members and on the selfish and particularistic relations among them. By 1928, he had devised a rough outline of inner-Party rectification or thought remolding. Mao then attempted to establish the principles for the selection and training of leaders, whom he designated "cadres" in contrast to the rank-and-file Party members. Cadres were to be organized more rigorously than the general members and were to be given wide discretionary powers to carry out tasks in their areas of responsibility. Although Party members technically selected and controlled "their" cadres, Mao regulated the apparatus of the Party's leadership elite, including their selection, training, and practical operation, without recourse to membership sanction. Not until 1956—at its Eighth National Party Congress—did the elite set up a regular schedule for congresses of Party-member representatives, but the Central Committee has not adhered to schedule and makes only nominal gestures in the direction of membership control.

Aided by German military advisers, the Kuomintang soundly defeated the Communists in the Chinese Soviet Republic during the Second Revolutionary Civil War. The Japanese movement into North China, however, coincided with the Communist retreat to Yenan and presented the Party with a remarkable opportunity to gain mass support without competition from the Kuomintang, which the Japanese had displaced. The full-scale war against Japan followed the arrival of the remnants of the Long March in Yenan and the abortive effort to establish a united front with the Kuomintang. Chinese Communist leaders deftly mined the emotions of personal suffering and hate aroused against the Japanese and on these emotions rebuilt their shattered forces.

During the early years of the war against Japan, the Party built its military and political forces and summarized and codified the lessons of the previous period in training cadres and members and in mass-line operation. To indoctrinate new members in these lessons and to thwart undesirable tendencies in the Party, the Communist leaders in 1941 inaugurated a study campaign and from 1942 to 1944 carried on a "thought reform" or rectification movement, in the course of which the Maoist leadership utilized "small-group" meetings to insure intensive surveillance of individual members. By its skillful use of indoctrination techniques to instill commitment and weed out the less qualified, the Party elite combined rapid numerical growth with high individual standards. Cadres selected during this period staffed the Party and the military apparatus throughout the final stages of the war with Japan and then during the post-1945 campaigns against the Kuomintang. And it was these cadres who took the major posts when in 1949 the Kuomintang was defeated, control of China passed to the Communists, and Chiang Kai-shek fled to Taiwan (Formosa). A key postvictory problem—one that is emphasized in the final five selections in this chapter and in Chapter 2—has been the maintenance of high standards of commitment and fervor in a period devoid of revolutionary conflict. Older Party members were raised with rifles in their hands and with their lives at stake, and the passing of these conditions has created the task of transmitting the revolution to the next generation.

The period from 1945 to 1949, the Third Revolutionary Civil War, marked a critical transformation in the Chinese Communist Party's thought about its mission in China and in the world. During these years, Communist leaders formed decisive attitudes toward the United States, neutralist or nonaligned nationalists, and the Soviet Union. For the first time, the Party faced the fact that conditions for exercising power differ fundamentally from conditions required to compete for power, and attitudes of the Party's leadership changed markedly as the need to establish order was recognized. Where scapegoats were relatively abundant in the previous periods, the Party now had to stand accountable to the Chinese people for failures and continued chaos. The writings of Mao Tse-tung for these years (the final volume thus far published in the English-language series of his *Selected Works*) reflect his compromises and shifts to account for the change in the Party's role. These writings illuminate key conceptual problems that have confronted the Party for the past fourteen or more years in its attempt to exercise power for economic and social development.

The three periods that currently divide the years after 1949 and the establishment of the Chinese People's Republic may be analyzed in terms of this attempt to exercise Party power. During the first period (1949–1952), one of reconstruction and consolidation, the Chinese Communists retained their militant hostility formed in the years of revolutionary struggle. They eliminated peasants classified as "landlords" through executions, imprisonment, and confiscations, although they remained ambivalent toward some "landlord-type" elements—especially industrialists, intellectuals from the landlord class, and some religious figures who were also landlords—whose knowledge or position was important for the restoration of the shattered economy and demoralized society. In this first period, the Chinese entered the Korean War against the forces of the United Nations and freely challenged newly formed governments in Asia by their open support of peasant revolutions fought according to the principles of the "Chinese model." Domestically, economic and social programs restored internal stability and prewar production levels, and the Communist Party leaders then set their sights on the transformation of China into an advanced industrial nation.

The second period, the years from 1953 to 1957, marked the end of the reconstruction phase and the launching of the "transition to socialism." These years correspond to the First Five-Year Plan that, with Soviet help, sought to lay the preliminary basis for industrialization. The Chinese Communists linked the systematic building of power and industrial facilities and the opening up of new sources of raw material with the planned transition of the rural and urban economy to collective and socialist forms. This transitional process can best be seen in the countryside. The initial step in the rural transformation began with mutual-aid teams that were first organized seasonally and then permanently in order to pool manpower, tools, seeds, and farm animals. State agencies favored these teams in arrangements for credits and the purchase of goods, and these advantages, when regularized and enlarged with the formation of small (or "lower-level") agricultural producers' cooperatives between 1953 and 1955, constituted an effective assault on the rich peasants. Careful, balanced planning characterized economic and social projects in this period, and the dominant "tone" of Party policies was reflected in a relatively lenient attitude toward the remaining businessmen and "bourgeois" intellectuals and in the moderate foreign policy announced at the Bandung Conference in 1955.

The tempo of the second period, however, picked up during the last two years. In the winter of 1955–1956, the Party hastened the transformation of the lower-level cooperatives into an advanced or "higher-level" form in which most peasants could participate regardless of land holdings and from which they would derive income commensurate with the amount of labor they had performed. In contrast, the mutual-aid teams and lower-level cooperatives distributed income on the basis of the land pooled. With the higher-level form, the Chinese Communists sought to destroy the middle peasantry as a class. The rapid 1955–1956 movement into higher-level cooperatives brought Chinese agricultural organization to the approximate level of collectivization achieved in the Soviet Union. The Communists in China had moved cleverly and decisively and had avoided most of the violent repercussions that had accompanied the similar drives toward collectivization in Soviet Russia and eastern Europe. Although the Party's rural programs systematically impoverished the rich and middle peasants, the more than 70 per cent of the rural population in the poor and landless categories had been aided and could be counted on to support the higher-level organization. The success in rural areas, moreover, was duplicated in the cities where Party cadres substantially completed the socialization of industrial and business enterprises by early 1956.

A general atmosphere of success and self-congratulation prevailed at the Party's Eighth National Congress held in September 1956. At this congress, the Party elite formalized its present leadership machinery and wrote the Constitution that was to guide the next phase of policy operation. The reports of this congress, however, reflected a certain dissatisfaction with the motivations and qualifications of new members, and decisions followed to revitalize many revolutionary systems and doctrines that had gradually fallen into disuse over the years. From the postcongress discussions came the landmark decisions to launch the 1957–1958 rectification campaign—which blossomed into the fateful "hundred flowers" adventure when extended in the spring of 1957 to intellectuals and non-Communist "democrats"—and thence the bold political line that was to set the tone for the third period, the "general line of socialist construction."

The pressures behind the dramatic inauguration of the general line, the "great leap forward," and finally the rural people's communes—the vaunted three red banners—in 1958 remain unclear. Although the consolidation of higher-level collectives into mammoth communes was realized more on paper and in slogans than in fact, furious activity attended the initial effort. Many facile explanations have been offered to clarify the reasons for the abandonment of a gradual, balanced approach, but most of these assume that the Chinese Communists fully understood the complex implications of the 1955–1956 developments, of the completion of the First Five-Year Plan and the requirements for the next plan to begin in 1958, and of the state of morale and social cohesion following the 1957–1958 rectification campaign. We know that indecision and argument existed within the highest echelons of the Party elite, but no reliable evidence has yet come to light to demonstrate that cliques or factions were important in the debate or even that they existed. The orbiting of the Soviet sputnik in late 1957 and the subsequent Chinese demand for a more provocative bloc policy toward the American "paper tiger" roughly coincided with the more intensive Chinese appraisals of the objectives of their Second Five-Year Plan as well as with their experiences in massive construction projects for water conservation and flood control and with their optimistic assessment of social engineering in the wake of the "hundred flowers" and antirightist campaigns in 1957. Out of the complex developments of the winter of 1957–1958 emerged the decisions for the "great leap forward." Through the successful implementation of these decisions, the central leadership hoped to attain the level of industrialization and social reorganization necessary to "usher in communism" within a "few years." The Party placed full faith in the political leadership of its cadres and in the "energy and will of the masses" to overcome all difficulties, and it sloganized the new "general line of socialist construction" as "going all out and pressing ahead consistently to achieve greater, faster, better, and more economical results." In the "great-leap" period, which has yet to end formally, the image of the past revolutionary drama gripped the mind of the Party. Reenacted in its new setting, that drama and its actors appeared strangely unreal.

The third and present period (1958–   ) thus remains the least understood because of its uncertain origins and because the failures in agriculture and commune organization have forced the Communists to withhold vital sources of information from reports designed for export. We know that the commune movement rapidly lost momentum in the course of the production disasters of 1959, 1960, and 1961 and that the production team —the form of rural organization equivalent to the 1954 lower-level cooperative—has now assumed the dominant position in ownership, distribution, accounting, and production (see Chapter 9 for details). Rural disorganzation demolished the Party's dreams of an early "transition to communism," and agricultural production failures forced major cutbacks in industrial targets. As sensitivities increased during the years of domestic crisis, the Chinese Communists stubbornly clung to their more virulent propositions concerning international politics and progressively alienated Communist-bloc leaders, including the Soviet leadership itself. In October and November 1962, the strains in the Communist alliance sharply intensified when the Chinese bitterly condemned Soviet actions in Cuba and invaded Indian-held border regions on the vast Himalayan front. The final two selections of this chapter outline the developments of the "great-leap" period, and subsequent chapters examine the ramifications of this remarkable period in detail.

Good Facts and Bad Facts

Teng T'o • The study of history in China began a long time ago and has a fine tradition. If we count from the time when Confucius wrote *Spring and Autumn Annals* 2,700 years ago, it began 300 years before the days of the Greek historian Herodotus, whom the Europeans call the father of the study of history in the world. Throughout the dynasties, China produced many distinguished historians who made important contributions to the development of the study of history. However, the deduction of objective laws from the complicated course of the development of the history of mankind and the conversion of the work of historical research into a branch of science began with Marx and Engels. . . .

As people understand and master better and better the laws governing the development of history, and more and more self-consciously put into effect these laws in guiding the practice of social reforms, the importance of the science of history also be-

From Teng T'o, "The Thought of Mao Tse-tung Opens the Way for the Development of China's Science of History," Li-shih yen-chiu [Historical Research], No. 1, February 15, 1961.

comes more and more obvious. Generally speaking, the task of
this science is not only to explain society correctly, but also to
help people to reform society, as is "the task of a philosopher not
only to explain the world, but also to reform it," to use the
words of Karl Marx. Here, we should establish the fact that the
science of history is a practical science and revolutionary, and,
therefore, the work of research on the science of history must
comply with revolutionary requirements. Even when capitalism
was still on the rise, Marx already saw that it was doomed to
extinction. He found the objective laws governing the development of society and thus established scientific socialist theories.
The Marxists are entirely different from all historians of the
past in their attitude toward research on social history. The
latter often claimed that their research work consisted merely in
recording and arranging historical facts, as if they were "just"
and "impartial." In fact, however, this claim was only a cover
under which they imparted to the masses of the people the reactionary concept of history. Such being the case, it goes without
saying that, as dictated by their class interests, their historical
research served only the purpose of the exploiting class to maintain its rule. Facts show that the science of history, like all other
social sciences, has a distinctive class nature and partisan nature
plus a strong political character. Differences in class standpoint,
viewpoint, and method in research on history will lead to definitely different results of research.

Seven Congresses to Victory

People's China • The Chinese Communist Party was founded in
Shanghai on July 1, 1921. This First National Congress was attended by twelve delegates, including Mao Tse-tung, Tung Pi-wu,
Ho Shu-heng, Ch'en T'an-ch'iu, representing the 57 Communists
at that time. The Party was founded on the basis of the Marxist
groups which had been formed in many cities and among Chinese
students abroad in 1920, the year after the May 4 Movement. [On
May 4, 1919, students demonstrated against the alleged betrayal
by the Versailles Conference in giving China's Shantung Penin-
sula to Japan. Many of these students joined the revolutionary

*"From the First to the Seventh National Congress of the Chinese Communist
Party," People's China, No. 18, September 16, 1956.*

movement and later gravitated into the Chinese Communist Party.]

Having agreed on an analysis of the current political situation, the congress decided that the fundamental task of the Party was to fight for the dictatorship of the proletariat, but that, in the meantime, it must call on the proletariat to participate in the bourgeois-democratic revolution. It was decided that the organization of the Party should be modeled on the pattern of the Bolshevik Party in Russia. The congress also elected a Central Working Department as its leading organ, composed of the Secretary and the Directors of Organization and of Propaganda. Ch'en Tu-hsiu was elected Party Secretary.

In July 1922, the Party held its Second National Congress [in Shanghai]. This was attended by twelve delegates representing 123 members. The Party Manifesto drawn up by this congress declared that the ultimate task of the Chinese Communist Party was "to organize the proletariat to wage the class struggle and establish a dictatorship of workers and peasants, to abolish the private ownership of property, and gradually attain a Communist society." It also pointed out that, in the meantime, "it is the capitalist imperialists and the feudal forces of the warlords and bureaucrats who have brought the greatest misery to the Chinese people (be they capitalists, workers, or peasants). Therefore, the democratic revolutionary movement against these two forces is of the greatest importance." This manifesto, however, did not mention either the need for proletarian leadership of the democratic revolution or the need for agrarian reform.

Between January 1922 and February 1923, there was a great upsurge of the working-class movement led by the Party. All the workers' strikes, however, were suppressed by the imperialists and warlords and ended in failure. The Party began to realize that in the struggle against the reactionary forces, the Chinese working class must ally itself with the peasants, the petty bourgeoisie, and the bourgeois democrats.

In June 1923, the Party held its Third National Congress [in Canton]. This gave serious attention to the question of setting up a revolutionary united front starting from the cooperation between the Kuomintang and the Chinese Communist Party. It was attended by thirty members (27 of them were delegates) representing 432 Communists.

There were heated debates at this congress on the question

of the united front. Ch'en Tu-hsiu held the view that the bourgeois-democratic revolution should be led by the bourgeoisie, so
"all work should be turned over to the Kuomintang," and that
the proletariat should know its place and only play an auxiliary
role; that the proletariat would have to wait until a bourgeois
republic had been established and capitalism had developed further before it could start the second revolution, establish the dictatorship of the proletariat, and build socialism. Chang Kuo-t'ao,
on the other hand, objected to the principle of cooperating with
the Kuomintang; he thought that it was not capable of carrying
through the democratic revolution and that only the proletariat
and the Communist Party could carry it through. The congress
criticized and rejected both these views; it agreed on the principle
of establishing a revolutionary united front and decided that
members of the Communist Party might join the Kuomintang
as individuals so as to reorganize it into a democratic revolutionary alliance of workers, peasants, urban petty bourgeoisie, and
national bourgeoisie, but that the political and organizational
independence of the Communist Party should be preserved.

It was at this congress that Mao Tse-tung was elected to the
Central Committee of the Party.

Dr. Sun Yat-sen (1866–1925) reorganized the Kuomintang
with the help of the Communist Party. In January 1924, the
Kuomintang held its first national congress. It declared its loyalty
to the new Three People's Principles (San Min Chu Yi) and the
Three Policies of alliance with Soviet Russia, cooperation with
the Communists, and help to the workers and peasants. As a
result of Kuomintang-Communist cooperation, the revolution
began to advance with great rapidity.

In January 1925, the Party held its Fourth National Congress
[in Shanghai]. This was attended by twenty delegates representing 950 members. This congress pointed out the significance of
working-class leadership in the democratic revolution and the
formation of the worker-peasant alliance. It called on the whole
people to join the "movement for convocation of a National
Assembly," a rapidly growing movement which opposed the rule
of the warlords and demanded a democratic government. The
congress criticized both "left" and right mistakes in united front
work during the previous year; decided that the Party must lead
the workers into action in the national revolutionary movement
and that the anti-imperialist struggle must be combined with

economic struggle. It also decided to mobilize as many peasants as possible to take part in political and economic struggle. However, in regard to the peasants, the only slogan it put forward was to "oppose illegal taxation." It also made the wrong decision that it was "not proper to leave it to the peasants themselves to decide whether or not to launch the movement to reduce rents." It was also resolved to set up Party organizations throughout the country.

On May 30, 1925, a nationwide anti-imperialist patriotic movement [consisting of demonstrations, strikes, and boycotts] broke out in Shanghai.

In July 1926, the National Revolutionary Army set out from the revolutionary base in Kwangtung on the Northern Expedition against the warlords. It soon occupied the Yangtze Valley.

On April 12, 1927, Chiang Kai-shek, Commander-in-Chief of the National Revolutionary Army, betrayed the revolution and set up a government in Nanking as a center of opposition to the revolutionary government in Wuhan.

On April 27, the Party held its Fifth National Congress [in Wuhan]. This was attended by eighty delegates representing 57,967 members. At that time, the Communist Youth League already had a membership of 35,000, the trade unions, 2,800,000, and the Peasants' Associations, 9,720,000. These organizations were all led by the Party. In Hunan and Hupeh, the peasants had risen in a spontaneous struggle to divide up the land.

The congress criticized Ch'en Tu-hsiu's right opportunism, pointing out that as a result of his mistakes, in the first place, the Party in the past two years had neglected the struggle against the bourgeoisie for leadership of the revolution and, secondly, that the Party had not fought to settle the peasants' demand for land. It held that the betrayal of the revolution by the bourgeoisie had not weakened the revolution, and that the Party should appeal to the peasants and the petty bourgeoisie with demands for agrarian revolution and the establishment of a democratic regime. In regard to the agrarian revolution, the congress advocated that land rented out by the big landlords should be confiscated and handed over to the peasants.

Mao Tse-tung attended the congress but was deprived of the right to vote by the Ch'en Tu-hsiuites. His important *Report of an Investigation into the Peasant Movement in Hunan*, written in March 1927, was suppressed.

Ch'en Tu-hsiu declared that he accepted the congress resolution denouncing his opportunist mistakes. He was reelected as General Secretary of the Party. After the congress, however, instead of carrying out the resolutions it had passed, he continued to pursue the erroneous policy of class capitulation.

In July of that year, following in the wake of Chiang Kai-shek, the Wang Ching-wei clique in the Kuomintang which had taken the reins of power in the Wuhan government also betrayed the revolution.

On August 1, Chou En-lai, Chu Teh, Yeh T'ing, Ho Lung, and others led part of the National Revolutionary Army, which was under the influence of the Communist Party, in an armed uprising at Nanchang.

On August 7, the Central Committee of the Party held an emergency meeting, now known as the "August the Seventh Conference." This was attended by twenty-two delegates, including Ch'ü Ch'iu-pai, Mao Tse-tung, and Teng Chung-hsia. This conference denounced Ch'en Tu-hsiu's right opportunism in forthright terms and expelled him from the Central Committee of the Party. It also laid down the policy of overthrowing the reactionary rule of the Kuomintang by armed uprisings and leading the peasants to carry out the agrarian revolution.

In October, Mao Tse-tung established the first revolutionary base in the countryside in the Chingkangshan area on the borders of Kiangsi and Hunan Provinces. In April of the following year the revolutionary troops under Chu Teh joined forces with those under Mao Tse-tung at Chingkangshan.

In November 1927, the Central Committee of the Party called an enlarged meeting of the provisional Political Bureau. Ch'ü Ch'iu-pai, who was the leading member of the Party, presided over this meeting. It was characterized by the growth of "left" deviations which had resulted from opposition to the right deviations at the August the Seventh Conference. It adopted a wrong policy of "left" adventurism. This policy caused heavy losses to the Party. It was only stopped when subjected to criticism in April 1928.

In July 1928, the Party held its Sixth National Congress [in Moscow]. This summed up the experience gained in the First Revolutionary Civil War (1925–1927) and defined the tasks and tactics of the Party in the new phase of the struggle that had opened. The congress correctly stated that Chinese society was then still in a semifeudal and semicolonial state, so the Chinese revolution was still a bourgeois-democratic revolution in nature. It decided that the fight against imperialism and for the carrying out of the agrarian revolution were the two most important tasks at that time. It pointed out that another revolutionary upsurge was bound to come, that the current political situation was the trough between two revolutionary waves, and that the primary task of the Party was to win over the masses.

This congress liquidated Ch'en Tu-hsiu's right opportunist mistakes and also criticized the error of "left" adventurism. However, it failed to make a proper estimate of the importance of the revolutionary bases in the countryside, of the protracted nature of the democratic revolution, and of the characteristics of the national bourgeoisie in China. As a result it still emphasized "leadership in the cities" and regarded the national bourgeoisie as "one of the most dangerous enemies" of the revolution. After the congress, the Central Committee, which was still in the hands of the "left" elements, continued to stay in the cities.

Between 1928 and 1930, Mao Tse-tung, Chu Teh, and other Communists established the central revolutionary base with Juichin in Kiangsi as its center. It was at this time that Mao Tse-tung wrote his important *Why Can China's Red Political Power Exist?* and *A Single Spark Can Start a Prairie Fire*. He thus showed both in theory and practice how the question of revolutionary bases in the countryside could be solved.

In May 1930, a civil war flared up between Chiang Kai-shek and the warlord Yen Hsi-shan and his then ally Feng Yü-hsiang. In June the Political Bureau of the Central Committee of the Party came under the leadership of Li Li-san. For the second time, the wrong line of the "left" opportunists was adopted. Arguing that the situation was ripe, they demanded the organization of general uprisings in key cities and the launching of a general offensive against such cities by all Red Army forces. This wrong line was corrected in September of the same year by the plenary session of the Central Committee presided over by Ch'ü Ch'iu-pai. Admitting his mistakes, Li Li-san left his leading post on the Central Committee, but the wrong line had already caused the Party heavy losses.

In January 1931, the fourth plenary session of the Central Committee elected by the Sixth National Congress met, and the Central Committee of the Party for the third time fell under the sway of "left" policies. This time the "left" deviation was carried on by the doctrinaires [the so-called "28 Bolsheviks" brought back to China by Comintern agent Pavel Mif] headed by Wang Ming (Ch'en Shao-yü) and Po Ku (Ch'in Pang-hsien). These wanted to wage a struggle against the upper strata of the petty bourgeoisie and the bourgeoisie as a whole; they dreamt of organizing uprisings in the key cities; they set little store by the revolutionary bases in the countryside and the military struggle waged by the Red Army; they were sectarian in their approach to the organizational work of the Party.

In September the "Mukden Incident" marked the start of the Japanese imperialists' seizure of northeast China, but Chiang Kai-shek continued his policy of "nonresistance." By the following January, the Japanese imperialists had occupied the whole of northeast China [Manchuria]. The movement to resist Japanese aggression and save the country surged up throughout the nation. The conflict between the Chinese people and the Japanese imperialists overshadowed the class struggle inside China. The doctrinaires in the Central Committee of the Party, however, continued to lay the main emphasis on class contradictions inside the country and refused to form a national united front against Japanese aggression.

In November, the Central Workers' and Peasants' Democratic Government [Chinese Soviet Republic] with Mao Tse-tung as its Chairman was formed at Juichin, Kiangsi. It called on the whole population to arm themselves and fight against Japanese aggression.

Between 1931 and the early part of 1933, the "left" elements in the Party opposed the policy advocated by Liu Shao-ch'i, of making use of all legal possibilities and conserving and accumulating the strength of the revolutionary forces. As a result of the adventurist policies they carried out, the underground organizations of the Party in the Kuomintang-controlled areas were almost utterly destroyed. By the early part of 1933, even the provisional Central Committee of the Party could not maintain itself there and was compelled to move to the central revolutionary base.

From October 1930 to March 1933, the central revolutionary base, under the leadership of Mao Tse-tung, Chu Teh, and other comrades, smashed four encirclement campaigns launched by Chiang Kai-shek. During this period, democratic state power was soundly established in the base and good progress was made with various constructive activities.

The provisional Central Committee of the Party arrived at the central revolutionary base in January 1933. Here the "left" elements elbowed aside Mao Tse-tung's leadership, especially his leadership in the Red Army, and imposed and carried out their own wrong policies.

In October, Chiang Kai-shek unleashed his fifth encirclement campaign with a force of a million men. As a result of the wrong leadership given by the "left" elements, the Red Army was defeated.

In October 1934, the Central Red Army retreated from its bases and began the Long March. In January 1935, it had reached Tsunyi in Kweichow Province.

At Tsunyi the Party held an enlarged conference of the Political Bureau of the Central Committee. This was known as the Tsunyi Conference, and was of great significance in the history of the Chinese revolution. The conference, with the support of the great majority of comrades present, removed the "left" opportunists from the Party leadership and formed a new leadership headed by Mao Tse-tung. It also decided that the Red Army should continue its march to the north to fight against Japanese aggression.

In October 1935, the Central Red Army arrived in northern Shensi. In December, the "December the Ninth Movement" led by the Party started a new upsurge throughout the country of the democratic movement for resistance to Japanese aggression.

In the latter part of the same month, following a resolution passed at the conference held by the Political Bureau of the Central Committee of the Party at Wayaopao, Mao Tse-tung delivered a report entitled *On the Tactics of Fighting Japanese Imperialism* at a conference of Party activists held at the same place on December 27. In this report he dealt fully with the possibility and importance of reestablishing a national united front with the national bourgeoisie against Japanese aggression, and emphasized the leading role the Party should play in that front. He also drew attention to the protracted nature of the Chinese revolution and criticized the narrow, "closed-door" sectarianism and revolutionary impetuosity which had prevailed in the Party for a long time—the main reason for the severe setbacks which the Party and Red Army suffered between 1927 and

1934 during the Second Revolutionary Civil War.

In July 1937, the War of Resistance to Japanese Aggression broke out.

In April 1945, the Party held its Seventh National Congress in Yenan. By that time, the Party already had a membership of 1,210,000. The anti-Japanese bases led by the Party had a population of 95 million. The prestige and influence of the Party in the Kuomintang-controlled area was growing daily.

At the seventh congress Mao Tse-tung delivered a political report entitled *On Coalition Government,* Chu Teh a military report entitled *The Battle Front of the Liberated Areas,* and Liu Shao-ch'i a report on the revision of the Party Constitution [entitled *On the Party*]. In his report, Mao Tse-tung pointed out that the general program of the Party in the period of the bourgeois-democratic revolution was to build up a new democratic society following victory in the war of resistance; that its principal specific program was to complete the defeat of the Japanese aggressors, abolish the Kuomintang's one-party dictatorship (*i.e.,* the dictatorship of the big landlords and big bourgeoisie), and form a democratic coalition government. The congress unanimously agreed that Mao Tse-tung's teaching concerning the Chinese revolution—integrating Marxist-Leninist theory with revolutionary practice in China—should be the guiding line of the Party. The Seventh Party Congress bore witness to the unity of the Party and prepared the Party for victory.

In August 1945, China celebrated victory in the War of Resistance to Japanese Aggression.

In July 1946, the War of Liberation began.

On October 1 [1949], the People's Republic of China was founded. This marked the completion in the main of the first stage of the Chinese revolution, the bourgeois-democratic revolution led by the Party. The second stage of the revolution, the socialist revolution, began.

Same Party, New Role

Mao Tse-tung • From 1927 to the present the center of gravity of our work has been in the villages—gathering strength in the

From Mao Tse-tung, *"Report to the Second Plenary Session of the Seventh Central Committee of the Communist Party of China"* [*March 5, 1949*], in Selected Works, *Vol. IV (Peking: Foreign Languages Press, 1961).*

villages, using the villages in order to surround the cities, and then taking the cities. The period for this method of work has now ended. The period of "from the city to the village" and of the city leading the village has now begun. The center of gravity of the Party's work has shifted from the village to the city. In the south the People's Liberation Army will occupy first the cities and then the villages. Attention must be given to both city and village, and it is necessary to link closely urban and rural work, workers and peasants, industry and agriculture. In no circumstances should the village be ignored and only the city be given attention; such thinking is entirely wrong. Nevertheless, the center of gravity of the work of the Party and the army must be in the cities; we must do our utmost to learn how to administer and build the cities. In the cities we must learn how to wage political, economic, and cultural struggles against the imperialists, the Kuomintang, and the bourgeoisie and also how to wage diplomatic struggles against the imperialists. We must learn how to carry on overt struggles against them, we must also learn how to carry on covert struggles against them. If we do not pay attention to these problems, if we do not learn how to wage these struggles against them and win victory in the struggles, we shall be unable to maintain our political power, we shall be unable to stand on our feet, we shall fail. After the enemies with guns have been wiped out, there will still be enemies without guns; they are bound to struggle desperately against us; we must never regard these enemies lightly. If we do not now raise and understand the problem in this way, we shall commit very grave mistakes. . . .

Very soon we shall be victorious throughout the country. This victory will breach the eastern front of imperialism and will have great international significance. To win this victory will not require much more time and effort, but to consolidate it will. The bourgeoisie doubts our ability to construct. The imperialists reckon that eventually we will beg alms from them in order to live. With victory, certain moods may grow within the Party—arrogance, the airs of self-styled hero, inertia and unwillingness to make progress, love of pleasure, and distaste for continued hard living. With victory, the people will be grateful to us and the bourgeoisie will come forward to flatter us. It has been proved that the enemy cannot conquer us by force of arms. However, the flattery of the bourgeoisie may conquer the weak-willed in our ranks. There may be some Communists, who were not conquered by enemies with guns and were worthy of the name of heroes for standing up to these enemies, but who cannot withstand sugar-coated bullets; they will be defeated by sugar-coated bullets. We must guard against such a situation. To win countrywide victory is only the first step in a long march of ten thousand *li*. Even if this step is worthy of pride, it is comparatively tiny; what will be more worthy of pride is yet to come. After several decades, the victory of the Chinese people's democratic revolution, viewed in retrospect, will seem like only a brief prologue to a long drama. A drama begins with a prologue, but the prologue is not the climax. The Chinese revolution is great, but the road after the revolution will be longer, the work greater and more arduous. This must be made clear now in the Party. The comrades must be taught to remain modest, prudent, and free from arrogance and rashness in their style of work. The comrades must be taught to preserve the style of plain living and hard struggle. We have the Marxist-Leninist weapon of criticism and self-criticism. We can get rid of a bad style and keep the good. We can learn what we did not know. We are not only good at destroying the old world, we are also good at building the new. Not only can the Chinese people live without begging alms from the imperialists, they will live a better life than that in the imperialist countries.

Foundations of Power

Mao Tse-tung • Before the May 4 Movement of 1919 (which occurred after the first imperialist world war of 1914 and the Russian October Revolution of 1917), the political leaders in the Chinese bourgeois-democratic revolution were the Chinese petty bourgeoisie and bourgeoisie (represented by their intellectuals). At that time, the Chinese proletariat had not yet appeared on the political scene as an awakened and independent class force; it participated in the revolution only as a follower of the petty bourgeoisie and the bourgeoisie. The proletariat at the time of the Revolution of 1911, for instance, was such a class.

From Mao Tse-tung, On New Democracy [*January 1940*] (*Peking: Foreign Languages Press, 1954*). *Although written more than 9 years before the Communist victory on the mainland, the passages given here were used as the basic rationale for the organization of political power in 1949.*

After the May 4 Movement, although the Chinese national bourgeoisie continued to participate in the revolution, the political leaders of China's bourgeois-democratic revolution belonged no longer to the Chinese bourgeoisie, but to the Chinese proletariat. By that time the Chinese proletariat, owing to its own maturity and the influence of the Russian revolution, had rapidly become an awakened and independent political force. The slogan "Down with imperialism," together with the thoroughgoing program of the entire bourgeois-democratic revolution of China, was proposed by the Chinese Communist Party, and the agrarian revolution was carried out by the Chinese Communist Party alone.

Being a bourgeoisie in a colonial and semicolonial country and under the oppression of imperialism, the Chinese national bourgeoisie, even in the era of imperialism, retains at certain periods and to a certain degree a revolutionary quality which enables it to fight against foreign imperialism and the home governments of bureaucrats and warlords (instances of the latter can be found in the periods of the Revolution of 1911 and of the Northern Expedition), and ally with the proletariat and the petty bourgeoisie to oppose the enemies it sets itself against. This is the point where the Chinese bourgeoisie differs from the bourgeoisie of old tsarist Russia. Since tsarist Russia was itself already a country of militarist and feudalist imperialism which encroached upon other countries, the Russian bourgeoisie had no revolutionary quality to speak of. There the task of the proletariat was to oppose the bourgeoisie, not to unite with it. Since China is a colony as well as a semicolony encroached upon by others, her national bourgeoisie has at certain periods and to a certain degree a revolutionary quality. Here the task of the proletariat is to attach due importance to the revolutionary quality of the national bourgeoisie and establish with it a united front against imperialism and the governments of bureaucrats and warlords.

But, at the same time, just because the Chinese national bourgeoisie is a bourgeois class in a colony and semicolony, it is extremely flabby politically and economically, and it possesses another character, namely, a proneness to compromise with the enemy of the revolution. Even when it takes part in a revolution, it is unwilling to break completely with imperialism and is moreover closely related to exploitation by land rent in rural areas; thus it is neither willing nor able to overthrow imperialism thoroughly, much less the feudal forces. . . .

On the one hand, the possibility of participating in the revolution; and on the other hand, the proneness to compromise with the enemy of the revolution—these constitute the dual character of "one person filling two posts" of the Chinese bourgeoisie. This dual character was also shown by the bourgeoisie in European and American history. When confronted with a formidable enemy, they unite with the workers and peasants to oppose the enemy, but when the workers and peasants are awakened, they unite with the enemy to oppose the workers and peasants. This is the general rule governing the bourgeoisie in every country of the world, but the trait is even more pronounced among the Chinese bourgeoisie.

It is quite evident that whoever in China can lead the people to overthrow imperialism and the feudal forces will win the people's confidence, because the mortal enemies of the people are imperialism and the feudal forces, especially imperialism. Today, whoever can lead the people to drive out Japanese imperialism and bring about a democratic government will be the savior of the people. History has proved that the Chinese bourgeoisie is unable to fulfill this responsibility which consequently cannot but fall on the shoulders of the proletariat.

Therefore, under all circumstances, the proletariat, the peasantry, the intelligentsia and other sections of the petty bourgeoisie in China are the basic forces determining her fate. These classes, some already awakened and others on the point of awakening, will necessarily become the basic component parts of the state structure and of the structure of political power of the democratic republic of China with the proletariat as the leading force. The democratic republic of China which we now want to establish can only be a democratic republic under the joint dictatorship of all anti-imperialist and anti-feudal people led by the proletariat, that is, a new-democratic republic. . . .

On the one hand, this new-democratic republic is different from the old European-American form of capitalist republic under bourgeois dictatorship, for such [an] old democratic republic is already out of date; on the other hand, it is also different from the socialist republics of the type of the U.S.S.R., republics under the dictatorship of the proletariat; such socialist republics are already flourishing in the Soviet Union and moreover will be established in all the capitalist countries and undoubtedly [will] become the dominant form of state structure and of political power in all industrially advanced countries. Yet, during a given historical period, they are not yet suitable for the revolution in colonial and semicolonial countries. Therefore, the form of state to be adopted by the revolution in colonial and semicolonial countries during a given historical period can only be a third one, namely, the new-democratic republic. This is the form for a given historical period and therefore a transitional form, but an unalterable and necessary form. . . .

What is under discussion here is the question of "state system." Though this question of the state system has been wrangled over for several decades since the end of the Manchu dynasty, it is still not clarified. Actually it is simply the question of the status of various social classes in the state. The bourgeoisie, as a rule, conceals the status of classes and uses the term "citizenship" as a dodge to bring about the dictatorship of one class. Such concealment is not at all beneficial to the revolutionary people, and the matter must be explained clearly to them. The term "citizenship" may be employed, but it does not include the counterrevolutionaries and collaborators. A [joint] dictatorship of all revolutionary classes [namely, the workers, peasants, petty bourgeoisie, and national bourgeoisie] over the counterrevolutionaries and collaborators is the kind of state [system] we want today. . . .

As to the question of "political structure," it is one of the forms of the structure of political power, the form adopted by certain social classes in establishing their organs of political power to oppose their enemy and protect themselves. Without an adequate form of political power there would be nothing to represent the state. China can now adopt a system of people's congresses—the people's national congress, the people's provincial congresses, the people's county congresses, the people's district congresses, down to the people's township congresses—and let these congresses at various levels elect the organs of government.* But a system of really universal and equal suffrage, irrespective of sex, creed, property, or education, must be put into practice so that the organs of government elected can properly represent each revolutionary class according to its status in the state, express the people's will and direct revolutionary struggles and embody the spirit of new democracy. Such a system is democratic centralism. Only a government of democratic centralism can fully ex-

---

* This system of congresses was not established until 1954. For details, see below, Chapter 7.

press the will of all the revolutionary people and most powerfully fight the enemies of the revolution. The spirit of "not to be monopolized by a few" must be embodied in the organizations of the government and the army; without a genuinely democratic system such an aim can never be attained, and that would mean a discrepancy between the political structure and the state system.

Mao Tse-tung • The first of July 1949 marks the fact that the Chinese Communist Party has already run a course of twenty-eight years. Like a human being, a political party has its childhood, youth, manhood, and old age. The Chinese Communist Party is no longer a child or a lad in his teens but has reached manhood. When a man reaches old age, he will die; the same is true of a party, for when classes disappear, all instruments of class struggle—the party and the state machine—will become less and less useful or necessary and gradually wither away along with the fulfillment of their historical mission, and human society will move to a higher stage. We form the very opposite of the political parties of the bourgeoisie. They are afraid to speak of the elimination of classes, state power, and parties. We, on the contrary, openly declare that we are striving hard precisely to create the conditions that will hasten the elimination of these things. The Communist Party and the state power of the people's dictatorship constitute such conditions. . . .

"Don't you want to eliminate state power?" Yes, we do, but not now; we cannot yet afford to do that. Why? Because imperialism still exists, and within our country reactionaries and classes still exist. Our present task is to strengthen the people's state machine—principally the people's army, the people's police, and the people's courts—so that the national defense can be consolidated and the people's interests protected. Given these conditions, China, under the leadership of the working class and the Communist Party, can develop steadily from an agricultural country into an industrial country and from a new democratic into a socialist and Communist society, in order to eliminate classes and achieve world communism. The state machine, including the army, the police, and the courts, is the instrument with which one class oppresses another. It is an instrument of oppression against all hostile classes; it means violence and is

From Mao Tse-tung, On People's Democratic Dictatorship [*June 30, 1949*] (*Peking: Foreign Languages Press, 1959*).

certainly not anything "benevolent." "You are merciless." Quite so. We definitely do not adopt a benevolent policy toward the reactionary activities of the reactionaries and the reactionary classes. Our benevolent policy applies only to the people, not to the reactionary activities of the reactionaries and reactionary classes that are outside the ranks of the people. . . .

To sum up our experiences and bring them into focus: We must have the people's democratic dictatorship led by the working class (through the Communist Party) and based upon the alliance of workers and peasants. This dictatorship must unite with all international revolutionary forces. This is our formula, our principal experience, our main program.

Lessons from a Sometime Comrade

People's Daily • What is the fundamental experience of the Soviet Union in revolution and construction? In our opinion, the following, at the very least, should be considered fundamental:

1. The advanced members of the proletariat organize themselves into a Communist Party which takes Marxism-Leninism as its guide to action, builds itself up along the lines of democratic centralism, establishes close links with the masses, strives to become the core of the laboring masses, and educates its Party members and the masses of people in Marxism-Leninism.

2. The proletariat, under the leadership of the Communist Party, rallying all the laboring people, takes state power from the bourgeoisie by means of revolutionary struggle.

3. After the victory of the revolution, the proletariat, under the leadership of the Communist Party, rallying the broad mass of the people on the basis of a worker-peasant alliance, establishes a dictatorship of the proletariat over the landlord and capitalist classes, crushes the resistance of the counterrevolutionaries, and carries out the nationalization of industry and the step-by-step collectivization of agriculture, thereby eliminating the system of exploitation, private ownership of the means of production, and classes.

4. The state, led by the proletariat and the Communist Party,

From an editorial in Jen-min jih-pao [People's Daily], *December 29, 1956,* *translated in* The Historical Experience of the Dictatorship of the Proletariat (*Peking: Foreign Languages Press, 1959*).

leads the people in the planned development of socialist economy and culture, and on this basis gradually raises the people's living standards and actively prepares and works for the transition to Communist society.

5. The state, led by the proletariat and the Communist Party, resolutely opposes imperialist aggression, recognizes the equality of all nations, and defends world peace; firmly adheres to the principles of proletarian internationalism, strives to win the help of the laboring people of all countries, and at the same time strives to help them and all oppressed nations.

What we commonly refer to as the path of the October Revolution means precisely these basic things, leaving aside the specific form it took at that particular time and place. These basic things are all universally applicable truths of Marxism-Leninism.

In the course of revolution and construction in different countries there are, besides aspects common to all, aspects which are different. In this sense, each country has its own specific path of development. . . . But as far as basic theory is concerned, the road of the October Revolution reflects the general laws of revolution and construction at a particular stage in the long course of the development of human society. . . .

Challenge to Mao: "The Kao-Jao Row"

Communist Party Resolution • The National Conference of the Communist Party of China heard a report by Comrade Teng Hsiao-p'ing, on behalf of the Central Committee, concerning the anti-Party bloc of Kao Kang and Jao Shu-shih, and unanimously expressed support for the measures taken by the Political Bureau of the Central Committee after the fourth plenary session of the Seventh Central Committee in regard to this question.

Kao Kang's anti-Party activities had a fairly long history. The facts brought to light before and after the fourth plenary session of the Seventh Central Committee of the Party held in February 1954 proved that, from 1949 on, Kao Kang carried on conspiratorial activities aimed at seizing leadership in the Party and the state. In Northeast China [the chief industrial region and

---

"Resolution on the Anti-Party Bloc of Kao Kang and Jao Shu-shih" [*March 31, 1955*], Documents of the National Conference of the Communist Party of China, March 1955 (*Peking: Foreign Languages Press, 1955*).

the staging area for Chinese "volunteers" in the 1950–1953 Korean War] and other places, he created and spread many rumors slandering the Central Committee of the Party and lauding himself, with the aim of sowing discord and dissension among the comrades and stirring up dissatisfaction with the leading comrades of the Central Committee of the Party; he thus carried on activities to split the Party and, in the course of these activities, formed his own anti-Party faction. In their work in the northeast area, the anti-Party faction formed by Kao Kang violated the policy of the Central Committee of the Party, tried its utmost to belittle the role of the Party, and to undermine solidarity and unity in the Party, regarding the northeast area as the independent kingdom of Kao Kang. After Kao Kang was transferred to work in the central organs in 1953 [as a vice premier and member of what is now called the Standing Committee of the Political Bureau], his anti-Party activities became even more outrageous. He even tried to instigate Party members in the army to support his conspiracy against the Central Committee of the Party. For this purpose he invented the utterly absurd "theory" that our Party consisted of two parties—one, the so-called "Party of the revolutionary bases and the army," the other, the so-called "Party of the white areas"—and that the Party was created by the army. He himself claimed to be the representative of the so-called "Party of the revolutionary bases and the army" and thus entitled to hold the major authority, and advocated that both the Central Committee of the Party and the government should be reorganized in accordance with his plan, and that he himself should be for the time being general secretary or vice chairman of the Central Committee of the Party and Premier of the State Council. After a serious warning was given to the anti-Party elements by the fourth plenary session of the Seventh Central Committee of the Party, Kao Kang not only did not admit his guilt to the Party, but committed suicide as an ultimate expression of his betrayal of the Party.

Jao Shu-shih was Kao Kang's chief ally in his conspiratorial activities against the Party. It has been fully established that in the ten years between 1943 and 1953 Jao Shu-shih resorted on many occasions to shameless deceit in the Party to seize power. During his tenure of office in East China, he did his utmost to adopt in the cities and countryside a rightist policy of surrender to the capitalists, landlords, and rich peasants. At the same time, he did everything possible to protect counterrevolutionaries in defiance of the Central Committee's policy of suppressing them. After his transfer to the Party Center in 1953, Jao Shu-shih thought that Kao Kang was on the point of success in his activities aimed at seizing power in the Central Committee. Therefore, he formed an anti-Party bloc with Kao Kang and used his office as Director of the Organization Department of the Central Committee to start a struggle with the aim of opposing leading members of the Central Committee, and thus actively carried out activities to split the Party. From the time of the fourth plenary session of the Seventh Central Committee of the Party up to the present, Jao Shu-shih has never shown any signs of repentance, and still persists in an attitude of attacking the Party.

The Eighth Party Congress:
Crisis in Political Leadership

Liu Shao-ch'i • During the period from the Seventh [1945] to the Eighth National Congress of the Party, along with the victory of the revolution and the changes that have taken place in the situation of our country, there have also been great changes in the Party itself. It is now a party that leads the state power over the whole country, and it enjoys very high prestige among the masses of the people. The Party organization has grown; it has a membership of 10,730,000, of whom 14 per cent come from the ranks of the workers, 69 per cent from the peasantry, and 12 per cent from the intellectuals. Party organizations are spread throughout the country, and among the various nationalities as well. The overwhelming majority of Party members have been tempered in great revolutionary struggles. Even the new members who joined the Party after 1949—and who constitute more than 60 per cent of the membership—are, in the main, outstanding and active elements who have come forward in the mass revolutionary struggles and in socialist labor over the last few years. On the whole, the Party is more closely bound to the masses of the people; it has gained richer and more comprehen-

From Liu Shao-ch'i, "The Political Report of the Central Committee of the Communist Party of China" [September 15, 1956], Eighth National Congress of the Communist Party of China, Vol. I (Peking: Foreign Languages Press, 1956).

sive experience in its work; and never before has its unity been as strong as it is today.

As we have said before, the cause of socialism in our country cannot do without the dictatorship of the proletariat which is realized through the leadership of the party of the proletariat— the Communist Party. The strength of leadership of the Chinese Communist Party lies in the fact that it is armed ideologically with Marxism-Leninism, is correct in its political and organizational lines, rich in experience in struggle and in work, skilled in crystallizing the wisdom of the people of the whole country and turning that wisdom into one united will and disciplined action. And not only in the past, but in the future too, the leadership of such a party is essential in order to insure that our country can deal effectively with complex domestic and international affairs. This view is shared by all sections of the people and democratic parties in our country as a result of their experience in life.

Nevertheless, in the work of our socialist construction there are comrades, though very few, who have tried to weaken the leading role of the Party. They confuse the question of the Party giving leadership to various spheres of state affairs in regard to principles and policies with the question of purely technical matters; they think that since the Party is still a layman in the technical side of these things, it should not exercise leadership over such work, while they themselves can go on taking arbitrary action. We have criticized this wrong viewpoint. In all work the Party should and can play a leading role ideologically, politically, and in matters of principle and policy. Of course, that does not mean that the Party should take everything into its own hands or interfere in everything. Neither does it mean that it should be content with being a layman in things it does not understand. The Party asks its cadres and members to study painstakingly in order to master the things they do not understand in their work. For the more we study, the better will we be able to lead. . . .

To enable our Party to continue to maintain its correct and sound leadership in the future, the main thing is to see to it that Party organizations and Party members make fewer ideological mistakes. There are struggles in our Party between correct ideology and wrong ideology and between the correct line and the wrong line. . . . In order to prevent mistakes, therefore, the basic thing is to acquire an accurate knowledge of objective reality and correctly differentiate between right and wrong.

Teng Hsiao-p'ing • A great change has also come about in the situation of our Party. The Communist Party of China is now a party in power, playing the leading role in all the work of the state. Party organizations have spread to every city and town, to every county and district, to every major enterprise, and among the various nationalities. Now, the Party membership is nine times what it was at the time of the Seventh Congress, and nearly three times what it was in 1949 at the time of our nationwide victory. Furthermore, the majority of our Party members are now working in government offices, economic and cultural establishments, and people's organizations at all levels. All these changes make it imperative for us to pay the greatest attention to strengthening the Party's organizational and educational work among the membership.

As a party in power our Party has been confronted with a fresh test. Generally speaking, our Party has stood the test in the past seven years. Our country has made remarkable progress in every sphere, and the overwhelming majority of our Party members are working hard and doing well at their respective posts. But the experience of these seven years has also shown us that, with the Party in power, our comrades are liable to be tainted with bureaucracy. Both for Party organizations and individual members the danger of drifting away from reality and from the masses has increased rather than decreased. Any such drifting away is bound to give rise to errors of subjectivism, that is, errors of doctrinairism and empiricism, and such errors have increased rather than decreased in our Party compared with the situation of a few years ago.

The position of the Party as a party in power can also easily breed arrogance and self-complacency among the membership. Some Party members become puffed-up over the smallest success in their work, and tend to look down upon others, upon the masses, upon non-Party personalities, as though the mere fact of being Party members makes them stand head and shoulders above non-Party people. Some, fond of showing off as leader, order the masses about from above, and are reluctant to consult them in

From Teng Hsiao-p'ing, "Report on the Revision of the Constitution of the Communist Party of China" [September 16, 1956], ibid.

their work. This is in fact a tendency towards narrow sectarianism, a dangerous tendency which leads to the most serious isolation from the masses.

In view of this situation, the Party must pay constant attention to combating subjectivism, bureaucracy, and sectarianism, and must always guard against the danger of drifting away from reality and from the masses. Therefore, apart from strengthening the ideological education of its members, the Party has an even more important task, namely, to strengthen the Party's leadership in various ways and to make appropriate provisions in both the state and the Party systems for a strict supervision over our Party organizations and Party members.

Rectification as a Response

Central Committee Directive • In the past few years, in the Party there has been a new growth of bureaucracy, sectarianism, and subjectivism which depart from the masses and reality. Therefore, the Central Committee considers it necessary, on the basis of the policy of "proceeding from the desire for unity, and through criticism and self-criticism, achieving new unity on a new basis," to launch within the Party once again an extensive, thoroughgoing rectification campaign against bureaucracy, sectarianism, and subjectivism, and to raise the Marxist ideological level of the whole Party and improve the working style so as to conform with needs of socialist transformation and construction.

This campaign should be guided ideologically by the reports delivered by Comrade Mao Tse-tung on behalf of the Central Committee of the Party at the enlarged Supreme State Conference in February [*On the Correct Handling of Contradictions Among the People,* see pages 98–105] and at the National Conference on Propaganda convened by the Central Committee in March this year, and should at present center on correctly handling contradictions within the ranks of the people.

The two reports delivered by Comrade Mao Tse-tung have been relayed to broad sections of the cadres and intellectuals and will be relayed to all Party members and the people. The two reports relayed have given rise to enthusiastic discussions both

From Chinese Communist Party Central Committee, "Directive Concerning the Campaign to Rectify Working Style," April 27, 1957.

within and outside the Party. As far as our Party is concerned, this is, in fact, the beginning of the campaign.

Party committees at all levels should organize studies of these two reports, and summarize and improve the work in their own areas, departments, and organizations in accordance with the basic ideas in the two reports and by reference to a number of other relevant documents.

In the course of this study, the leading organs and cadres at all levels should mainly review how contradictions within the ranks of the people are being dealt with and how the Party policies, "Let many flowers blossom, let diverse schools of thought contend," "long-term coexistence and mutual supervision," and "building the country on industry and thrift" are being executed; investigate the bureaucracy which has brought isolation from the masses of the workers, peasants, students, and intellectuals, the sectarianism, which does not proceed from unity with our 600 million people, unity with the democratic parties and the broad non-Party masses, and unity with the whole Party and soldiers, subjectivism which does not proceed from the actual situation; and finally, they should faithfully carry out the directive of the Central Committee concerning "correctly handling the question of contradictions within the ranks of the people." . . .

This campaign should be a movement of ideological education carried out seriously, yet as gently as a breeze or a mild rain. It should be a campaign of criticism and self-criticism carried to the proper extent. Meetings should be limited to small-sized discussion or group meetings. Comradely heart-to-heart talks in the form of conversations, namely exchange of views between individuals, should be used more, and large meetings of criticism or "struggle" should not be held. Criticism should be boldly encouraged when it is done at discussion or group meetings or in the course of individual talks. The principle of "telling all that you know, and telling it without reservation; blaming not the speaker but heeding what you hear; correcting mistakes if you have committed them and avoiding them if you have not" should be firmly adhered to. One should not justify everything concerning himself and reject criticism by others. On the other hand, the critics should be encouraged to be true to facts and make concrete analyses in order to avoid complete negation of everything done by the person criticized, which will become one-sided and exaggerated criticism. Everyone should listen with an open mind to the opinion of others and enthusiastically take part in expressing his opinions of others. But criticism should not be imposed upon a person who does not accept it. Whenever possible, the necessary conclusions should be drawn about some of the arguments involving matters of principle, but the right to reserve differences must be permitted. In the course of the campaign, those found to have committed mistakes, big or small, except for serious cases of offenses against the law or discipline, are all to be exempted from organizational disciplinary measures. They are to be given positive and patient help to achieve the aim of "taking warning from the past in order to be more careful in the future and treating the illness in order to save the man."

Non-Party people who wish to participate in the rectification campaign should be welcomed. But this should be done on an entirely voluntary basis, and no coercion is allowed. They should be permitted to withdraw freely at any time.

In order to strengthen the contact between the Party and the broad mass of working people and to change thoroughly the situation where many of those in leading positions are separated from the masses, it is necessary, while the rectification campaign is being conducted, for the whole Party to advocate and encourage that leading personnel who hold key positions at all levels in the Party, in the government, and in the military service and who are fit for physical labor should devote part of their time to engaging in physical labor with the workers and peasants. This measure should be gradually made into a permanent system. . . . The present task of the Party is, on the one hand, to organize studies in the rectification of the working style, to raise the ideological understanding within the Party, and to correct the shortcomings and mistakes in work. On the other hand, it is to preserve in full and also carry forward, in actual life, the Party's excellent tradition of working hard and perseveringly to overcome difficulties, and then to proceed to establish a basic system under which the mental work of leading personnel in the Party and government organs is integrated with physical labor, so that they may be closely knitted with the masses.

The Summing Up

Liu Shao-ch'i • We are gathered here today to celebrate the 40th anniversary of the founding of the Communist Party of China.

The forty years since the founding of the Communist Party of China have been years during which our Party has led the people of the whole country in heroic struggles and in achieving great victories, years during which Marxism-Leninism has spread widely in China and has won great victories.

Before the founding of the Communist Party of China, the Chinese people waged a long struggle against imperialism and feudalism, with new fighters always stepping forward as others fell, a struggle that moves us to song and tears. However, they never attained genuine victory. It was not until Marxism-Leninism spread to China following the Great October Socialist Revolution in Russia that the Chinese people found the best theoretical weapon for their liberation. The Communist Party of China wielded this weapon and formulated the correct objectives, policies, and methods for the struggle to liberate the Chinese people. From then on the march of the Chinese people from victory to victory has been irresistible.

During these forty years, the Communist Party of China, together with the Chinese people, has accomplished a great deal. To sum up, what has been accomplished consists mainly of two important things:

First, we carried out the people's democratic revolution in China. Because of its weakness, the Chinese national bourgeoisie could not lead China's bourgeois-democratic revolution to victory. The responsibility of leading this revolution had to be shouldered by the proletariat. . . .

Second, we have been carrying out the socialist revolution and socialist construction in China. We have been doing this for the past twelve years and we are continuing to do it. The founding of the People's Republic of China marked the beginning of the transition from the democratic to the socialist revolution. The Chinese people's democratic state power is in

From *Liu Shao-ch'i*, Address at the Meeting in Celebration of the 40th Anniversary of the Founding of the Communist Party of China [*June 30, 1961*] (*Peking: Foreign Languages Press, 1961*).

essence the dictatorship of the proletariat. In the past twelve years, we have basically completed the socialist revolution and have achieved immense successes in socialist construction. A very long time is still required to build China into a great socialist country with modern industry, modern agriculture, and modern science and culture. And a longer historical period is required to realize the transition from socialism to communism. Nevertheless, anyone can see that the socialist system is already established in this great land of China and that China is no longer a stagnant country but is forging ahead vigorously. . . .

In every historical period of our Party it has been the leader of our Party, Comrade Mao Tse-tung, who has stood at the very forefront and who has been the most able in integrating the universal truth of Marxism-Leninism with the concrete practice of China.

Confronted with the extreme complexity of the Chinese revolution, Comrade Mao Tse-tung correctly posed and resolved a series of theoretical and tactical problems, thus enabling the Chinese revolution to steer clear of one shoal after another and to capture one position after another. . . .

After the establishment of the People's Republic of China we carried out the antifeudal land reform in the newly liberated areas, and at the same time we waged the great struggles to suppress counterrevolutionaries and to resist U. S. aggression and aid Korea; thereby we further cleared the way for the socialist revolution and for socialist construction in our country.

Guided by the general line and the various specific policies for the period of transition to socialism which were laid down by the Party's Central Committee headed by Comrade Mao Tse-tung, our socialist revolution may be said to have proceeded comparatively rapidly and smoothly.

On the socialist transformation of agriculture: We applied Lenin's theory of the worker-peasant alliance under the dictatorship of the proletariat and his theory of agricultural cooperation; we summed up the experience we had gained in our revolutionary base areas in the movement for agricultural mutual aid and cooperation; and in accordance with the concrete conditions of our country after liberation, we relied on the poor peasants and lower middle peasants, united firmly with the rest of the middle peasantry, used various transitional forms, and thus enabled our agriculture to change from an individual economy to a socialist collective economy.

On the socialist transformation of industry and commerce of the national bourgeoisie: We applied Marx's idea that in certain conditions the proletariat may adopt a policy of buying out the bourgeoisie and Lenin's ideas concerning the policy of state capitalism under proletarian dictatorship; we summed up our Party's experience in its industrial and commercial policies in the revolutionary base areas; and in accordance with the concrete conditions of our country after liberation, we carried out the combined policy of utilizing, restricting, and transforming capitalist industry and commerce and used various forms of state capitalism, ranging from the lower to the higher, in order to achieve this transformation. . . .

The struggle as between the socialist and the capitalist road has not ended with the basic completion of the socialist revolution in the ownership of the means of production, and this struggle will go on for a long time especially on the political and ideological fronts. . . .

Today our country is still economically backward. Imperialism continues to bully us. The people of our country urgently demand an end to this backwardness. There is not the slightest doubt that our Party's general line for socialist construction [which is: to go all out, aim high, and achieve greater, faster, better, and more economical results] conforms to the aspirations of the whole people.

Guided by the Party's general line for socialist construction, our country has made big leaps forward for three consecutive years beginning with 1958. Meanwhile, in our countryside there have emerged the people's communes formed by agricultural cooperatives joining together. Thus the general line, the big leap forward and the people's commune have become the three red banners that are leading the Chinese people.

During the three years of the big leap forward, the key targets set for industry in the Second Five-Year Plan [1958–1962] have been fulfilled ahead of schedule, a fairly large modern industrial base has been built, and consequently the productive capacity of the basic industries has increased two or more times. In agriculture, water conservancy projects have been undertaken extensively, and thus conditions essential for the future development of agricultural production have been created. In the fields of culture and education there has also been great progress over the last three years. . . .

Our general line is developed and perfected through practice, and the various specific policies and specific measures essential for its realization have also to be developed and perfected gradually through practice. During the big leap forward of the last three years we have had tremendous achievements, and the general line and the various specific policies and measures have all been developed. At the same time, there have also been quite a few shortcomings in our work which, together with the serious natural calamities of the two successive years, have given rise to some temporary difficulties. In a large country like ours with a population of 650 million, a country that is economically and culturally backward, it would be inconceivable for such a new undertaking as socialist construction to proceed without shortcomings, without running into any difficulty. Historical experience has proved that no difficulty, no shortcoming, can frighten us; on the contrary, we have always steeled ourselves and become stronger and more correct in the course of extending our achievements and overcoming all kinds of difficulties and shortcomings. . . .

In order to do a good job in the interests of the great unity of the whole people and in the interests of socialist construction, all members of our Party must, under the leadership of the Central Committee, raise their ideological and political level further, perfect the Party organizations, and strengthen the unity of the Party.

Our Party now has more than 17 million members. Eighty per cent of them have joined the Party since the founding of the People's Republic of China, and 70 per cent have joined since 1953. They are the Party's new blood but lack experience, and many of them have not yet had systematic Marxist-Leninist education. Those who joined the Party before liberation have gone through sanguinary revolutionary struggles and are now the backbone of our Party, but while familiar with revolution they have not yet had adequate experience in socialist construction. Therefore, all Party members, whether old or new, have a serious task before them, that is, they must learn socialist construction conscientiously and systematically.

Crisis and Resolve at the Tenth Plenum

Communist Party Communiqué • The tenth plenary session notes with satisfaction that since the ninth plenary session held in [January] 1961, and particularly since the beginning of this year, the work done by the whole Party in implementing the policy of readjustment, consolidation, filling out, and raising standards in the national economy and in strengthening the agricultural front has yielded remarkable results. Despite the serious natural disasters for several consecutive years and the shortcomings and mistakes in the work, the condition of the national economy last year was slightly better than the year before, and this year is again slightly better than that of last year.

In agriculture, the actual harvest of summer crops this year has shown a slight gain over that of last year, and the yield of autumn crops is also expected to register an increase. This is the result of carrying through the Party's series of policies concerning the rural people's communes and thus giving play to the advantages of the collective economy of the people's communes.

In industry, positive results have been achieved through the adoption of effective measures of readjustment. The output of production in support of agriculture, light industrial products using industrial products as raw materials, many handicrafts, and some badly needed heavy industrial products has registered a considerable increase during the January–August period as compared with the corresponding period of last year. Many enterprises have improved their management, their products are of a higher quality and cover a greater range, their production costs have been cut down, and their labor productivity has been raised.

In the field of commerce there are also new improvements, and the supply of commodities is slightly better than before.

All this shows that, both in the towns and countryside, our economic conditions are getting better and better with each passing day.

It should be pointed out that some of our work is not well done. For instance, because of the incompetence of the leading

From *Communiqué of the Tenth Plenum* (*meeting in Peking, September 24–27, 1962*) *of the Eighth Central Committee of the Chinese Communist Party, September 28, 1962.*

cadres, some production teams, some factories, and some business establishments have produced less or become unwelcome to the masses. We should endeavor to change this state of affairs and improve the work of those units without delay.

The people of our country have always united closely around the Central Committee of the Party and Comrade Mao Tse-tung. Even when confronted with serious difficulties at home and from abroad, the broadest masses and cadres of our country have always firmly believed in the correctness of the general line for socialist construction, the big leap forward, and the people's communes—the three red banners. Giving full play to the glorious tradition of working hard and building the country with diligence and thrift, and to the militant spirit of relying on our own efforts and working with vigor for the country's prosperity, they have actively grappled with the difficulties and scored brilliant achievements under the leadership of the Party and the people's government.

The Chinese People's Liberation Army and the public security forces are strong and reliable armed forces of the people. Our country has also a heroic militia force of vast numbers. They have performed well their glorious task of defending the motherland, the people's labor, and the socialist system. At all times they are vigilantly guarding the frontiers of our great motherland and protecting public order and stand ready to smash the aggressive and sabotage activities of any enemy.

Tested in all these struggles, our country is worthy of being called a great country, our people a great people, our armed forces great armed forces, and our Party a great Party.

The imperialists, the reactionaries of various countries, and the modern revisionists gloated over the temporary difficulties encountered by the Chinese people, and they wantonly vilified China's general line for socialist construction, the big leap forward, and the people's communes, striking up an anti-Chinese chorus which was sensational for a time. U. S. imperialism instigated the Chiang Kai-shek gang entrenched in Taiwan to plot vainly an invasion of the coastal areas of the mainland. At home, those landlords, rich peasants, and bourgeois rightists who have not reformed themselves and the remnant counter-revolutionaries also gloated over our difficulties and tried to take advantage of the situation. But the imperialists and their running-dogs in China and abroad completely miscalculated. All their criminal activities have not only further exposed their hideous features but have heightened the socialist and patriotic fervor of our people in working vigorously for the prosperity of our country. Our people have resolutely smashed and will continue to smash every one of their scheming activities be it intrusion, provocation, or aggression, or subversion within our state or our Party.

The tenth plenary session of the Eighth Central Committee points out that throughout the historical period of proletarian revolution and proletarian dictatorship, throughout the historical period of transition from capitalism to communism (which will last scores of years or even longer), there is class struggle between the proletariat and the bourgeoisie and struggle between the socialist road and the capitalist road. The reactionary ruling classes which have been otherthrown are not reconciled to their doom. They always attempt to stage a comeback. Meanwhile there still exist in society bourgeois influence, the force of habit of the old society, and the spontaneous tendency toward capitalism among part of the small producers. Therefore, among the people, a small number of persons, making up only a tiny fraction of the total population, who have not yet undergone socialist remolding, always attempt to depart from the socialist road and turn to the capitalist road whenever there is an opportunity. Class struggle is inevitable in these circumstances. This is a law of history which has long been elucidated by Marxism-Leninism. We must never forget it. This class struggle is complicated, tortuous, with ups and downs, and sometimes it is very sharp. This class struggle inevitably finds expression within the Party. Pressure from foreign imperialism and the existence of bourgeois influence at home constitute the social source of revisionist ideas in the Party. While waging a struggle against the foreign and domestic class enemies, we must remain vigilant and resolutely oppose in good time various opportunist ideological tendencies in the Party. The great historic significance of the eighth plenary session of the Eighth Central Committee held in Lushan in August 1959 lies in the fact that it victoriously smashed attacks by right opportunism, *i.e.*, revisionism, and safeguarded the Party line and the unity of the Party. Both at present and in the future, our Party must sharpen its vigilance and correctly wage a struggle on two fronts, against revisionism and against dogmatism. Only thus can the purity of Marxism-Leninism be always preserved, the unity of the Party constantly strengthened, and the fighting power of the Party continuously increased.

The tenth plenary session holds that the urgent task facing the people of our country at present is to carry through the general policy of developing the national economy with agriculture as the foundation and industry as the leading factor, as put forward by Comrade Mao Tse-tung, attach first importance to the development of agriculture, correctly handle the relationship between industry and agriculture, and resolutely readjust the work of the industrial departments according to the policy of making agriculture the foundation of the national economy.

Chapter 2

Communist Party Leaders

THE CHINESE COMMUNISTS call their leaders *cadres* (*kan-pu*), the
designation Mao had adopted when he was reformulating
Party principles after the 1927 debacle. Within the Party, a cadre
is an official who exercises leadership through his position on a
committee or in an authoritative post in one of the secretariats,
departments, or bureaus beneath the committee. Each Party
committee—from those at the local levels to those at the county,
special district, provincial, and central levels or the equivalent—
includes one or more "leading cadre" responsible for the overall
operation of that committee and all subordinate committees.
Other members of the committee are referred to as "working
cadres" or simply "cadres." Outside the Party, cadres hold positions of leadership in the state, military, commune, industrial,
educational, and "people's" organizations, and as such they need
not be Party members.

At the zenith of the leadership apparatus stands the Party
Central Committee (94 members and 93 alternates), which brings
together the principal "leading cadres" for all China. Elected by
the National Party Congress, the Central Committee met ten
times in plenary session from September 1956 to September 1962.
It has the power to elect the membership of the central Party
organs, including the Political Bureau, the Standing Committee of
the Political Bureau, the Secretariat, and the Central Control
Commission. Also elected by the Central Committee, the Chairman
of the Party, Mao Tse-tung, reigns supreme as "Party leader."
Mao's role demands both awe and obedience, and his official authority merges with the charismatic appeal of his personal power.
With his deputies within the all-powerful Standing Committee

of the Political Bureau—Liu Shao-ch'i, Chou En-lai, Chu Teh, Ch'en Yün, Lin Piao, and Teng Hsiao-p'ing—Mao guides the fate of the Chinese nation.

The seven-man Standing Committee forms the leadership nucleus for the somewhat larger Political Bureau (19 members, 6 alternates). The Political Bureau directs the daily work of the Chinese polity through an administrative chain under the Secretariat (10 members, 3 alternates) and through the policy command chain of lower-level bureaus and committees. Led by Secretary General Teng Hsiao-p'ing, the Secretariat coordinates administrative work through a General Office and distributes the work functionally to departments (Communications Work, Finance and Trade Work, Industrial Work, International Liaison, Organization, Propaganda, Rural Work, Social Affairs, and United Front Work) and committees (especially those for Military Affairs, Women, Central State Organs, and Party Organs Directly under the Central Committee). This functional apparatus prepares reports for higher-level policy discussion and decision, makes policy decisions in limited functional areas, and supervises the implementation of Party policies in state organs at all levels, in the army, in mass organizations (for example, the Young Communist League, Young Pioneers, Democratic Federation of Women, trade unions, and non-Communist parties), in schools, industrial enterprises, and communes. The Political Bureau enforces responsive service and discipline through a discipline control apparatus under the direction of the Central Control Commission (enlarged in September 1962; now more than 17 members, 2 alternates).

In theory, the central leadership apparatus, and especially the Central Committee, is responsible to the general Party membership, which expresses its will through congresses. In practice, however, the congresses, which meet infrequently, have been little more than sounding boards for Political Bureau policies and convocations for morale and propaganda purposes.

The initial selections in this chapter elaborate the basic Communist doctrines on Party leaders and cadres. From this background on the general elite, the selections turn more specifically to the "Party leader"—that is, to Mao Tse-tung and his chosen successor, Liu Shao-ch'i. The selections picture Mao as early as the pivotal post-1927 period and reveal the many dimensions of his official personality. The steadfast leader, the skillful organizer, the fatherly officer who scorns ostentation and flattery, the practical peasant, the athlete, the all-wise scholar, and the creative intellectual vie for attention in the Party-sponsored image of Mao Tse-tung. Now 70, Mao's "real" personality lies submerged in the depths of praise and publicity; his public and private selves have fused. Yet, through the years of fawning attention, the Party has maintained that Mao has successfully withstood the temptations of public hero worship and thereby sidestepped Stalin's cardinal sin, the cult of individual personality.

Mao consciously attempts to symbolize the "unique contribution" of the Chinese revolution to international communism and foreign "national liberation movements" and has increasingly devoted his efforts to fortifying the symbolic myth. Stepping down from the chairmanship of the Chinese People's Republic in favor of Liu Shao-ch'i in 1959, Mao has remained aloof from the economic calamities and policy failures. He has issued only vague, brief statements in recent years and has not delivered a major address since the 1957 *On the Correct Handling of Contradictions Among the People*. Rumors persist that illness and advancing years have seriously impaired Mao's health, but somehow he continues to greet selected foreign delegations and to chair important meetings.

His eventual death may not long precede that of Liu Shao-ch'i. Probably in his middle or late sixties, Liu remains Mao's chief lieutenant, and together Mao and Liu personify the distinguishing characteristics of the senior Chinese Communist elite: shared revolutionary experiences, remarkable personal careers, long and tested service, and advancing age. Liu's biography, however, does not duplicate Mao's. Trained in the Soviet Union, Liu returned to China as a dynamic and sometimes doctrinaire young leader. No task proved too challenging for Liu, whose principal early experiences were gained in China's struggling trade-union movement. In the years after 1927—in the course of wide travels throughout China—Liu operated in the Communist underground and accepted vital organizational and propaganda tasks. When the Red Army retreated on the Long March, he stayed behind, and in the course of the war against the Japanese operated in the no-man's-land of Central China, a prized target for Japanese and Kuomintang agents. Liu manifests less of the common peasant and more of the professional revolutionary and remains a greater enigma than does Mao. Selections in this chapter and Liu's writings elsewhere in the book penetrate that enigma somewhat.

So pervasive has been the influence of Mao and Liu that this book might have been subtitled "The Thought of Mao Tse-tung and Liu Shao-ch'i." No two men have left such an imprint on Chinese Communist doctrine or indeed on modern China itself. They share the central responsibility for the Communist elite's major legacy to the next generation of leaders: the doctrine of revolutionary operation and the practical system of ideological training. The final selection (page 75) places the fate of that legacy in doubt.

The Role of the Leader

Teng Hsiao-p'ing • While recognizing that history is made by the people, Marxism never denies the role that outstanding individuals play in history; Marxism only points out that the individual role is, in the final analysis, dependent upon given social conditions. Likewise, Marxism never denies the role of leaders in political parties. In Lenin's famous words, the leaders are those who are "the most authoritative, influential, and experienced." Undoubtedly, their authority, their influence, and their experience are valuable assets to the Party, the class, and the people. We Chinese Communists can fully appreciate this from our own experiences. Of course, such leaders emerge naturally from the midst of the mass struggles and cannot be self-appointed. Unlike the leaders of the exploiting classes in the past, the leaders of the working-class party stand not above the masses, but in their midst, not above the Party, but within it. Precisely because of this, they must set an example in maintaining close contact with the masses, in obeying the Party organizations and observing Party discipline. Love for the leader is essentially an expression of love for the interests of the Party, the class, and the people, and not the deification of an individual. An important achievement of the 20th Congress of the Communist Party of the Soviet Union [at which Stalin was denounced by Khrushchev]

From Teng Hsiao-p'ing, "Report on the Revision of the Constitution of the Communist Party of China" [*September 16, 1956*], Eighth National Congress of the Communist Party of China, *Vol. I* (*Peking: Foreign Languages Press, 1956*).

lies in the fact that it showed us what serious consequences can follow from the deification of the individual. Our Party has always held that no political parties and no individuals are free from flaws and mistakes in their activities. and this has now been written into the General Program of the draft Constitution of our Party [see below, Chapter 4, pages 120–121]. For the same reason, our Party abhors the deification of the individual. At the second plenary session of the Seventh Central Committee held in March 1949—that is, on the eve of the nationwide victory of the people's revolution—the Central Committee, at the suggestion of Comrade Mao Tse-tung, made a decision prohibiting birthday celebrations for Party leaders and the use of Party leaders' names to designate places, streets, and enterprises. This has had a wholesome effect in checking the glorification and exaltation of individuals. The Central Committee has always been against sending to the leaders messages of greetings or telegrams reporting successes in work. Likewise, it has been against exaggerating the role of leaders in works of art and literature. Of course, the cult of the individual is a social phenomenon with a long history, and it cannot but find certain reflections in our Party and public life. It is our task to continue to observe faithfully the Central Committee's principle of opposition to the elevation and glorification of the individual and to achieve a real consolidation of the ties between the leaders and the masses so that the Party's democratic principle and mass line will be carried out to the full in every field.

The Elite: Party Cadres

Mao Tse-tung • The Chinese Communist Party is a party at the head of a great revolutionary struggle in a nation of several hundred millions of people and cannot fulfill its historical task without a large number of leading cadres who combine ability with character. Because in the last seventeen years our Party has nurtured quite a number of competent leaders, our members have formed nuclei in every field—military, political, and cultural work, Party affairs, and mass movement; this is a glory to the Party and a glory to the whole nation. But the present frame-

From Mao Tse-tung, The Role of the Chinese Communist Party in the National War [*October 1938*] (*Peking: Foreign Languages Press, 1956*).

work is not yet strong enough to support the vast edifice of our struggle, and we still have to rear large numbers of capable people. Since many active people have emerged and will continue to emerge from the great struggle of the Chinese people, our responsibility is to organize them, nurture them, take good care of them, and make proper use of them. Once the correct political line has been determined, the cadres will become the decisive factor. Hence to rear large numbers of new cadres according to plan is our fighting task.

We should be concerned not only about Party cadres but also about non-Party cadres. There are many capable people outside the Party and the Party should not leave them out of account. . . .

We must know how to judge cadres. We must not confine our view to a short period or a single instant in a cadre's life, but should look at his life and work as a whole; this is the principal method of judging cadres.

We must know how to employ cadres. The responsibilities of the leadership boil down chiefly to two things: to devise ways and means and to employ cadres. Things like making plans and decisions, giving orders and directives, etc., belong to the sphere of "devising ways and means." To realize all these "devices" we must unite the cadres and urge them to work for them, and this belongs to the sphere of "employing cadres." On the problem of employing cadres, there have been in our national history two opposing lines: the line of "employing only the worthy," and the line of "employing only the near and dear." The former is the practice of the honest and the latter that of the dishonest. . . .

We [Mao is reporting to the Central Committee] must know how to take care of cadres. There are several ways of taking care of them. First, to give them guidance. This means, on the one hand, to allow them a free hand in their work so that they will have the courage to assume responsibilities themselves and, on the other, to give them timely directions so that they can put forth their creative power on the basis of the Party's political line. Secondly, to elevate them. This means giving them opportunities to learn and educating them, so that they can raise their theoretical understanding and working ability to a higher level. Thirdly, to check up on their work, help them to sum up their experiences, encourage their achievements, and correct their mistakes. To assign work to cadres without checking up on it, and to pay attention to them only when they commit serious mistakes, is certainly not to take good care of cadres. Fourthly, to employ generally the method of persuasion toward cadres who have erred and to help them to correct their mistakes. Only in the case of those who have committed serious mistakes and yet do not accept guidance should the method of struggle be used. [Despite this 1938 statement, later "struggle" using the rectification method of "unity-criticism-unity" became a regular form of inner-party life. See below, Chapter 6, pages 143–149.] Patience is necessary; it is wrong to label people "opportunists" or lightly to "start struggles" against them. Fifthly, to help them in their difficulties. When cadres are faced with difficult problems, such as illness, difficulties in living conditions or family problems, we must see to it that all possible help is given to them. Such are the ways to take good care of cadres.

Liu Shao-ch'i • It can be seen from our [1945] Party Constitution that the leading bodies of our Party at all levels are of tremendous importance for the Party and its cause. Since the leading bodies of the Party at all levels are composed of cadres, the problem of cadres is therefore a problem of vital importance.

The cadres of the Party are the nucleus of the Party leadership and of the Chinese revolution. Everyone knows that "cadres decide everything." Without cadres, it would be impossible to carry out our Party Program and policy through the masses, or achieve the emancipation of the Chinese people. Large numbers of cadres have been steeled in the course of our Party's heroic struggles during the past twenty-four years. In the interests of the people's emancipation, they have demonstrated the noblest revolutionary qualities of the Chinese people in their self-sacrifice, their profuse creative power, and their perseverance. They are, as Comrade Mao Tse-tung puts it, "the treasures of the nation and pride of the whole Party." But for the sacrifices and efforts of a great many of our cadres in the past, the people's cause would not have achieved so much as it has today. If there are no concerted efforts of the entire body of our cadres in the future, the cause of the people's emancipation will not be able to attain complete victory. Hence the problem of cadres of the Party

From *Liu Shao-ch'i*, On the Party [*May 14, 1945*] (*Peking: Foreign Languages Press, 1950*).

is virtually an all-decisive issue in the cause of the Chinese people. Any comparatively serious mistake on this issue would impair the Chinese people's cause.

Our cadres come from the masses and work among the masses. They should be the leaders of the masses of the people and at the same time carry out the mass line. They are the nucleus of leadership among the masses, emerging from the struggles of the masses and in turn directing the struggles of the masses. The cadres are therefore that part of the masses who deserve our special regard. It is precisely because of our regard for the masses and their cause that we particularly think highly of their cadres. Our regard for cadres starts from our regard for the masses. It is not isolated from that viewpoint, nor is it a matter merely for its own sake. Therefore, cadres who have isolated themselves from the masses or who, instead of serving the masses well, have done harm to the masses do not deserve our regard. The Party must reform such cadres by strict education. Thus one of the most important criteria for appraising cadres lies in their mass standpoint and mass line and in the intimacy of their connections with the masses.

Coming from different walks of life our cadres generally are of two categories: those of worker and peasant origin and those of student and intellectual origin. However, both categories fight and work for a common goal. Of these two categories the first makes up the majority of our cadres. In the first category itself, the cadres of peasant origin constitute the majority. This fact proves that our Party is the vanguard of the working class of China. In the entire history of China only a party like ours has been able to educate and train up thousands upon thousands of distinguished cadres from among the ordinary workers and peasants. It is only under our Party's education and encouragement that they have achieved such a development today as heroes of the nation's cause. This is to the credit of our Party, and Marxism-Leninism—the Thought of Mao Tse-tung.

Each of these two categories of our Party cadres has both merits and defects which ought to be developed or eliminated as the case may be. The worker-peasant cadres should endeavor to maintain and broaden their connections with the masses and their popular style of work. Meanwhile they should overcome their cultural and theoretical deficiencies. The intellectual cadres on the other hand should foster factual and mass standpoints, eliminate their idealistic standpoint and their lack of regard for labor, for workers and peasants, and strive to mix . . . with the masses of workers and peasants.

Both categories are indispensable to the success of the cause of the Chinese people's emancipation, and neither can be dispensed with. . . .

In each of these two categories there is a distinction between old and new cadres, with the latter in the majority. Most of the cadres who joined our Party after the beginning of the Anti-Japanese War [1937–1945] have done splendid work for the people, undergone excellent training, and become well experienced in the struggles. Our Party has been constantly reinforced with large numbers of new cadres. It is only with such reinforcements of new cadres that the cause of our Party may succeed. The relationship between the new and old cadres, that is, the proper attitude to be adopted by each toward the other, is a problem of constant importance within our Party. . . .

Cadres also differ from each other owing to the difference in the nature, record, and location of their work in the course of the revolution, resulting in the distinction between the military and the civilian cadres, between the cadres of one army and those of another, between the cadres of one place and those of another, between the cadres of one department and those of another, between local cadres and those from outside, etc. Each of these cadres is versed in a certain field of revolutionary work but weak in others, and each has his merits and defects. Therefore, they ought to respect, help, and learn from each other, instead of meeting each other with contempt, complaint, or friction. Comrade Mao Tse-tung has stressed the proper relationship between these cadres . . . , and every cadre and Party member must act accordingly. Only with a high degree of solidarity and cooperation between these cadres in all circumstances can our common cause be advanced.

The cadre policy of our Party and of Comrade Mao Tse-tung is, above all, a policy of solidarity among the cadres, between the worker-peasant cadres and intellectual cadres, between the old and new cadres, between cadres in different fields, between the cadres in different places of work, and between cadres of the entire Party. Hence, anything which stands in the way of solidarity ought to be overcome.

On what basis should the solidarity of our cadres be built

up? What impedes their solidarity?

Our Party is neither a family body nor a trade guild. It is a revolutionary political party welded by a common ideology and political program. The solidarity of our cadres is consequently neither unprincipled nor founded on the interests or feelings of personal life, but based on Marxist-Leninist ideological unity, on a common faith in and a common program for the cause of the Chinese people's emancipation, on the correct line of the Central Committee of the Party, and under the correct leadership of the Central Committee and of Comrade Mao Tse-tung. Therefore so long as we are united ideologically, so long as we have the same faith and program to serve the people, and so long as we all support and carry out the line of the Central Committee and fight hand in hand under the leadership of the Central Committee and Comrade Mao Tse-tung, then irrespective of what kind of cadres we are or what place or field of work we are assigned to, we must unite. There is no reason why we should not. Petty differences in personal life and in sentiment shall no longer be permitted to sow discord among us. This is the firm foundation of the solidarity and unity of the entire Party and of all cadres.

Teng Hsiao-p'ing • Truly, if we make strict demands on every rank-and-file Party member, we need to make still more strict demands on the Party cadres. Since the key functionaries in the Party organizations at all levels enjoy greater confidence from the Party and the people, then obviously they have a greater responsibility to the Party and the people than the rank-and-file members. According to a rough estimate, there are altogether over 300,000 Party cadres of and above the rank of county Party committee members. The quality of the work of these 300,000-odd people is of decisive significance to the cause of the Party. These cadres more than others should learn never to become separated from the masses, never to feel self-complacent, never to be afraid of difficulties, and always to be ready to accept criticism from below, to ceaselessly improve their work, and to patiently educate those who are working under their leadership through their personal example.

It would be superfluous to explain the fact that since the

From Teng Hsiao-p'ing, "Report on the Revision of the Constitution of the Communist Party of China," op. cit.

Seventh Congress [in 1945], especially since 1949, there has been a great increase in the number of Party cadres. Nevertheless, there is a universal feeling that there are not enough of them. This shows that there are serious defects in the selection and promotion of cadres. The chief of these is that even today in selecting cadres many comrades still take "seniority" as the criterion. Older Party members with a rich store of experience are undoubtedly a valuable asset to the Party. But we should be committing a very serious mistake if we set store by this asset to the exclusion of everything else, because our revolutionary work is developing all the time and the number of cadres required is constantly increasing, while the number of old Party members is necessarily on the decrease. This being so, if we do not resolutely and confidently employ carefully selected new cadres, what other outcome can there be except harm to the cause of the Party and the people?

In order to keep up with the rapid development of the cause of the Party and the people, one of the important tasks the Party has is to train and promote large numbers of new cadres and help them to familiarize themselves with their work and build a comradely relationship with the older cadres, a relationship of unity and solidarity and of learning from one another. The Party must pay particular attention to the training of cadres to master production technique and various branches of professional knowledge, because cadres with such qualifications are the basic force for the building of socialism. In all localities our Party must train native cadres who are familiar with local conditions and have close ties with the local people. In national minority areas the Party must do its utmost to train cadres belonging to the nationalities there. Our Party must be very firmly resolved to train and promote women cadres and help and encourage them to advance unceasingly, since women form one of the greatest reservoirs of Party cadres.

In the Party's work of cadre administration, an important improvement in the last few years has been the dividing up of administration work so that each division covers groupings of certain ranks and departments and is thus coordinated with the work of political and professional inspection and supervision. The Party should strive to improve its administrative work further in this direction, so that the cadres at all posts and in all departments will be under the careful supervision of the

Party and receive concrete help from it, and the quality of cadres themselves will thus be constantly raised. This is also an essential prerequisite for steadily raising the quality of all Party members.

In the Image of Mao

Han Wei • After evacuating Ch'aling, we reached Huk'ou where we checked our units. We had lost many soldiers; in our platoon, there were seven or eight casualties; we also wasted much ammunition. After a rest, the units suddenly changed direction by marching south, and the pace of the march also accelerated. We couldn't help muttering: "To the south is Kwangtung where a main army of the enemy is stationed. Why should we march southward in such haste?" While we were still doubting, an order came: "Commissar Mao has arrived; all units return to Huk'ou and encamp!" * Early the following morning, we assembled at a grassy yard in the southern part of Huk'ou. We were speculating that Commissar Mao may have some directions which would expose the riddle of the [events of the] previous night. We waited tensely and eagerly.

Comrade Mao was standing in front of the rank-and-file, his eyes surveying the vicinity sharply. He said: "Some of the wavering elements in our ranks have been frightened by the White terror." Our hearts jumped; we stood quietly and tensely listened. He gestured toward several of the cadres in the front and continued: "Your regimental commander, vice commander, and chief of staff have deceived their superiors and subordinates and want to bring you to surrender to the warlord Fang Ting-ying [in Kwangtung]." His words shocked us. There was a hush in the ranks. We suddenly understood why our units were marching southward, and why Comrade Mao Tse-tung had rushed here. We all indignantly scolded the renegades. Comrade Mao immediately dismissed them and ordered their arrest and trial at the revolutionary tribunal. After that, the units were ordered to Lungt'u in the Chingkang Mountains.

* Although "commissar" has been retained in this passage, the actual title used at this time was "Party representative." Some confusion is inevitable on titles, since the term "political commissioner" or "commissar" was adopted in 1929. Han Wei is describing events which occurred in late 1927.

From Jen-min jih-pao [People's Daily], *June 23, 1961.*

At Lungt'u, Comrade Mao Tse-tung first of all comforted the units by commending our stubbornness in fighting. He then asked if it was right to fight this battle. We had been thinking that with results such as these this war shouldn't have been fought. However, what could we do if we didn't fight? We had no answer. Continuing, Comrade Mao Tse-tung said: "Fighting is like a business deal, if there is money to be made, do it; if we have to lose money, then don't do it. Now, the enemy is strong, and we are weak. We can't use the old strategy which is to become fat by swallowing big mouthfuls. There is no usual pattern in war. We must be adept in basing our actions on the actual conditions of the enemy and ourselves in order to change our idea of strategy. Under the principle of eliminating the enemy and preserving ourselves, we must abandon the old tactics." He also talked about the problem of "walking." Even a two- or three-year-old child can learn to walk, but in fighting, walking is a big subject! He gave an example: "There was previously an old bandit in the Chingkang Mountains who engaged in fighting the 'government soldiers' for several decades." He summed up the experience: "Never fight; just learn to run in circles. Of course, when bandits run in circles, it is passive. It is not for the purpose of eliminating the enemy in order to expand their own base. We should make an amendment: Be adept in making circles, as well as in fighting. The purpose of taking a circuitous route is to avoid the strong and to attack the weak in order to annihilate the enemy and to consolidate our bastion. When the formidable enemy arrives, we should, first of all, take him for a walk for a few rounds, and after he has shown his vulnerable points, we must grasp firmly and strike fiercely, so that we can defeat him and get his arms." Finally, he [Mao] said smilingly: "When we can win, we will fight; if not, we will run. If there is profit, we do it; if we have to lose money, we don't. This is our strategy." Of course, then I couldn't comprehend Chairman Mao's tactical ideology very deeply, though I was already aware that the old tactics were no longer viable, and changes must be effected.

Colonel Ch'en Chang-feng • I was posted as a bugler with the headquarters of the Fourth Army of the Chinese Workers' and

From Ch'en Chang-feng, On the Long March with Chairman Mao (*Peking: Foreign Languages Press, 1959*).

Peasants' Red Army, under the command of Comrade Chu Teh. Later I became an orderly. One afternoon at the end of March 1930, when the headquarters was in Paisha Village, Yungfeng County, Kiangsi, Adjutant Officer Liu told me that I would be transferred. At that time, I did not fully understand the meaning of the word "transferred." So I asked him what it meant.

"Transferred means that you'll change your place of work," said Liu, looking at me intently as if there were something important which he could not tell me at once.

"Where'll I be transferred to?" I asked Liu again. I wasn't too pleased because I was well satisfied where I was.

"You'll go to the Front Committee as orderly for Commissar Mao," he said with a smile.

I knew the Front Committee of the Chinese Communist Party, but who Commissar Mao was, I wasn't quite clear. He must be a leading officer, I reckoned, otherwise he couldn't have an orderly. But what sort of man was he? Was he good tempered?

Adjutant Liu, seeing my hesitation, patted me on the shoulder and said encouragingly: "You're a lucky little devil. Commissar Mao is a wonderful man. You'll certainly have a wonderful future if you work with him!" Then he handed me a letter of introduction, told me to pack up my things and be off. . . .

The Front Committee was in the same village, so I was soon there. I was a bit nervous. A comrade named Wu took me to the Commissar. He lived in a typical Kiangsi wooden house with two rooms, one a bedroom and the other an office. We entered through the bedroom. In it was an ordinary wooden bed covered with a cotton sheet. It didn't even have a pillow. I grew less nervous. Judging from the room, the Commissar must be living as simply as all of us, I thought. Two men were talking together in the office. Comrade Wu indicated the man in the chair and whispered: "That's Commissar Mao." I looked at him curiously. His gray uniform was the same as ours. The only difference was that the pockets on his coat seemed to be especially large. His black hair contrasted sharply with his fair complexion. Maybe he was a bit too thin. His eyes seemed to be very big and keen. He seemed to be about forty at most [actually Mao was 37 in 1930]. Talking to a man opposite him, he gesticulated with his hands; his voice was gentle. Although I didn't understand what he was talking about, I felt he was very sincere.

Ho Te-ch'üan • In 1944 I was a Communist Party member. Our Party cell included Comrades Mao Tse-tung, Liu Shao-ch'i, Chu Teh, K'o Ch'ing-shih, and Li Fu-ch'un. At the first session of our Party cell, the Chairman proposed that I be elected head of the cell; other comrades agreed to the proposal. A little embarrassed, I declined the offer several times. The Chairman then told me: "The organizational principle of the Party is subordination of a minority to a majority. Since all want you to be the head, you should try. If you have difficulties, all will try to overcome them." At that session of the Party cell, I became head of the cell.

The Chairman called me to his office one day and said: "Cell head, I have not yet given you a report. . . ."

"You are Chairman; no need to report," I said feeling restrained.

"No! Within the Party all are members without distinction of ranks. Since you are head of the cell, you are my leader." The Chairman was quite serious. It was the first time I saw him with so serious a manner.

I was speechless and, after a while, the Chairman told me: "From now on if I forget to make a report, you should come to me and criticize me."

From Jen-min jih-pao [People's Daily], *November 13, 1958.*

Hung Ch'i • How busy indeed is the life of our respected and beloved leader Chairman Mao! He spends most of his time attending meetings. Important meetings very frequently last until two o'clock in the morning and are then followed by smaller ones. When these meetings have broken up, he still keeps on chatting with various leaders. When he works, the Chairman makes no distinction between day and night. Sometimes, he works continuously for over thirty hours. When it is late at night, he works attentively by lamplight. After about one hour's work, he will stand up and walk around. After six or seven hours' work, he will go to the courtyard for a stroll and exercise a bit.

The Chairman reads documents with the greatest attention. He carefully analyzes every sentence and every word. He draws a lot of strokes, circles, and dots on the documents. He divides some of the sentences into several sections by means of different signs and adds the figures 1, 2, 3, 4, etc. Sometimes, he will delete

From Kung-jen jih-pao [Daily Worker], *January 15, 1959.*

a few things. Very often, he enriches the contents by numerous supplements.

Each year the Chairman spends a great deal of time in visiting factories, cooperatives, government offices, schools, and the armed forces. He approaches the broad masses of the people, tries to understand their work and life, asks their opinions, raises many problems for discussion with them, and helps them in different ways.

The Chairman also pays great attention to physical exercise. His most frequent forms of exercise are walking, mountain climbing, and swimming. In 1953, he climbed 35 mountains and did not give up even when it rained. As far as climbing is concerned, the Chairman is even more capable than we youngsters are!

He was already a good swimmer in his childhood. Even though he is over 60, this has not changed. Everywhere he goes, if conditions permit, he always spends some time swimming. During the period of the Nanning Conference in January 1958, though he was so busy he had to eat his meals in the conference hall, he still found time to swim twice in the Yung River where the water temperature was only 17 degrees.

Ch'en Po-ta • Comrade Mao Tse-tung's greatest contribution to the Chinese revolution is his correct and living synthesis of the universal truth of Marxism-Leninism with the actual practice of the Chinese revolution, which has resulted in the solution of a series of problems in the Chinese revolution. He has further developed the science of Marxism-Leninism with reference to the conditions in China and in the East, thereby leading the Chinese people's revolution to victory.

Comrade Mao Tse-tung says: "The theory of Marx, Engels, Lenin, and Stalin is a 'universally applicable' truth."

However, to correctly apply their theory to China and to transform it into an invincible power of the masses, it is essential to make constant efforts to clear away ideological obstacles and to wage ideological struggles, and bitter struggles at that. For 30 years Comrade Mao Tse-tung has waged unceasing and irreconcilable struggles against various reactionary ideologies outside the Party and against opportunism which took various forms inside the Party. . . . In the course of this series of struggles, Comrade

From Ch'en Po-ta, Mao Tse-tung on the Chinese Revolution [July 1951] (Peking: Foreign Languages Press, 1953).

Mao Tse-tung has proved himself a great master in propagating and applying the revolutionary theories of Marx, Engels, Lenin, and Stalin. The series of struggles which he conducted have served to strengthen and consolidate the Communist Party of China. . . .

It is precisely by relying upon the creative power of the revolutionary masses of China, by relying upon the many-sided, complex experiences of the Chinese revolution (it is precisely on this basis) that Comrade Mao Tse-tung has developed Marxism-Leninism, forcing every kind of nonsense aimed at vitiating or distorting Marxism-Leninism to declare its bankruptcy before the masses. . . .

Without doubt, the very fact that the Chinese people under the leadership of the Chinese working class rose to struggle and have recently won great victories is a fresh confirmation of the large-scale, outstanding victory of Marxism-Leninism in the East; a confirmation that the teachings of Marx, Engels, Lenin, and Stalin are a universal, all-powerful science applicable everywhere without exception; and a confirmation that Comrade Mao Tse-tung, the leader of the Communist Party of China, has applied this science to the conditions of China and developed it with very brilliant success.

The Heir Apparent, Liu Shao-ch'i

Peking Review • At four o'clock in the morning of September 14, [1922], a locomotive at the Anyüan railway station broke the predawn quiet with a long blast on its whistle. Answering whistles came from the repair works and the Pafangching pit. The whistle blasts lasted fully five minutes. This was the call to the miners and railway workers to unite and wage a struggle against the bureaucrat-capitalists—the running-dogs of imperialism.

The great Anyüan strike which shook the country was on! . . .

By the 17th, all the schemes which the bureaucrat-capitalists had so painstakingly worked out to break the strike had failed. Led by the [Anyüan Miners' and Chuchow-Pinghsiang Railway Workers] club, the workers fought on doggedly throughout that

From Peking Review, *No. 42, October 19, 1962.*

fourth day of the strike. They were bitterly incensed at the capitalists for still refusing to accept their terms. There was talk everywhere about closing down the boiler room at the Pafangching pit; every coalface and most of the shafts would be flooded if the boiler room stopped working for even a single hour.

The mine owners were apprehensive at the news that the strikers were planning to close down the boiler room. Furthermore, the Japanese imperialists were at that time pressing the bureaucrat-capitalists hard for coal. With the consent of the brigade commander, Li Hung-cheng, they therefore sent a letter to the club offering to hold talks with representatives of the workers. On receiving the letter, the club gave Liu Shao-ch'i full authority to discuss terms with the enemy. . . .

Liu Shao-ch'i walked upstairs [to Li Hung-cheng's office in the mining administration's office building]. When he came to the door of the conference room, the two armed guards outside were fidgeting and holding their rifles tightly. Sitting in a chair facing the door of the room was Li Hung-cheng, chief of the martial law command; judging from his appearance, this sternlooking man with the upturned moustaches was clearly an old fox. To his left and right sat a representative of the mine and railway administrations. . . . The whole place looked more like a courtroom than a conference room.

On entering, Liu Shao-ch'i examined it calmly and then proceeded to the "guest seat" and sat down. . . . The atmosphere was tense. The din of the crowd was audible every now and then. Unable to contain himself any longer, Li Hung-cheng, twisting his moustache, turned to Liu Shao-ch'i with a very clumsy question: "Why did you people of the club incite the workers to revolt?"

Liu Shao-ch'i kept his presence of mind, stated the reasons for the strike, and, having completed his statement, challenged the enemy, asking gravely: "Now is this a talk or a hearing? Do you want to settle the issue or do you want to complicate it?" . . .

The martial law commander felt that Liu Shao-ch'i's question had insulted his dignity. His face contorted, he banged the table with his fist and declared with all the authority he could muster: "If this revolt continues, the representative of the workers will be the first one to pay the penalty and die!" At this, his guards straightened their backs, and took tighter hold on their rifles, ready to obey his command.

Liu Shao-ch'i was undaunted. He slowly stood up and calmly but with great firmness told his opponents: "These are the just demands of more than 10,000 workers. You may make mince-meat of me but the question will remain unsolved." . . .

Downstairs, the workers' shouts became louder and louder. Shu Hsiu-tai and the representative of the administration went to the veranda to try to quiet the crowd. Nobody listened to them and they shouted themselves hoarse. When the workers saw the two of them appear in the veranda they yelled even louder—it was like a roaring wave, an irresistible torrent drowning the voices of the capitalists. Shu Hsiu-tai, afraid of the angry crowd, ran back to the conference room and appealed to Liu Shao-ch'i: "Representative Liu, please go and help restore order; there's nothing that cannot be talked over."

Lieutenant General Yang Hsiu-shan • The military area command [in 1942] sent us an emergency telegram saying that Comrade Liu Shao-ch'i had spent several nights at P'ingch'uan and could no longer conceal himself. The telegram ordered us to try all possible means to receive Comrade Liu Shao-ch'i that night. This telegram increased our sense of responsibility and our anxiety as well. . . . I walked forward and before long I saw security guards in plainclothes accompanying Comrade Liu Shao-ch'i and our soldiers escorting several comrades on horseback. . . . I had not met Comrade Liu Shao-ch'i before, but I walked toward them and said "Leader, you must have had a hard time."

The comrade on horseback immediately halted his horse and began to dismount. Immediately, judging by his genial face, I knew that he was Comrade Liu Shao-ch'i, whom we had long hoped to meet.

I walked toward him in haste and, supporting him with my hands, said: "Please don't dismount. . . ."

Before I finished my words, he had already dismounted and shook my hands warmly.

Comrade Liu Shao-ch'i wore a long gown made of green cloth and disguised himself as a merchant. He was so thin, his eyes brilliant with kindly radiance, and he was so calm. After a long march, sneaking through the blockade lines of the enemy and marching for 10,000 *li* under the moon, he showed not the slight-

From Chung-kuo ch'ing-nien pao [China Youth News], *June 6, 1961.*

est sign of fatigue on his face. Seeing that he had only a light, long gown, I took off my overcoat in haste and handed it to him saying: "Leader, you must feel cold. Please put it on!"

Taking a look at me, Comrade Liu Shao-ch'i asked: "How about you?"

"Me? I am wearing enough clothes. And I am younger. . . ." I was afraid that Comrade Liu Shao-ch'i would not wear it, so in haste I told him all the plausible reasons.

Smiling and nodding his head, Comrade Liu Shao-ch'i said: "Oh, younger than I! Good!" But he did not put on the overcoat. Instead, he turned and gave it to one of his followers. Smiling, he said to me: "Let's go!" At that moment, I did not know what to say. Fortunately, Comrade Ma Sen handed his own overcoat to Comrade Liu Shao-ch'i and persuaded him to put it on. Smiling, Comrade Liu Shao-ch'i said: "We have taken two overcoats from you within a minute!" But, he put it on at long last.

His geniality and amiability at once swept formalities overboard.

Liu Wei-kung • I am the grandniece of Liu Shao-ch'i. . . . I lived in Peking for eight years without a break. In the summer of 1957, I was graduated from the Peking Experimental Middle School. During my school days, I had a great interest in machinery, and wanted to become a mechanical engineer so that I could contribute my bit to the industrial construction of our motherland. I had dreamed of happy times in the department of mechanical engineering since the day I sat for university matriculation. In the latter part of August, I received a note from the Student Enrollment Committee for Institutions of Higher Learning in the North China Area informing me that I was not accepted. I was greatly upset. After several days of pondering over this matter, I decided to go to Canton where my father was posted to catch up with my studies.

I called on my grandfather [meaning Liu Shao-ch'i, her granduncle] on the evening of September 3. Grandpa, wearing glasses, was reading documents. He asked me to sit beside him when he saw me enter. He glanced over the *Liberation Army Pictorial* I was holding. Turning to me, he probably noticed I was upset. "What are you going to do now that you have not been accepted?"

From Wen-hui pao [Cultural Exchange News], April 15, 1958.

he asked with obvious concern.

"I do not know which road to take. I am asking you for advice!" I said, feeling embarrassed about telling him my plans.

"My idea is that you go back to your native place to do farm work and become a modern peasant," he cut in bluntly. "The countryside now needs young intellectuals with culture!"

I knew that grandpa had read my mind. Staring at him in silence, I thought: "The same line of talk. I have had enough of it!"

"After a couple of years of training in the countryside, you should then compare yourself with your schoolmates who have gone on to college," grandpa said in a milder tone. "You will not be worse than they are."

"I have not been to college myself," grandpa added after a moment's pause. "Neither has Chairman Mao. But, we are not inferior to those who have been to college. Knowledge in the world stems from two sources, natural science and social science. And, these can only be acquired in actual work and training."

Taking another look at me, grandpa went on: "Revolutionaries of our older generation are willing to hand over our enterprise to those sincerely serving the laboring people, and to those who deeply understand workers and peasants without caring about personal gain."

I listened and listened, feeling more upset than the day I flunked the matriculation. I felt my cheeks burning and ashamed. Privately, I had made up my mind to become somebody among the upcoming generation.

"The reason I want you to go back to your native place to do farm work is that more people are becoming primary school teachers or are going to state-owned farms where working conditions are better," grandpa said in a quiet, sober tone. "Very few people, however, have gone back to their native places where the hardships and problems are relatively greater. To forge and train oneself, one should go to the places beset with greater hardships." Then, grandpa added after pausing a moment: "Things in the countryside will be easier to handle with the influx of large numbers of youth with culture [i.e., those who are literate]. It will also be easier to spread advanced agricultural skills. Once in the countryside, you should learn modestly and honestly from the peasants. As far as the countryside is concerned, your culture [educational level] is higher. Other people might ask you to do lighter work at higher wages. You must not do that. You must learn to till the land and win the glorious appellation 'peasant.' "

After listening to grandpa's talk, I gave up the idea of going to Canton to catch up with my studies. "You must not seek fine appearances in the countryside," grandpa told me in high spirits when he noticed my mind was made up. "You must share the hardships and joys with the peasants. Let calluses grow on your hands and feet, and get a dark tan on your face."

Not long afterward, I left Peking for my native village. On the trip, I constantly recalled grandpa's words: "Sentiments are of a class nature. What the United States is happy about we are not, and what the U.S. is not happy about, we are. You will be happy about going back to your native place." . . .

I, who shunned physical labor and was not able to distinguish one crop from another, have been educated by grandpa. To meet the pressing needs of the motherland, I have become the first generation modern peasant in the new China.

A Revolutionary Outlook for Tomorrow's Elite?

Central Committee Directive • The Central Committee of the Communist Party of China today issued a directive on leading personnel at all levels taking part in physical labor. The text follows: . . .

The Party's Central Committee hereby calls to the attention of all Party comrades that over the past 30 years and more our Party has struggled together with the masses under difficult conditions and achieved great victory in revolution. The large-scale class struggle has now been concluded in the main. The arduous task now facing us is to build our country into a great socialist state having modern industry and agriculture. In order to achieve this task, it is imperative for us to carry forward our Party's tradition of keeping in close touch with the masses and working hard under all conditions. This excellent tradition will be carried forward by the system of leading cadres at all levels participating in physical labor so as gradually to combine mental and physical work. It is also an objective of the current rectification campaign. During the 10 years of civil war from 1927 to 1936, many of our

---

From Chinese Communist Party Central Committee Directive of May 14, 1957.

Party cadres and commanders and fighters of the worker-peasant Red Army devoted part of their time to participating in productive labor. During the war of resistance to Japanese aggression, mass-production campaigns were carried out among the troops, government departments and schools in Yenan, and other resistance war bases. Many leading cadres took part in agricultural work, and others joined in handicrafts. These production campaigns greatly improved relations between the leaders and the masses, strengthened the respect for labor of the many cadres and intellectuals, and helped production in the liberated areas. Not a few comrades who were influenced by the thinking of the exploiting classes of the old society have now forgotten this excellent tradition, and they look down on physical labor. A concern for fame, advantage, and position is growing among them. In addition, some people hope to get away from production, and once they do so they are reluctant to return to it. This is a very dangerous tendency. It is necessary for the Party to wage a resolute struggle against this tendency.

As the number of working personnel in all of China who have departed from production work is comparatively large, it is impossible for them to take part in physical labor all at once. With the exception of cadres at the basic levels, all of whom should take an active part in physical labor, participation in some physical labor is confined to only a minority of leading personnel in units above the county levels at the outset. But in principle, all Communists irrespective of their position and seniority should assume similar and equal work as ordinary laborers. . . . This is a great test for Communists: whether they can work for the Party's general task under the new historical conditions. The Party's Central Committee is confident that all Party comrades can stand this test.

Chao Han • In order to build and consolidate their political power, all classes must have their own ruling persons. Apart from cadres, the question of state power cannot be fully settled. In order to build and consolidate its state power, the working class, too, must have its leading persons and must organize and train its cadres. The proletarian revolution is the most profound and most thoroughgoing revolution in human history. It is not a

From Hung-ch'i [Red Flag], *No. 12, June 16, 1962.*

revolution that substitutes one form of exploitation for another form of exploitation but one aimed at eliminating all systems of exploitation and all exploiting classes. On no account may the working classes achieve their objective simply by taking hold of the ready-made state machinery, but must completely smash the old state machinery and build a new state machinery. Having seized state power, the working class is required to foster large numbers of cadres for political power construction, economic construction, and cultural and educational construction in order to carry out the socialist revolution, undertake socialist construction, and build a new society as never before [witnessed] in human history. When the working class was oppressed, it was not possible for it to prepare such cadres in adequate numbers. The socialist state should unite with, educate, and transform the talented persons of the old society on the one hand, and foster large numbers of new cadres on the other. Thus the question of cadres confronting the working classes after victory in the revolution is a difficult organizational task unprecedented in human history.

Ch'en Yi • At present, there is a current slogan among the students: "One must be thoroughly red and deeply specialized." If by "thoroughly red" we mean that one is an ideological specialist and "deeply specialized" a technical specialist, then they are difficult to achieve at the same time. We shouldn't explain "thoroughly red and deeply specialized" in that way. During an earlier period, many organizations called those who devoted themselves to their own work and rarely participated in political activities by the name "white specialists." This is not right and should be corrected. Now our nation is in great need of a large number of specialists. If they can devote themselves to their work in order to contribute more to our socialist reconstruction, to our fatherland, and to our people, this is certainly welcome. Not only should we not object to it, but we should also give them a more suitable atmosphere in which to work so that they can do their work better.

We cannot gauge how "red" or how "white" a person is merely by looking at how much political activity he engages in.

From *Ch'en Yi, "Address Before the Graduates of Higher Institutes in Peking"* [*August 10, 1961*] in Jen-min shou-ts'e 1961 [1961 People's Handbook] (*Peking: Ta-kung pao she, 1961*).

Some persons require more time to do their work; others are not extremely interested in politics and therefore spend less time in political activities. But, if they can accomplish things within their own fields and contribute to our socialist construction, I think they should not be criticized even if they do not participate in a great deal of political activity. The truly white specialists are only those who are forever antagonistic toward the people and utilize their special work to carry on anti-party and counterrevolutionary activities. Since the liberation and after the subjugation of the counterrevolutionaries, the disciplinary and anti-rightist movements, these people have greatly decreased in number. If we do not draw a clear line, and everywhere try to criticize the "white specialist's route," it will affect the positiveness of many other specialists. The learning of specialized knowledge will also be retarded. This certainly is disadvantageous to our mission. . . .

It is impossible to hope that every youth will, within a short time, become a high-level Marxist. We must remember that the concepts of the old society still exert profound influences upon the people. When we deal with the thought problems of youth, we must adopt a patient, educational attitude. We must not take any shortcuts. Chairman Mao has taught us that we should unify all those who can be unified and mobilize all the positive elements in our nation to build socialism. We should carefully remember Chairman Mao's teaching. The more people we can unify, the more prosperous will be our cause.

Talking about the student cadres, your thought level, work attitude, and working methods must still be constantly raised. You cannot say that you have entirely discarded individualism. Using myself as an example, I can say that my own thoughts are pretty complicated. There are [in my thoughts] Communist ideology, the philosophy of Confucius and Mencius, and also capitalist thought. I have participated in the revolution for forty years, and still it cannot be said that I am "thoroughly red." I can only say that the Communist ideology has gained the uppermost part of my thoughts. But it is still possible that I have not completely driven away the philosophy of Confucius and Mencius and the capitalist thoughts. Therefore, in using the simple, executive method, and hoping to solve the thought problem in a few sessions of criticism, we are not employing the method of Marxism-Leninism. I therefore hope that all the comrades in the Party, the Young Communist League, and in our institutes of higher learning will pay more attention to this problem.

I want to say a few words about those youths who came from the exploiting class. Concerning them, we should not unilaterally emphasize their family origin. They are different from the founders of their families. A youth cannot help whether he came from an exploiting family or a worker-peasant family. Being born in the exploiting class does not hinder his becoming a revolutionary. Many leaders in our Party Central Committee came from the upper or middle classes. Those who came from the families of workers and peasants are very few. Nevertheless, this fact did not hinder their becoming leaders of our Party. Therefore, to over-emphasize birth, family, and "background theory" is incorrect. At the same time, we have already had twelve years of liberation. Certainly the situation is greatly different from that of the early period of liberation. . . .

Finally, a few words about the problem of your assignment. It is based on the needs of our nation, your volition, and your specialities. You should obey your assignment. I hope you will go to the poorest areas. Some of you have the idea of "four to and four not to," and this is bad. ["Four to and four not to" means to the higher levels and not the lower levels, to the big and not the small, to the city and not the villages, to the south but not the north.] You should go wherever your fatherland needs you. You should go to the poorest and most difficult places and get your training there. Your thought level and ideological level are not high enough. Your technical level is insufficient. Whatever training and knowledge you have received at your schools are still not enough. . . .

Chapter 3

Ideology

THE CHINESE COMMUNISTS perpetuate Marxist and Chinese traditions when they attempt to integrate and unify all reality as well as the knowledge of that reality. They interpret this "holistic," though flexible, doctrine of "objective reality" with distinctive fervor, however, and confute their opponents with missionary zeal. From the Chinese viewpoint, ideology alone differentiates Communists from all others in the political marketplace, and ideological principles as interpreted by the Chinese provide the point of departure for their decisions and judgments. In the first instance, therefore, Marxism-Leninism comprises a set of methodological statements for the "scientific analysis" of reality and, in the second instance, on the basis of this analysis, Marxism-Leninism "guides the revolutionary struggles of the proletariat" as operational signposts and a program of action.

The key elements that may be abstracted from this Chinese Communist ideology pertain to individuals and to general social groups. Marxism-Leninism examines both the differences and the interrelationships between these two elements, holding, for example, that the individual's perception of "true" objective reality must be expressed in his style of action. Those who correctly grasp the totality of the objective world will work unselfishly for society as a whole and particularly for its most advanced, integrative segment, the working class. According to Mao's definition of "theory and practice," however, the valid "perception" of the working class can come only from practice as a worker, and thus, almost as an act of faith, work on behalf of the proletariat must precede the individual's comprehension of the real meaning or purpose of his action. Thus conceived, the paradox of theory and practice appears to demand the intrusion of an advanced intelligence to direct practice toward the correct understanding of totality. Needless to say, Mao holds that the individual must follow the guidance of the most perceptive section of the working class to adopt those actions that will insure correct thought. In short, for a person to think properly, he must be led by the Chinese Communist Party.

Faithful adherence to Party policy gradually rewards the novice with a deeper awareness of objective reality itself. He "understands" that the essence of all reality is the "contradiction." Contradictions form the building blocks of all that he perceives and comprehends. Fundamental to any concept is the contradiction it incorporates. The contradiction may be simple—male and female, plus and minus, offense and defense—or it may be complex—class struggle, state power, mathematical relativity. The individual who truly comprehends contradictions and who seeks to resolve the central contradictions that arise in his own life will adopt a manner of behavior modeled on Party leaders whose insight he has come to respect. In particular, he must consciously reflect the struggle and tension implicit in contradictory reality. He must make judgments with the air of a man who knows the truth and who suspects all who cannot yet comprehend what he knows. The Party has stipulated that an individual at this stage of intellectual development is ready for admission to the elite.

What is the relevancy of ideology to actual Party policies and practices? Is it merely window dressing for the use of naked, opportunistic power? This question can be explored in many ways and has been extensively debated. In general, Mao's writings make fairly clear the Communist position on this point. His reasoning goes something like this: Practice underlies thought; those who have already attained "advanced" thought must guide the practice of those who have less-advanced thought; practice should continue to change commensurate with changes in objective reality, and those with advanced thought are enabled to anticipate opportunities for new practice prior to impending "objective" changes; and the most advanced must take advantage of the new opportunities in order to retain their relative excellence. An important corollary to this line of reasoning states that those who are advanced must also guide objective reality by a manipulation of practice and an experimentation with new forms conceived by the leadership elite. Thus the making and taking advantage of new opportunities has been incorporated into the ideology itself. In the debate against alleged Soviet opportunism, the Chinese in 1963 said:

> While adhering to policies based on principle, the party of the proletariat must also exercise flexibility. In revolutionary struggle, it is wrong to refuse to adjust to changing circumstances or reject roundabout ways of advance. The difference between Marxist-Leninists and the opportunists and revisionists is that the former stand for flexibility in carrying out policies based on principle, while the latter practice a flexibility which is actually the abandonment of principled policies.

This discussion could be expanded, moreover, to show how the formulation of ideology takes cognizance of mistakes and states that the correction of mistakes—which are inevitable—sustains the progressive status of the elite. That the Party alone can determine opportunities, "principled" policies, and mistakes renders it ideologically infallible no matter what it does.

Although its most important functions may relate to the indoctrination of new recruits and the maintenance of the myth of leadership infallibility, Chinese Communist ideology is not simply a meaningless façade. If it did nothing more than impose a style of operation on Party novitiates and lend credence to the assertion that the Party alone can and should lead, ideology would remain an important aspect of Chinese politics. But Communist ideology also provides a common approach and a common language that bind all echelons of the elite and speed reliable communications. Equally important, the Chinese Communists appear to believe that the real world has the exact dimensions and nature they perceive in the course of ideological study and struggle, and they have manipulated Chinese society according to their perception of China and their ideological goals for it. In part, their running dispute since 1958 with the Soviet Union and their long-standing antagonism toward the "Tito clique" hinge on their rigid conception of the present world struggle and on the consequent importance of Communist Party leadership and revolutionary pressure.

Whether the "originality" of Chinese Communist ideology constitutes "good Marxism" is frequently debated, and the selections in this chapter will not resolve that debate. The Chinese have chosen their points of emphasis from the varied and sometimes contradictory statements of the Communist writers from Marx through Stalin and from their own unique experiences from 1921 to the present. They state that their selections and adaptations add up to an original contribution—although, taken individually, most of their central propositions can be traced to major Marxist writers, particularly to Engels and Lenin. However important it may be as an intellectual exercise, the debate over Mao Tse-tung's originality should not mask the fact that Chinese Communist ideology—whatever its origins may be—comprises a significant body of thought and belief that guides the actions of Chinese leaders. Although some aspects of the Sino-Soviet controversy may be clarified by comparisons of Chinese and Soviet interpretations of Marxist-Leninist classics, Chinese writings on ideology need no such recourse, for in themselves they constitute an important source for understanding the Chinese mind and strategies.

Menshevism and Bolshevism in the Chinese Revolution

Liu Shao-ch'i • During these twenty-two years [since the founding of the Party in 1921], our Party's experience of struggle has been most rich and varied. I cannot now describe [these struggles] in great detail. But of all these experiences, which is the most important? I consider the most important of all these experiences is that concerning the question as to what is a true Marxist, what is a true Bolshevik. Everybody knows that only Marxism can save China. In China there are many people who claim to be Marxists. But what is true Marxism and what is a true Marxist? What is pseudo-Marxism and what is a pseudo-Marxist? This has been a question which for many years has never been completely solved among the revolutionary masses of China and inside the Communist Party.

There is a difference between true and false Marxism, between true and false Marxists. This difference is not determined by subjective standards and claims by various individuals but by

From Liu Shao-ch'i, "Liquidate the Menshevist Ideology Within the Party" [July 1, 1943], appendix in his On Inner-Party Struggle (Peking: Foreign Languages Press, n.d.).

objective standards. If our Party members do not understand the objective standard which differentiates true from false Marxists, and unconsciously and blindly follow pseudo-Marxists in the revolution, nothing could be more dangerous. This lesson is the most painful of the many painful lessons our Party has learned. . . .

The first group are pseudo-Marxists. They are the Mensheviks and opportunists. They usually confine themselves to outward acceptance, to ceremonial avowal of Marxism, but are unable to grasp the essence of Marxism or translate it into reality. They convert it into formulas and dogmas. In their work, they do not base their activities on experience, on what practical work teaches, but on books. In deciding what instructions to give or what policies to pursue they do not draw upon these from an analysis of actual realities, but from books, from historical analogies or parallels.

There are discrepancies between their words and deeds. They talk Marxism, but what they actually do is entirely non-Marxist. The development of objective facts time and again betrays them, leaving them in despair and frustration.

The other group are genuine Marxists. They are Leninists and Bolsheviks. They apply Marxism and translate it into reality. They lay stress on finding ways and means of applying Marxism that best answer the situation and on changing these ways and means in accordance with changing conditions. In deciding what instructions to give or directions to pursue, they do not derive these from historical analogies or parallels, but from investigation and study of prevailing conditions. In their work, they do not base their activities on quotations and maxims, but on practical experience and test their every step by experience, learning from their mistakes and teaching others to advance their work.

There is no discrepancy between words and deeds in this group. They talk Marxism and what they do is also Marxist. They not only interpret the world, but lay greatest emphasis on changing the world. They always preserve the living, revolutionary force of Marxism. . . .

Master scientific Marxism-Leninism, eradicate the remnants of opportunism inside the Party, and we will be invincible.

Method and Purpose

Mao Tse-tung • Pre-Marxist materialism failed to understand the dependence of knowledge upon social practice, in other words, the dependence of knowledge upon production and class struggle, because it examined the problem of knowledge apart from man's social nature and his historical development.

To begin with, the Marxist regards man's productive activity as the most fundamental practical activity, the determinant of all his other activities. Man in the process of knowing, chiefly through his activity in material production, gradually understands nature's phenomena, characteristics, laws, and the relations between himself and nature; and through productive activity he also gradually understands in varying degrees certain human relations. No such knowledge can be acquired apart from productive activity. In a classless society every person, as a member of society, joins with his fellow members, enters into certain relations of production with them, and engages in productive activity to meet the needs of material life. In the various kinds of class society, on the other hand, members of all classes also enter, in different ways, into certain relations of production and engage in productive activity to meet the needs of material life. This is the primary source of man's knowledge.

Man does not confine his social practice to production but engages in many other forms of activity, such as class struggle and political activity, scientific and artistic pursuits, and, as a social being, takes part in all spheres of practical social life. Thus his knowledge consists not only in knowing things through material life, but also in knowing in varying degrees the various kinds of human relations through political and cultural life, both being closely connected with material life. Among these relations class struggle in its various forms exerts a particularly profound influence on the development of his knowledge. In a class society everyone lives as a member of a particular class and every mode of thought is stamped with the brand of a class.

The Marxist holds that productive activity in human society

From Mao Tse-tung, On Practice [*July 1937*] (*Peking: Foreign Languages Press, 1958*).

develops step by step from a lower to a higher level, and consequently man's knowledge, whether of nature or of society, also develops step by step from a lower to a higher level, that is, from the superficial to the profound, and from the one-sided to the many-sided. For a very long period in history man had only a one-sided understanding of social history because, on the one hand, the biased views of the exploiting classes constantly distorted social history and, on the other, small-scale production limited man's outlook. It was not until the modern proletariat emerged along with the big forces of production, that is, large-scale industry, that man could acquire a comprehensive, historical understanding of the development of society and turn this understanding into a science, the science of Marxism.

The Marxist holds that man's social practice alone is the criterion of the truth of his knowledge of the external world. In fact, knowledge becomes verified only when, in the process of social practice, that is, of material production, class struggle, or scientific experiment, man achieves his anticipated results. If man wants to achieve success, that is, to get the anticipated results in his work, he must make his ideas correspond to the laws of the objective world; otherwise he will fail in practice. The failure will teach him a lesson, make him alter his ideas to fit in with the laws of the objective world so that he can turn failure into success; that is what is meant by "failure is the mother of success," or "a fall into the pit, a gain in your wit."

The theory of knowledge of dialectical materialism raises practice to first place, holds that knowledge is absolutely inseparable from practice, and repudiates all theories which deny the importance of practice or separate knowledge from practice. Thus Lenin said: "Practice is higher than (theoretical) knowledge because it has not only the virtue of universality, but also the virtue of immediate reality."

Marxist philosophy, or dialectical materialism, has two outstanding characteristics: one is its class nature, its open declaration that dialectical materialism serves the proletariat; the other is its practicality, its emphasis on the dependence of theory on practice and on practice as the foundation of theory which in turn serves practice. The truth of a piece of knowledge or a theory is judged not by our subjective feelings about it, but by its objective result in social practice. Social practice alone is the criterion of truth. To make practice the point of departure is the first and basic feature of the theory of knowledge of dialectical materialism.

But how in the last analysis does man's knowledge arise from practice and in turn serve practice? The answer will become clear if we examine the process of knowing.

In practice, man at first notices only the appearance of various things, their separate aspects, their external relations. Take for instance the visitors to Yenan on an observation tour. In the first day or two, they see Yenan's topographical features, streets, and houses; they meet a good number of people, attend banquets, evening parties, and mass meetings; they listen to various talks and read various documents; all these constitute the appearance of things, their separate aspects and external relations. This is called the perceptual stage of knowledge, namely, the stage of perception and impression. That is, various things in Yenan affect the sense organs of the visitors, give rise to their perceptions, and leave on their minds many impressions, together with a general idea of the external relations between these impressions; this is the first stage of knowledge. At this stage, man cannot as yet form profound concepts or draw logical conclusions.

As social practice continues, with the frequent repetition of such perceptions and impressions, a sudden change or leap takes place in the process of knowing, resulting in the forming of concepts. Concepts no longer represent the appearance of things, their separate aspects, or their external relations, but grasp their essence, their totality, and their internal relations. Conception and perception differ not only in quantity but also in quality. Proceeding further and employing the method of judgment and inference, we can then draw logical conclusions. What is described in the *Tale of the Three Kingdoms* as "knitting the brows one hits upon a stratagem," or in common parlance as "let me think it over," refer to the process of manipulation of concepts in the mind to form judgments and inferences. This is the second stage of knowledge. . . .

If a man wants to know one or several things at first hand, it is only through taking part personally in the practical struggle to change reality, to change those things, that he can come into contact with their appearance; and it is only through taking part personally in the practical struggle to change reality that he can discover and grasp their essence. This is the path to knowledge along which everyone actually travels, though some people deliberately distort the facts and deny it. The most ridiculous person is the know-all who, having picked up a smattering of second-hand knowledge, poses as the world's wise man number one; this merely shows that he has misjudged his own ability.

The question of knowledge is one of science, and there must not be the least trace of insincerity or conceit; what is required is exactly the opposite—sincerity and modesty. If you want to acquire knowledge you must take part in the practice of changing reality. If you want to know the taste of a pear, you must change the pear by eating it as food. If you want to know the composition and properties of atoms, you must make experiments in physics and chemistry to change the state of atoms. If you want to know the theory and methods of revolution, you must join the revolution.

All genuine knowledge comes from firsthand experience. But man cannot have firsthand experience in everything; as a matter of fact, most of our knowledge comes from secondhand experience, for instance, from the knowledge obtained in ancient times and foreign lands. The ancients and foreigners, on their part, acquire such knowledge from firsthand experience; if such knowledge which is their firsthand experience also fulfills the condition of "scientific abstraction" . . . and scientifically reflects objective things, then it is reliable, otherwise it is not. Hence a man's knowledge consists only of two parts, firsthand experience and second-hand experience. And what is secondhand experience to me is of course firsthand experience to someone else. Consequently, considered as a whole, knowledge of whatever kind is inseparable from firsthand experience. . . .

But the process of knowing does not end here. Should the dialectical-materialist process of knowing stop at rational knowledge, it has covered only half the problem. And so far as Marxist philosophy is concerned, it has covered only the less-important half. From the point of view of Marxist philosophy the most important problem consists not merely in understanding the laws of the objective world and thereby becoming capable of explaining it, but in actively changing the world by applying the knowledge of these laws. From the Marxist viewpoint, theory is important, and its importance is fully shown in Lenin's statement: "Without a revolutionary theory there can be no revolutionary movement." But Marxism emphasizes the importance of theory precisely and only because it serves as a guide to action. If we have a correct theory, but merely chatter about it, pigeonhole it, and do not put it into practice, then that theory, however good, has no importance.

Knowledge begins with practice, reaches the theoretical level through practice, and then returns to practice. The active function of knowing not only manifests itself in the active leap from perceptual to rational knowledge, but also—and this is the more important—in the leap from rational knowledge to revolutionary practice. The knowledge which enables us to grasp the laws of the world must be redirected to the practice of changing the world, that is, it must again be applied in the practice of production, of revolutionary class struggle and revolutionary national struggle as well as in the practice of scientific experimentation. This is the process of testing and developing theory, the continuation of the whole process of knowing. . . .

However, man's process of knowing is never completed. As any event, whether in the natural or social world, advances and develops through its internal contradictions and struggles, the process of knowing it must also advance and develop accordingly. In terms of social movement, not only must a true revolutionary leader be adept at correcting his ideas, theories, plans, or programs when they are found to be wrong, as we have seen, but he must also, when a certain objective event has already advanced and developed from one stage to another, be adept at making himself and all his fellow revolutionaries advance and revise their subjective ideas accordingly, that is to say, he must propose new revolutionary tasks and new working programs corresponding to the changes in the new situation. In a revolutionary period the situation changes very rapidly; if the knowledge of revolutionaries does not change rapidly in accordance with the changed situation, they will be unable to lead the revolution to victory. . . .

Common to idealism, mechanistic materialism, opportunism, and adventurism is the breach between the subjective and the objective, the separation of knowledge from practice. The Marxist-Leninist theory of knowledge, which is distinguished by its emphasis on social practice as the criterion of scientific truth, resolutely opposes these wrong ideas. The Marxist recognizes that in the absolute, total process of the development of the universe, the development of each particular process is relative; hence, in the endless flow of absolute truth, man's knowledge of the particular process at each given stage of development is only relatively true. The sum total of innumerable relative truths makes up the absolute truth. The development both of the objective process and of the process of knowing is full of contradictions and struggles. All the dialectical movements of the objective world can sooner or later be reflected in man's knowledge. As the process of emergence, development, and disappearance in social practice is infinite, so is the process of emergence, development, and disappearance in knowledge. As the practice directed toward changing objective reality on the basis of definite ideas, theories, plans, or programs advances further each time, knowledge of objective reality also deepens each time. The process of change in the objective world will never be completed, nor will knowledge of truth through practice. Marxism-Leninism has in no way summed up all knowledge of truth, but is ceaselessly opening up, through practice, the road to the knowledge of truth. . . .

At the present stage of social development, the responsibility for correctly understanding and changing the world has, by historical necessity, fallen upon the shoulders of the proletariat and its party. This process of the practice of changing the world, determined on the basis of scientific knowledge, has already reached an historic moment in the world and in China, unique in human history, when the darkness in the world and in China is being completely dispelled and a world of light such as never before existed is being ushered in.

The struggle of the proletariat and revolutionary people in changing the world consists in achieving the following tasks: to remold the objective world as well as their own subjective world —to remold their faculty of knowing as well as the relations between the subjective world and the objective world. Such a remolding has already been effected in one part of the world, the Soviet Union. The people there are still pushing forward this process. The people of China and the rest of the world are either passing, or will pass, through such a process. And the objective world which is to be remolded includes the opponents of remolding, who must undergo a stage of compulsory remolding before they can pass to a stage of voluntary remolding. When the whole of mankind remolds itself of its own free will and changes the world, the era of world communism will dawn.

Basic Reality, Mao's Yin and Yang

Mao Tse-tung • The law of contradiction, that is, the law of the unity of opposites in things, is the basic law in materialist dialectics. Lenin wrote: "In its proper meaning, dialectics is the study of the contradiction within the very essence of things." This law has often been described by Lenin as the essence or kernel of dialectics. Therefore, in studying this law, we cannot but touch upon a wide range of subjects and a great number of philosophical problems. If we get a clear notion of all these problems we shall have a thorough understanding of materialist dialectics. The problems are: two kinds of world outlook, the universality of contradiction, the particularity of contradiction, the principal contradiction and the principal aspect of a contradiction, the identity and struggle of the two aspects of a contradiction, the role of antagonism in contradiction. . . .

1. Two Kinds of World Outlook

In the history of human knowledge, there have been two different views on the laws of development of the world, two mutually opposed world outlooks: the metaphysical view and the dialectical view. Lenin said [in "On Dialectics"]: "The two basic (or two possible? or two historically observable?) conceptions of development (evolution) are: development as decrease and increase, as repetition, *and* development as a unity of opposites (the division of the one into mutually exclusive opposites and their reciprocal relation)." Here Lenin was referring to these two different kinds of world outlook.

In China as well as in Europe, metaphysics has for a long time formed part of the idealist world outlook and occupied a dominant position in human thought. In the early days of the bourgeoisie in Europe, materialism was also metaphysical. The Marxist materialist-dialetical world outlook emerged because in many European countries social economy had entered the stage of highly developed capitalism, the productive forces, the class struggle, and the sciences had all advanced to a level unprecedented in history, and the industrial proletariat had become the greatest

From *Mao Tse-tung*, **On** Contradiction [*August 1937*], *rev. trans. (Peking: Foreign Languages Press, 1958).*

motive force in historical development. Then among the bourgeoisie, besides idealism which sheds all disguise and flaunts its
reactionary tendency, there also emerged vulgar evolutionism to
oppose materialist dialectics.

The metaphysical world outlook or the world outlook of vulgar evolutionism consists in adopting an isolated, static, and one-
sided view of the world. It regards all things in the world, their
forms and their species, as forever isolated from one another and
forever changeless. Whatever change there is can only be an increase or decrease in quantity or a change of place. Moreover,
the cause of such an increase or decrease or change of place does
not lie inside things, but outside them, that is, propulsion by
external forces. Metaphysicians hold that all varieties of things in
the world, as well as their characteristics, have remained unchanged ever since they came into being, and that any subsequent
change is a mere quantitative expansion or contraction. They
contend that a thing can only be repeatedly reproduced as the
selfsame thing forever and cannot change into something different. In their eyes, capitalist exploitation, capitalist competition,
the individualistic ideology in capitalist society, and so on, can
all be found in the slave society of antiquity, or even in prim-
itive society, and will remain forever unchanged. They trace
social development to conditions external to society, such as
geography and climate. They naïvely seek outside a thing for the
cause of its development and deny the theory advanced by materialist dialectics that such development is caused by contradictions inside the thing. . . .

Contrary to the metaphysical world outlook, the materialistic-
dialectical world outlook advocates the study of the development
of a thing from the inside, from its relationship to other things,
or in other words teaches that the development of a thing should
be regarded as its internal and necessary self-movement, that a
thing in its movement and the things round it should be regarded
as interconnected and interacting upon each other. The basic
cause of development of a thing is not external but internal and
lies in its internal contradictions. A thing moves and develops
because of such contradictions within itself. Contradictions within
a thing are the basic cause of its development, while its relationship with other things, their interconnection and interaction, is
a secondary cause. Thus materialist dialectics effectively combats
the theory of external causes, or of propulsion, advanced by

metaphysical mechanistic materialism and vulgar evolutionism. It is evident that purely external causes can only lead to mechanical motion, that is, to changes in size and quantity, but cannot explain why things are qualitatively different in a thousand and one ways and why one thing changes into another.

As a matter of fact, even the mechanical motion of a thing under external propulsion is also brought about through its internal contradictions. Mere growth in plants and animals and their quantitative development are also chiefly caused by their internal contradictions.

Similarly, social development is chiefly due not to external but internal causes. . . .

According to the viewpoint of materialist dialectics, changes in nature are chiefly due to the development of the internal contradictions in nature. Changes in society are chiefly due to the development of the internal contradictions in society, namely, the contradiction between the productive forces and the relations of production, the contradiction between the classes, and the contradiction between the old and the new; it is the development of these contradictions that impels society forward and causes the supersession of the old society by a new one. . . .

2. The Universality of Contradiction

For convenience in exposition, I shall start with the universality of contradiction, and then proceed to the particularity of contradiction. The universality of contradiction can be briefly dealt with because the concept has been widely accepted ever since the great creators and continuators of Marxism—Marx, Engels, Lenin, and Stalin—established the materialist-dialectical world outlook and applied materialist dialectics with remarkable success in analyzing human history and natural history, and in changing society and nature (as in the Soviet Union); but many comrades, especially the doctrinaires, are still not clear about the problem of the particularity of contradiction. They do not understand that the universality of contradiction resides in the particularity of contradiction. Nor do they understand the importance of studying the particularity of contradiction in things confronting us in order to guide us further in revolutionary practice. Therefore, this problem calls for special attention and needs to be explained fully. Accordingly, in analyzing the law of contradiction in things, we start with the universality of contradiction, then proceed with special care to the particularity of contradiction, and finally return to the universality of contradiction.

The universality or absoluteness of contradiction has a two-fold meaning. One is that contradiction exists in the process of development of all things and the other is that in the process of development of each thing a movement of opposites exists from beginning to end. . . .

In war, offense and defense, advance and retreat, victory and defeat are all contradictions. The one cannot exist without the other. The two sides, at once in conflict and in combination with each other, constitute the totality of war, impelling its development, and solving its problems.

Every difference in man's concepts should be regarded as reflecting an objective contradiction. Objective contradictions, reflected in subjective thinking, set going the movement of opposites in concepts, impel the development of thinking, and ceaselessly solve the problems of thought.

Opposition and struggle between different ideas constantly occur within the Party, reflecting contradictions between the classes and between the old and the new in society. If in the Party there were no contradictions and no ideological struggles to solve them, the life of the Party would come to an end.

It is thus already clear that in simple as well as complex forms of motion, in objective as well as ideological phenomena, universally and in all processes, contradiction exists. . . .

How does a new process begin? In this way: when the old unity and its constituent opposites yield place to a new unity and its constituent opposites a new process begins to succeed the old. The old process is completed and the new one begins. The new process itself contains new contradictions, which now begin their own development. . . .

3. The Particularity of Contradiction

As has been shown, the universality and absoluteness of contradiction means that contradiction exists in and runs through the whole process of development of all things. Let us now take up the particularity and relativity of contradiction.

This problem should be studied from several angles.

First, the contradiction in each form of motion of matter has its particularity. Our knowledge of matter is a knowledge of the forms of its motion, because there is nothing in the world except matter in motion and this motion must assume a certain form.

In considering each form of motion, we must take into account the features common to all forms. But what is especially important and constitutes the basis of our knowledge is that we must take note of the distinguishing features, namely, the qualitative difference between one form of motion and other forms. Only when we have done this can we distinguish between things. Any form of motion contains within itself its own particular contradiction. This particular contradiction constitutes the particular quality which distinguishes one thing from all others. This is the internal cause or, as it may be called, the basis of the thousand and one ways in which things are different from one another. Many forms of motion exist in nature, mechanical movement, sound, light, heat, electricity, decomposition, combination, and so on. All these forms are interdependent and each is qualitatively different from the other. The particular quality of a form of motion is determined by the particular contradiction inherent in that form. This holds good not only with nature but also with society and with thinking. Every form of society, every way of thinking has its particular contradiction and particular quality. . . .

Qualitatively different contradictions can only be solved by qualitatively different methods. For instance, the contradiction between the proletariat and the bourgeoisie is solved by socialist revolution; the contradiction between the broad masses of the people and the feudal system is solved by democratic revolution; the contradiction between colonies and imperialism is solved by national revolutionary war; the contradiction between the working class and the peasantry in socialist society is solved by collectivization and mechanization of agriculture; the contradiction within the Communist Party is solved by criticism and self-criticism; the contradiction between society and nature is solved by the development of the productive forces. Processes change, old processes and old contradictions disappear, new processes and new contradictions emerge, and the methods of solving contradictions differ accordingly. There is a basic difference between the contradictions solved by the February Revolution and the October Revolution in Russia, as well as between the methods used to solve them. The use of different methods to solve different contradictions is a principle to be strictly observed by Marxist-Leninists. The doctrinaires do not abide by this principle; ignoring the differences between the various revolutionary situations, they do not understand that different methods should be used to solve different contradictions, but uniformly adopt what they imagine to be an unalterable formula and inflexibly apply it everywhere, a procedure which can only bring setbacks to the revolution or make a sorry mess of what could have been done well. . . .

Superficiality is evinced when a person considers neither the characteristics of a contradiction as a whole nor those of each of its aspects, denies the necessity of deeply probing into and minutely studying the characteristics of the contradiction, but would proceed to solve the contradiction (to answer a question, to settle a dispute, to perform a task, or to direct a military operation) after only a cursory glance from a distance. Such practice never leads to anything but trouble. . . .

In the movement of opposites in the whole process of development of a thing, we must notice not only the special features of the interconnections and conditions of each aspect, but also the special features of every stage in the process of development.

The basic contradiction in the process of development of a thing, and the nature of the process determined by this basic contradiction, will not disappear until the process is completed; but the conditions at each stage of this long process often differ from those at another stage. This is because, although the character of the basic contradiction in the development of a thing or the nature of the process has not changed, yet at the various stages in the long process the basic contradiction assumes an increasingly intensified form. The process is marked by stages among the numerous big and small contradictions determined or influenced by the basic contradiction, some become intensified, others are temporarily or partially solved or mitigated, and new ones emerge. If we do not pay attention to the stages in the process of development of a thing, we cannot properly deal with its contradictions. . . .

The relation between the universality and the particularity of contradiction is one between the common character and the individual character of contradictions. By the former we mean that contradictions exist in and run through all processes from beginning to end; contradictions are movements, things, processes, and thoughts. To deny contradiction is to deny everything. This is a truth applicable to all times and all countries without exception. Hence the common character or absoluteness. But this common character is contained in all individual characters; without individual character there can be no common character. If all individual characters were removed, what common character would remain? Individual characters arise because each contradiction is a particular one. All individual characters exist conditionally and temporarily, hence they are relative.

This principle of common character and individual character, of absoluteness and relativity, is the essence of the problem of the contradiction in things; to fail to understand it is tantamount to abandoning dialectics.

4. The Principal Contradiction and the Principal Aspect of a Contradiction

As regards the particularity of contradiction, there are still two points which require special analysis, the principal contradiction and the principal aspect of a contradiction.

Many contradictions exist in the development of a complex thing; among these, one is necessarily the principal contradiction whose existence and growth determines or influences the others.

For instance, in capitalist society, the two opposing forces, the proletariat and the bourgeoisie, form the principal contradiction; the other contradictions between the remnant feudal class and the bourgeoisie, the rural petty bourgeoisie and the bourgeoisie, the proletariat and the rural petty bourgeoisie, the liberal bourgeoisie and the monopolistic bourgeoisie, bourgeois democracy and bourgeois fascism, the capitalist countries themselves, imperialism and the colonies, are determined and influenced by this principal contradiction. . . .

As we have said, we cannot treat all contradictions in a process as being equal, but must distinguish between the principal and the secondary, and pay particular attention to grasping the principal. Now, in a given contradiction, whether principal or secondary, can we treat its two contradictory aspects as being equal? No. The development of the contradictory aspects in a contradiction is uneven. Sometimes there may appear to be a balance of forces, but that is only temporary and relative, while unevenness remains fundamental. Of the two contradictory aspects, one must be the principal and the other secondary. The principal aspect is that which plays the leading role in the contradiction. The quality of a thing is mainly determined by the principal aspect of the contradiction which has become dominant.

But this situation is by no means static; the principal and the nonprincipal aspects of a contradiction transform themselves into each other and the quality of a thing changes accordingly. In a certain process or at a certain stage in the development of a contradiction, the principal aspect is A and the nonprincipal aspect is B, but at another stage or in another process, the roles are reversed; this change is determined by the extent of the increase or decrease in the strength with which each of the two aspects struggles against the other in the development of a thing.

We often speak of "the old making room for the new." This is a universal and inviolable law. In this process, a thing is transformed into something else according to its nature and the conditions surrounding it by different forms of leap. Between the new and the old aspect of a thing there is a contradiction which gives rise to a series of intricate struggles. As a result, the new and minor aspect grows and becomes dominant while the old and major aspect dwindles and gradually approaches extinction. The moment the new aspect becomes dominant, the old thing changes qualitatively into the new thing. Thus the quality of a thing is mainly determined by the principal aspect of the contradiction that has become dominant. When the principal aspect of the contradiction which has become dominant undergoes a change, the quality of a thing changes accordingly. . . .

5. The Identity and Struggle of the Aspects of a Contradiction

Having understood the universality and particularity of contradiction, we must proceed to study the identity and struggle of the aspects of a contradiction.

Identity, unity, coincidence, interpermeation, interpenetration, interdependence, interconnection, or cooperation—all these different terms mean the same thing and refer to the following two conditions: first, each of the two aspects of a contradiction in the process of development presupposes its existence in the other aspect and both aspects coexist in an entity; second, each of the two contradictory aspects, according to given conditions, tends to transform itself into the other. This is what is meant by identity. . . .

The contradictory aspects in every process exclude each other, struggle with each other, and are opposed to each other. Such contradictory aspects exist in the development of all things in the world and in man's thought without exception. A simple process has only one pair of opposites, while a complex process has more.

Various pairs of opposites are in turn opposed to one another. In this way all things in the objective world and man's thought are formed and impelled to move.

Thus it appears that there is an utter lack of identity or unity. How then can we speak of identity or unity?

The fact is that a contradictory aspect cannot exist all by itself. If there is not the opposite aspect, each aspect loses the condition of its existence. Just imagine, can one of the aspects of a contradiction in things or in concepts exist apart from the other? Without life, there would be no death; without death, there would also be no life. Without above, there would be no below; without below, there would also be no above. . . .

But is it enough to say merely that the opposite aspects condition each other's existence, that is, their identity enables them to coexist in an entity? No. The matter does not end with their interdependence; what is more important is their transformation into each other. That is to say, each of the opposite aspects within a thing, owing to certain conditions, tends to transform itself into the other, to transfer itself to the position of its opposite. This is the second meaning of the identity of contradiction. . . .

All processes have a beginning and an end and transform themselves into their opposites. The stability of all processes is relative, but the mutability manifested in the transformation of one process into another is absolute.

The movement of all things assumes either one of the two forms: relative rest and conspicuous change. Both forms are caused by the struggle of the opposites within a thing. When the movement assumes the first form, it only undergoes a quantitative but not a qualitative change and consequently appears in a state of seeming rest. When it assumes the second form, it has already reached a certain culminating point of the quantitative change of the first form, caused the dissolution of the entity, produced a qualitative change, and consequently appears as conspicuous change. . . .

6. The Role of Antagonism in Contradiction

One of the questions concerning the struggle within the contradiction is: What is antagonism? Our answer is: Antagonism is one form of struggle within the contradiction, but not the only form.

In human history, class antagonism exists as a particular manifestation of the struggle within the contradiction. There is contradiction between the exploiting class and the exploited class, the two classes which, opposed as they are, coexist for a long time in the same slave, feudal, or capitalist society, and struggle with each other; but it is not until this contradiction has developed to a certain stage that the two classes adopt the form of open antagonism which develops into revolution. The transformation of peace into war in a class society is also a case in point. . . .

However, we must study the specific conditions of various kinds of struggle within the contradiction and should not inappropriately impose this formula on everything. Contradiction and struggle are universal, absolute, but the methods of solving them, that is, the forms of struggle, differ according to the nature of the contradictions. Some contradictions are characterized by open antagonism, others are not. Based on the specific development of things, some contradictions, originally not yet antagonistic, develop and become antagonistic, while others, originally antagonistic, develop and become nonantagonistic.

Social Realities of Socialism

Mao Tse-tung • Never has our country been as united as it is today. The victories of the bourgeois-democratic revolution and the socialist revolution, coupled with our achievements in socialist construction, have rapidly changed the face of old China. Now we see before us an even brighter future. The days of national disunity and turmoil which the people detested have gone forever. Led by the working class and the Communist Party, and united as one, our six hundred million people are engaged in the great work of building socialism. Unification of the country, unity of the people, and unity among our various nationalities—these are the basic guarantees for the sure triumph of our cause. However, this does not mean that there are no longer any contradictions in our society. It would be naïve to imagine that there are no more contradictions. To do so would be to fly in the face of objective reality. We are confronted by two types of social contradictions—contradictions between ourselves and the enemy and contradictions among the people. These two types of con-

From *Mao Tse-tung,* On the Correct Handling of Contradictions Among the People [*February 27, 1957*] (*Peking: Foreign Languages Press, 1957*).

tradictions are totally different in nature.

If we are to have a correct understanding of these two different types of contradictions, we must, first of all, make clear what is meant by "the people" and what is meant by the "enemy."

The term "the people" has different meanings in different countries, and in different historical periods in each country. . . . At this stage of building socialism, all classes, strata, and social groups which approve, support, and work for the cause of socialist construction belong to the category of the people, while those social forces and groups which resist the socialist revolution, and are hostile to and try to wreck socialist construction, are enemies of the people.

The contradictions between ourselves and our enemies are antagonistic ones. Within the ranks of the people, contradictions among the working people are nonantagonistic, while those between the exploiters and the exploited classes have, apart from their antagonistic aspect, a nonantagonistic aspect. Contradictions among the people have always existed. But their content differs in each period of the revolution and during the building of socialism. In the conditions existing in China today what we call contradictions among the people include the following: contradictions within the working class, contradictions within the peasantry, contradictions within the intelligentsia, contradictions between the working class and the peasantry, contradictions between the working class and peasantry on the one hand and the intelligentsia on the other, contradictions between the working class and other sections of the working people on the one hand and the national bourgeoisie on the other, contradictions within the national bourgeoisie, and so on. Our people's government is a government that truly represents the interests of the people and serves the people, yet certain contradictions do exist between the government and the masses. These include contradiction between the interests of the state, collective interests, and individual interests; between democracy and centralism; between those in positions of leadership and the led; and contradictions arising from the bureaucratic practices of certain state functionaries in their relations with the masses. All these are contradictions among the people. Generally speaking, underlying the contradictions among the people is the basic identity of the interests of the people. . . .

Since the contradictions between ourselves and the enemy and those among the people differ in nature, they must be solved in different ways. To put it briefly, the former is a matter of drawing a line between us and our enemies, while the latter is a matter of distinguishing between right and wrong. It is, of course, true that drawing a line between ourselves and our enemies is also a question of distinguishing between right and wrong. For example, the question as to who is right, we or the reactionaries at home and abroad—that is, the imperialists, the feudalists, and bureaucrat-capitalists—is also a question of distinguishing between right and wrong, but it is different in nature from questions of right and wrong among the people.

Ours is a people's democratic dictatorship, led by the working class and based on the worker-peasant alliance. What is this dictatorship for? Its first function is to suppress the reactionary classes and elements and those exploiters in the country who range themselves against the socialist revolution, to suppress all those who try to wreck our socialist construction; that is to say, to solve the contradictions between ourselves and the enemy within the country. For instance, to arrest, try, and sentence certain counterrevolutionaries, and for a specified period of time to deprive landlords and bureaucrat-capitalists of their right to vote and freedom of speech—all this comes within the scope of our dictatorship. To maintain law and order and safeguard the interests of the people, it is likewise necessary to exercise dictatorship over robbers, swindlers, murderers, arsonists, hooligans, and other scoundrels who seriously disrupt social order.

The second function of this dictatorship is to protect our country from subversive activities and possible aggression by the external enemy. Should that happen, it is the task of this dictatorship to solve the external contradiction between ourselves and the enemy. The aim of this dictatorship is to protect all our people so that they can work in peace and build China into a socialist country with a modern industry, agriculture, science, and culture.

Who is to exercise this dictatorship? Naturally it must be the working class and the entire people led by it. Dictatorship does not apply in the ranks of the people. The people cannot possibly exercise dictatorship over themselves; nor should one section of them oppress another section. Lawbreaking elements among the people will be dealt with according to law, but this is different in principle from using the dictatorship to suppress enemies of the people. What applies among the people is democratic centralism. Our Constitution lays it down that citizens of the People's Republic of China enjoy freedom of speech, of the press, of assembly, of association, of procession, of demonstration, of religious belief, and so on. Our Constitution also provides that organs of state must practice democratic centralism and must rely on the masses; that the personnel of organs of state must serve the people. Our socialist democracy is democracy in the widest sense, such as is not to be found in any capitalist country. Our dictatorship is known as the people's democratic dictatorship, led by the working class and based on the worker-peasant alliance. That is to say, democracy operates within the ranks of the people, while the working class, uniting with all those enjoying civil rights, the peasantry in the first place, enforces dictatorship over the reactionary classes and elements and all those who resist socialist transformation and oppose socialist construction. By civil rights, we mean, politically, freedom and democratic rights.

But this freedom is freedom with leadership and this democracy is democracy under centralized guidance, not anarchy. Anarchy does not conform to the interests or wishes of the people.

Certain people in our country were delighted when the Hungarian events [in 1956] took place. They hoped that something similar would happen in China, that thousands upon thousands of people would demonstrate in the streets against the people's government. Such hopes ran counter to the interests of the masses and therefore could not possibly get their support. In Hungary, a section of the people, deceived by domestic and foreign counter-revolutionaries, made the mistake of resorting to acts of violence against the people's government, with the result that both the state and the people suffered for it. The damage done to the country's economy in a few weeks of rioting will take a long time to repair. There were other people in our country who took a wavering attitude toward the Hungarian events because they were ignorant about the actual world situation. They felt that there was too little freedom under our people's democracy and that there was more freedom under Western parliamentary democracy. They ask for the adoption of the two-party system of the West, where one party is in office and the other out of office. But this so-called two-party system is nothing but a means of maintaining the dictatorship of the bourgeoisie; in no circumstances can it safeguard the freedom of the working people. As a matter of fact, freedom and democracy cannot exist in the abstract, they only exist in the concrete. In a society where there is class struggle, when the exploiting classes are free to exploit the working people the working people will have no freedom from being exploited; when there is democracy for the bourgeoisie there can be no democracy for the proletariat and other working people. In some capitalist countries the Communist Parties are allowed to exist legally but only to the extent that they do not endanger the fundamental interests of the bourgeoisie; beyond that they are not permitted legal existence. Those who demand freedom and democracy in the abstract regard democracy as an end and not a means. Democracy sometimes seems to be an end, but it is in fact only a means. Marxism teaches us that democracy is part of the superstructure and belongs to the category of politics. That is to say, in the last analysis, it serves the economic base. The same is true of freedom. Both democracy and freedom are relative, not absolute, and they come into being and develop in specific historical circumstances. Within the ranks of our people, democracy stands in relation to centralism, and freedom to discipline. They are two conflicting aspects of a single entity, contradictory as well as united, and we should not onesidedly emphasize one to the denial of the other. Within the ranks of the people, we cannot do without freedom, nor can we do without discipline; we cannot do without democracy, nor can we do without centralism. Our democratic centralism means the unity of democracy and centralism and the unity of freedom and discipline. Under this system, the people enjoy a wide measure of democracy and freedom, but at the same time they have to keep themselves within the bounds of socialist discipline. All this is well understood by the people.

While we stand for freedom with leadership and democracy under centralized guidance, in no sense do we mean that coercive measures should be taken to settle ideological matters and questions involving the distinction between right and wrong among the people. Any attempt to deal with ideological matters or questions involving right and wrong by administrative orders or coercive measures will not only be ineffective but harmful. We cannot abolish religion by administrative orders; nor can we force people not to believe in it. We cannot compel people to give up idealism, any more than we can force them to believe in Marxism. In settling matters of an ideological nature or controversial issues among the people, we can only use democratic methods,

methods of discussion, of criticism, of persuasion and education, not coercive, high-handed methods. In order to carry on their production and studies effectively and to order their lives properly, the people want their government, the leaders of productive work and of educational and cultural bodies, to issue suitable orders of an obligatory nature. It is common sense that the maintenance of law and order would be impossible without administrative orders. Administrative orders and the method of persuasion and education complement each other in solving contradictions among the people. Administrative orders issued for the maintenance of social order must be accompanied by persuasion and education, for in many cases administrative orders alone will not work.

In 1942, we worked out the formula "unity–criticism–unity" to describe this democratic method of resolving contradictions among the people. To elaborate, this means to start off with a desire for unity and resolve contradictions through criticism or struggle so as to achieve a new unity on a new basis. Our experience shows that this is a proper method of resolving contradictions among the people. . . .

The basic contradictions in socialist society are still those between the relations of production and the productive forces, and between the superstructure and the economic base. These contradictions, however, are fundamentally different in character and have different features from contradictions between the relations of production and the productive forces and between the superstructure and the economic base in the old societies. The present social system of our country is far superior to that of the old days. If this were not so, the old system would not have been overthrown and the new system could not have been set up. When we say that socialist relations of production are better suited than the old relations of production to the development of the productive forces, we mean that the former permits the productive forces to develop at a speed unparalleled in the old society, so that production can expand steadily and the constantly growing needs of the people can be met step by step. . . . Only socialism can save China. The socialist system has promoted the rapid development of the productive forces of our country—this is a fact that even our enemies abroad have had to acknowledge. . . .

To sum up, socialist relations of production have been established; they are suited to the development of the productive forces, but they are still far from perfect, and their imperfect aspects stand in contradiction to the development of the productive forces. There is conformity as well as contradiction between the relations of production and the development of the productive forces; similarly, there is conformity as well as contradiction between the superstructure and the economic base. The superstructure—our state institutions of people's democratic dictatorship and its laws, and socialist ideology under the guidance of Marxism-Leninism—has played a positive role in facilitating the victory of socialist transformation and establishment of a socialist organization of labor; it is suited to the socialist economic base, that is, socialist relations of production. But survivals of bourgeois ideology, bureaucratic ways of doing things in our state organs, and flaws in certain links of our state institutions stand in contradiction to the economic base of socialism. We must continue to resolve such contradictions in the light of specific conditions. Of course, as these contradictions are resolved, new problems and new contradictions will emerge and call for solution. For instance, a constant process of readjustment through state planning is needed to deal with the contradiction between production and the needs of society, which will long remain as an objective reality. Every year our country draws up an economic plan in an effort to establish a proper ratio between accumulation and consumption and achieve a balance between production and the needs of society. By "balance" we mean a temporary, relative unity of opposites. By the end of each year, such a balance, taken as a whole, is upset by the struggle of opposites, the unity achieved undergoes a change, balance becomes imbalance, unity becomes disunity, and once again it is necessary to work out a balance and unity for the next year. This is the superior quality of our planned economy. As a matter of fact, this balance and unity is partially upset every month and every quarter, and partial readjustments are called for. Sometimes, because our arrangements do not correspond to objective reality, contradictions arise and the balance is upset; this is what we call making a mistake. Contradictions arise continually and are continually resolved; this is the dialectical law of the development of things.

This is how things stand today: The turbulent class struggles waged by the masses on a large scale characteristic of the revolutionary periods have, in the main, concluded, but class struggle is not entirely over. While the broad masses of the people welcome the new system, they are not yet quite accustomed to it. Government workers are not sufficiently experienced, and should continue to examine and explore ways of dealing with questions relating to specific policies.

In other words, time is needed for our socialist system to grow and consolidate itself, for the masses to get accustomed to the new system, and for government workers to study and acquire experience. It is imperative that at this juncture we raise the question of distinguishing contradictions among the people from contradictions between ourselves and the enemy, as well as the question of the proper handling of contradictions among the people, so as to rally the people of all nationalities in our country to wage a new battle—the battle against nature—to develop our economy and culture, enable all our people to go through this transition period in a fairly smooth way, make our new system secure, and build up our new state.

The Party Must Lead

Liu Lan-t'ao • The Chinese Communist Party is the vanguard of the working class; it is composed of those from among the Chinese working class and laboring people who are most progressive, most outstanding, and most courageous and have a Communist outlook. It is the highest form of the class organization of the Chinese working class. The sacred duty of us Communists is to achieve the great goal of socialism and communism in China, and Marxism-Leninism is the guide to all our actions. Under the leadership of its Central Committee headed by Comrade Mao Tse-tung, our Party has consistently adhered to the policy of linking the universal truth of Marxism-Leninism with the concrete practice of the Chinese revolution. This enables our Party to get a really thorough grasp of the laws of social development and China's revolutionary struggle, correctly understand the development of the revolutionary situation and its changes, put forward new historical tasks in good time, formulate correct political and organizational policies, and guide the entire people in the advance from one revolutionary stage to another and from

From Liu Lan-t'ao, *"The Communist Party of China Is the High Command of the Chinese People in Building Socialism"* [*September 28, 1959*], in Ten Glorious Years (*Peking: Foreign Languages Press, 1960*).

victory to victory. History has proved that the Chinese Communist Party is the greatest and most glorious and most consistently correct revolutionary party in Chinese history, that it is a politically mature Marxist-Leninist party, that it alone is worthy of the high command in the revolutionary struggle and constructive work of the Chinese people. . . .

To insure the unified leadership of the Party we must persist in putting politics in command, fostering proletarian ideas, eliminating bourgeois ideas in all spheres of social endeavor, and guide all revolutionary work in accordance with the Marxist world outlook. Ideological and political work is always the soul and commander of all our work. Wherever the proletariat fails to take command the bourgeoisie will do so, and wherever the Party's ideological and political work is neglected and discarded, this will result in divorce from the masses, loss of bearings, and straying from the path. . . .

To insure the unified leadership of the Party, it is necessary for all revolutionary organizations, including government offices, army units, people's bodies, political and judicial organs like public security bureaus, courts and procuracies, and departments of finance, economy, culture, education, science, and public health, to be brought under the unified leadership of the Central Committee and the local committees at all levels (including the Party committees at the basic level) of the Party in their work and in the struggle to implement the general line and the fundamental tasks of the Party. Since the Chinese Communist Party is a tried and tested political party and the best representative of the people's interests, all revolutionary organizations have voluntarily accepted its leadership, for only in this way can they work under correct guidance, with a clear-cut goal, and give free play to their initiative in the common cause of the revolution.

Ideological Struggle and Personal Torment

Liu Shao-ch'i • Some people do not recognize the importance of increasing the speed of construction; they do not approve of the

From Liu Shao-ch'i, "*Report on the Work of the Central Committee of the Communist Party of China*" [*May 5, 1958*], in Second Session of the Eighth National Congress of the Communist Party of China (*Peking: Foreign Languages Press, 1958*).

policy of consistently achieving greater, faster, better, and more economical results, and they have raised various objections.

Some say that speeding up construction makes people feel "tense," and so it's better to slow down the tempo. But are things not going to get tense if the speed of construction is slowed down? Surely one should be able to see that a really terribly tense situation would exist if more than 600 million people had to live in poverty and cultural backwardness for a prolonged period, had to exert their utmost efforts just to eke out a bare living, and were unable to resist natural calamities effectively, unable to put a quick stop to possible foreign aggression, and utterly unable to master their own fate. It was to pull themselves out of such a situation, that the hundreds of millions of our people summoned up their energies to throw themselves, full of confidence, into the heat of work and struggle. This is simply normal revolutionary activity to which we should give our heartiest approval. This kind of "tension" is nothing to be afraid of.

Cheng Chih • Would the launching of struggles in succession make everybody tense and ill at ease? It is true that life is tense when a struggle is in progress. But we want to ask: Does it mean that we can be free from tension, become animated and lively, and feel at ease as long as there are not struggles?

Since class contradictions exist objectively, and they sometimes manifest themselves in a rather acute manner, with what devices can they be eased? Does it mean that they can be eased as long as struggles are not actively carried out? Definitely not, for the absence of struggles would aggravate the tension. . . .

It is not difficult for us to see here what was the stand taken by those who thought that the launching of struggles would make people tense and feel ill at ease. Why should they feel tense and ill at ease at a time when we hit back at the rightists, but not at a time when the rightists directed their rabid attack against the Party? Why should they feel tense and ill at ease at a time when we unfolded a struggle against right opportunism, but not at a time when the right opportunists attacked the Party's general line? It can thus be seen that the so-called tension and relaxed frame of mind are also [a form of] class consciousness. What makes

From Cheng Chih, "How We Should Deal with the Ceaseless Revolutionary Struggle on the Political and Ideological Front," Chung-kuo ch'ing-nien [China Youth], *No. 22, November 16, 1959.*

the bourgeoisie tense gives the proletariat a relaxed frame of mind, and vice versa. In order to ease the degree of tension gradually, the best way is to use struggle against struggle, and to eliminate class struggle with class struggle. By the time class struggle is eliminated in totality, all people will have a relaxed frame of mind.*

We also admit that as far as an individual is concerned, the participation in political campaigns, the unfolding of ideological struggles, and the review and criticism of one's own mistakes would bring mental agony. Sometimes, he would even suffer loss of sleep and appetite because of nervousness. But, provided he goes through the ideological struggle to enhance his consciousness, he will be able to realize his mistakes, and is bound to acquire another state of mind. He will feel that while the bitter sea had no bounds yesterday, the shore is near at hand today, and there is a bright future for him. He will naturally have no cause to become nervous.

On the other hand, if we shun the struggle out of fear of tension, we are just avoiding the discussion of our ailments with the doctor. Although we can thus have more leisure at our disposal for the time being, yet with the root of the ailment unremoved, it will erupt to give trouble in the long run, and, in the end, we will commit even greater mistakes politically, and suffer even greater agony. . . .

As a consequence, as far as the overwhelming majority of the people is concerned, the continued intensification of the revolutionary struggle will not engender the so-called condition of no escape for anybody, but will enhance the consciousness of the people, and make the ranks grow strong in battle. The key problem here is that people must be able to carry out self-consciously the political and ideological revolution continuously. Provided the people can carry out self-revolution unremittingly, they can forever hold pace with the wheel of time in firm strides.

* But, according to *Jen-min jih-pao* [*People's Daily*], April 5, 1956: ". . . not everybody will be perfect, even when a Communist society is established. By then there will still be contradictions among people, and there will still be good people and bad, people whose thinking is relatively correct and others whose thinking is relatively incorrect. Hence there will still be struggle between people, though its nature and form will be different from those in class societies."

Kan Feng • Often, due to carelessness or lack of strict self-discipline, some people, failing to resist the temptation of bourgeois thinking, end up on the road of moral decadence, then down that road they go. Since caution is a preventive measure, the importance of guarding the first line of defense has been stressed. The strengthening of disciplined thinking can develop immunity against bourgeois temptations. According to some recent letters received, some young comrades, who deeply regret and resent the moral stains on their character precipitated by carelessness in their struggle against bourgeois thinking, are at a loss concerning what to do. Those who are pessimistic and desperate say: "Such stains on the moral fiber can never be obliterated. My whole life is hopeless," or, "It is like a broken carrying-pole. You can mend it but you cannot use it any more." Those who are suspicious or oversensitive feel discriminated against by the [Youth League] organizations or by fellow comrades. When problems are discussed, they always think that they are being talked about. As for the few extreme ones, they adopt the attitude of going the whole hog. What is to be done when one's first line of defense has broken down? I feel we should cope with this problem the same way we treat sickness—preventive measures before getting sick and curative treatment when stricken. To adopt a pessimistic or hopeless attitude does not help in the least.

When a person has made a moral retreat and committed an error, does the stain last forever? Is it impossible for him to change for the better? Our answers are in the negative. After taking the first wrong step, along with regret and bitterness, there should be awakening. Then the feelings of remorse and self-resentment can be turned into strength for struggling, for tightening the second line of defense, and action to regain the first line. There must be resolute struggle against bourgeois thinking in order to reverse the downward moral trend and to turn defeat into victory. There is no alternative. The mistake of the past was a mistake, the question is how to correct it. A person who has erred morally is not necessarily a vicious person. With determined repentance and earnest efforts to improve, he can still cultivate

---

From Kan Feng, "After the Collapse of the First Line of Defense," Chung-kuo ch'ing-nien [China Youth], *No. 6, March 16, 1962.*

a good character. The conditions for removing the stigma are deep repentance and determination to make amends. With a heart brimming with contrition, he can cleanse the stain by correcting himself through his actions. The crux of the question is reform. This is the heart of the matter.

Chapter 4

The Party Structure

THE CONSTITUTION of the Communist Party of China formalizes the elite's concept of its mission, internal relationships, methods of operation, and hierarchy of authority. Based on the Constitution of 1945, the present Constitution was passed at the Eighth Party Congress in 1956. It provides the most important outline used by the elite in China to guide the Party's work and to indoctrinate those recruited to Party membership, although since 1956 Party leaders have emphasized the human dimension of the leadership structure rather than the formalistic details of bureaucratic charts and procedures.

Above its local level, the Party branch, which may be formed on the basis of residence or place of work, the Party is structured along geographical lines. The essential chain of command runs from the primary Party committee to committees at the county (or municipality), provincial (or autonomous regional), and national levels. For convenience, these levels or their equivalents may also establish subordinate bureaus or committees to coordinate local areas under their command, but only committees at the principal command levels are responsible to counterpart Party congresses. These congresses elect representatives to the next higher congress—that is, the individual Party member in the branch does not elect "his" representatives to provincial and national congresses—and elect the crucial committees at their respective levels. Composed of cadres, the committees constitute the real line of political authority. The composition of the Central Committee and the major organs that it elects and controls were examined in Chapter 2.

As the prototype for all "working-class" organizations in

China, the Communist Party structure follows the principle of democratic centralism. In addition to the well-known requirements that inferior levels and the "minority" obey senior levels and the "majority," the theory of democratic centralism adapts organization to process and action. It stipulates that members must participate actively within limits set by the central leadership and that in the process of decision-making cadres must en-

Numerical Growth of the Chinese Communist Party, *1921–1961*

	No. of members	Years covered	Avg. annual increase
First Revolutionary			
Civil War 1921–1927			
1921 (1st Congress)	57	—	—
1922 (2d Congress)	123	1	66
1923 (3d Congress)	432	1	309
1925 (4th Congress)	950	2	259
1927 (5th Congress)	57,967	2	28,508
1927 (after "April 12")	10,000	—	—
Second Revolutionary			
Civil War 1927–1937			
1928 (6th Congress)	40,000	1	30,000
1930	122,318	2	41,159
1933	300,000	3	59,227
1937	40,000	4	−65,000
War of Resistance to Japanese			
Aggression 1937–1945			
1940	800,000	3	253,333
1941	763,447	1	−36,553
1942	736,151	1	−27,296
1944	853,420	2	58,635
1945 (7th Congress)	1,211,128	1	357,708
Third Revolutionary			
Civil War 1945–1949			
1946	1,348,320	1	137,192
1947	2,759,456	1	1,411,136
1948	3,065,533	1	306,077
1949	4,488,080	1	1,422,547

	No. of members	Years covered	Avg. annual increase
People's Republic of China 1949–			
1950	5,821,604	1	1,333,524
1951	5,762,293	1	−59,311
1952	6,001,698	1	239,405
1953	6,612,254	1	610,556
1954	7,859,473	1	1,247,219
1955	9,393,394	1	1,533,921
1956 (8th Congress)	10,734,384	1	1,340,990
1957	12,720,000	1	1,985,616
1959	13,960,000	2	620,000
1961	17,000,000	2	1,520,000

Reprinted by permission from John W. Lewis, *Leadership in Communist China* (Ithaca: Cornell University Press, 1963), pp. 110–111.

courage the sharing of ideas and information before the policy is set as well as the active implementation of the policy after decision. To achieve genuine participation within guided limits, the Party leaders emphasize effective inner-group communications, especially regular meetings, reports, and follow-up supervision. The organizational use of such a process of decision-making presumably obviates the need for coercion, although the Party has established and recently strengthened its apparatus of discipline.

The key concept in the formulation of the Party's structure is membership solidarity. The Party highlights this concept for two reasons: Party members with different backgrounds and experiences have tended to form exclusive, independent groups; and in the very formation of unified group relationships Party members have often adopted the traditional "familylike" habits. Solidarity thus has meant both a Party-wide consensus or "comradeship" and individual commitment to the "collective" rather than to personal associates.

In addition to their attacks on localism, departmentalism, careerism, individualism, and other common deviations from Party solidarity, the Communist leaders have confronted the task of integrating the major "generations" that comprise the Party's membership. The table given above shows the growth of Party membership since 1921. According to Liu Shao-ch'i, more than 80 per cent of the more than 17 million members in 1961 joined the Party after 1949, and thus failed to share the critical revolutionary tradition with the senior membership. The division into revolutionary and postrevolutionary generations must be further subdivided to appreciate the pressures for disunity and diversity within the Party. From 1921–1927, the typical new Party member was an intellectual student; from 1928–1949, a peasant soldier; from 1950–1958, a young worker; and from 1958–1961, a village peasant. Viewed from the standpoint of major experiences, these Party members are also labeled as "Long March," "Yenan," and "new" members. By age divisions in 1956, the latest figures available, 24.83 per cent were 25 or younger, 67.54 per cent were between the ages of 26 and 45, and 7.63 per cent were above 46, but official reports indicate that only a small percentage of the first two age groups fought in the revolution. Despite the fact that the Party has conceived the development of genuine solidarity in terms of "education and persuasion," the obvious sources of disunity have required even greater emphasis on rigorous discipline and careful supervision.

Although the apparatus of the Chinese Communist Party may be depicted in the form of a pyramid rising from the base of Party members to the apex of the Standing Committee of the Political Bureau under Mao Tse-tung, certain elements in the Party apparatus make the pyramidal concept somewhat inaccurate. Certainly a small number of leading cadres controls a great many Party members who, in turn, regulate an even greater number of non-Party Chinese, but the actual form of organizational control emphasizes the "small group" rather than the large meeting, where decisions are announced without warning from the podium. Composed of fewer than 15 members, the small group personalizes the leadership apparatus at all levels of the "pyramid" and provides the framework for membership initiative and participation. In the Communist system an important element of reciprocity thus exists between the leaders and the led, and this binds the individual to the organizational life of the Party. Consequently, it has become almost impossible for a member simply to merge with the crowd and masquerade as an enthusiast without continuous participation and verbal commitment.

To achieve this level of organizational involvement, the Party requires that every Party member join a branch and participate in its activities and in the activities of one of the Party groups within the branch. Naturally, Mao Tse-tung is heralded as the outstanding branch member. The Party press has reported the details of Mao Tse-tung's branch life and has stressed that the secretary of the branch could "not have wished for a more dutiful member than Chairman Mao." In 1959, the Party was composed of 1,060,000 branches organized throughout China. The central figure in the branch is its secretary who has three principal and sometimes conflicting responsibilities. First, he must supervise the training and inner-Party activities of the Party members, guiding their performance and disciplining their conduct. Second, he is the last, and perhaps the most important, link in the cadre chain of command; he composes the reports on which later policies are based and directs his own cadres to implement policy measures. Last, he must maintain the Party as a force among the Chinese people and, specifically, within the individual residential or production unit on which the branch is based. The content of the organizational life within the branch will be examined in Chapter 5.

Constitution of the Communist Party of China

GENERAL PROGRAM

The Communist Party of China is the vanguard of the Chinese working class, the highest form of its class organization. The aim of the Party is the achievement of socialism and communism in China.

The Communist Party of China takes Marxism-Leninism as its guide to action. Only Marxism-Leninism correctly sets forth the laws of development of society and correctly charts the path leading to the achievement of socialism and communism. The Party adheres to the Marxist-Leninist world outlook of dialectical and historical materialism, and opposes the world outlook of idealism and metaphysics. Marxism-Leninism is not a dogma, but a guide to action. It demands that in striving to build socialism and communism we should proceed from reality, apply the principles of Marxism-Leninism in a flexible and creative way for the solution of various problems arising out of the actual struggle, and thus continuously develop the theory of Marxism-Leninism.

Full text of the Constitution of the Communist Party of China, adopted by the Eighth Party Congress, September 26, 1956.

Consequently, the Party in its activities upholds the principle of integrating the universal truths of Marxism-Leninism with the actual practice of China's revolutionary struggle, and combats all doctrinaire or empiricist deviations.

In the year 1949, after long years of revolutionary struggle and revolutionary wars, the Communist Party of China and the people of the whole country overthrew the rule of imperialism, feudalism, and bureaucrat-capitalism and founded the People's Republic of China—a people's democratic dictatorship led by the working class and based on the alliance of workers and peasants. Following this, the Party led the masses of the people in accomplishing the task of the democratic revolution in most parts of the country and achieving great successes in the struggle for the establishment of a socialist society. During the period of transition from the founding of the People's Republic of China to the attainment of a socialist society, the fundamental task of the Party is to complete, step by step, the socialist transformation of agriculture, handicrafts, and capitalist industry and commerce and to bring about, step by step, the industrialization of the country.

A decisive victory in every field has already been attained in the socialist transformation of our country. It is the task of the Communist Party of China by continuously adopting correct methods to transform what now remains of capitalist ownership into ownership by the whole people, transform what remains of individual ownership by working people into collective ownership by the working masses, uproot the system of exploitation, and remove all the causes that give rise to such a system. In the process of building up a socialist society, the principle "from each according to his ability, to each according to his work" should be brought into effect step by step; and all former exploiters should be reformed in a peaceful manner to become working people living by their own labor. The Party must continue to pay attention to the elimination of capitalist factors and influence in the economic, political, and ideological fields, and make determined efforts to mobilize and unite all the positive forces throughout the country that can be mobilized and united for the purpose of winning a complete victory for the great cause of socialism.

The victory of the socialist revolution has opened up illimitable possibilities for the gigantic development of the productive forces of society. It is the task of the Communist Party of China to develop the national economy in a planned way to bring about as rapidly as possible the industrialization of the country, and to effect the technological transformation of the national economy in a planned, systematic way so that China may possess a powerful modernized industry, a modernized agriculture, modernized communications and transport, and a modernized national defense. In order to achieve industrialization and bring about a continuous growth of the national economy, priority must be given to the development of heavy industry, and at the same time a due proportion must be maintained between heavy industry and light industry, and between industry as a whole and agriculture. The Party must do everything possible to stimulate the progress in China's science, culture, and technology so as to catch up with the world's advanced levels in these fields. The basic object of all Party work is to satisfy to the maximum extent the material and cultural needs of the people. Therefore, it is necessary that the living conditions of the people should, on the basis of increased production, gradually and continually improve. This is also a requisite for enhancing the people's enthusiasm for production.

Our country is a multinational state. Because of historical reasons, the development of many of the national minorities has been hindered. The Communist Party of China must make special efforts to raise the status of the national minorities, help them to attain self-government, endeavor to train cadres from among the national minorities, accelerate their economic and cultural advance, bring about complete equality among all the nationalities, and strengthen the unity and fraternal relations among them. Social reforms among the nationalities must be carried out by the respective nationalities themselves in accordance with their own wishes, and by taking steps in conformity with their special characteristics. The Party opposes all tendencies to great-nation chauvinism and local nationalism, both of which hamper the unity of nationalities. Special attention must be paid to the prevention and correction of tendencies of great-Hanism on the part of Party members and government workers of Han nationality.

The Communist Party of China must work untiringly to consolidate China's people's democratic dictatorship, which is the guarantee for the success of the socialist cause in China. The Party must fight for a fuller development of the democratic life

of the nation and strive for the constant improvement of its democratic institutions. The Party must work in every way to fortify
the fraternal alliance of workers and peasants, to consolidate the
united front of all patriotic forces, and to strengthen its lasting
cooperation with the other democratic parties as well as democrats without party affiliations. Since the imperialists and counterrevolutionary remnants are bent on undermining the cause of the
Chinese people, it is imperative for the Party to heighten its
revolutionary vigilance and wage severe struggles against those
forces which endanger our country's independence and security
and those elements who try to wreck socialist construction in our
country. The Party must work together with the people of the
whole country to bring about the liberation of Taiwan.

The Communist Party of China advocates a foreign policy
directed to the safeguarding of world peace and the achievement
of peaceful coexistence between countries with different systems.
The Party stands for the establishment and development of diplomatic, economic, and cultural relations between China and other
countries of the world and for the broadening and strengthening
of friendly relations between the Chinese people and the peoples
of all other countries of the world. The Party is resolutely opposed to any act of aggression against China by imperialist countries and to any imperialist plans for a new war; it supports all
efforts made by the peoples and governments of other countries
to uphold peace and promote friendly relations between nations
and expresses its sympathy for all struggles in the world against
imperialism and colonialism. The Party endeavors to develop and
strengthen China's friendship with all other countries in the camp
of peace, democracy, and socialism headed by the Soviet Union,
to strengthen the internationalist solidarity of the proletariat, and
to learn from the experiences of the world Communist movement.
It supports the struggle of the Communists, progressives, and the
laboring people of the whole world for the progress of mankind,
and educates its members and the Chinese people in the spirit of
internationalism, as expressed in the slogan "Proletarians of all
lands, unite!"

The Communist Party of China puts into practice all that it
advocates through the activity of the Party organizations and
membership among the masses and through the conscientious
efforts made by the people under its guidance. For this reason,
it is necessary to develop constantly the tradition of following the

mass line in Party work. Whether the Party is able to continue to give correct leadership depends on whether or not the Party will, through analysis and synthesis, systematically summarize the experience and opinions of the masses, turn the resulting ideas into the policy of the Party, and then, as a result of the Party's propaganda and organizational work among the masses, transform it into the views and action of the masses themselves, testing the correctness of Party policy, and supplementing and revising it in the course of mass activity. It is the duty of the Party leadership to insure that in the endless repetition of this process of "coming from the masses and going back to the masses" the Party members' level of understanding and that of the masses of the people are continually raised and the cause of the Party and the people is constantly advanced. The Party and its members must, therefore, maintain close and extensive ties with the workers, peasants, intellectuals, and other patriots and strive constantly to make such ties ever stronger and more widespread. Every Party member must understand that the interests of the Party and those of the people are one, and responsibility to the Party and responsibility to the people are identical. Every Party member must wholeheartedly serve the people, constantly consult them, pay heed to their opinions, concern himself with their well-being, and strive to help realize their wishes. Now that the Communist Party of China is a party in power, it must especially conduct itself with modesty and prudence, guard against self-conceit and impatience, and make the maximum effort in every Party organization, state organ, and economic unit to combat any bureaucratic practice which estranges the masses or leads to isolation from the realities of life.

The organizational principle of the Communist Party of China is democratic centralism, which means centralism on the basis of democracy and democracy under centralized guidance. The Party must take effective measures to promote inner-Party democracy, encourage the initiative and creative ability of all Party members and of all local and primary Party organizations, and strengthen the lively contact between the higher and lower Party organizations. Only in this way can the Party effectively extend and strengthen its ties with the masses of the people, give correct and timely leadership, and adapt itself flexibly to various concrete conditions and local characteristics. And only in this way can Party life be invigorated and the cause of the Party advance on an ever-wider scale and at an ever-greater pace. Only on this basis, furthermore, can centralism and unity of the Party be consolidated and its discipline be voluntarily, not mechanically, observed. Democratic centralism demands that every Party organization should strictly abide by the principle of collective leadership coupled with individual responsibility and that every Party member and Party organization should be subject to Party supervision from above and from below.

Democracy within the Party must not be divorced from centralism. The Party is a united militant organization, welded together by a discipline which is obligatory on all its members. Without discipline it would be impossible for the Party to lead the state and the people to overcome their powerful enemies and bring about socialism and communism. As the highest form of class organization, the Party must strive to play a correct role as the leader and core in every aspect of the country's life and must combat any tendency to departmentalism, which reduces the Party's role and weakens its unity. Solidarity and unity are the very life of the Party, the source of its strength. It is the sacred duty of every Party member to pay constant attention to the safeguarding of the solidarity of the Party and the consolidation of its unity. Within the Party, no action which violates the Party's political line or organizational principles is permissible, nor is it permissible to carry on activities aimed at splitting the Party or factional activities, to act independently of the Party, or to place the individual above the collective body of the Party.

No political party or person can be free from shortcomings and mistakes in work. The Communist Party of China and its members must constantly practice criticism and self-criticism to expose and eliminate their shortcomings and mistakes so as to educate themselves and the people. In view of the fact that the Party plays the leading role in the life of the state and society, it is all the more necessary that it should make stringent demands on every Party organization and member and promote criticism and self-criticism; and in particular, it should encourage and support criticism from below inside the Party as well as criticism of the Party by the masses of the people, and should prohibit any suppression of criticism. The Party must prevent and resist corrosion by bourgeois and petty bourgeois ways of thinking and styles of work and guard against and defeat any rightist or "leftist" opportunist deviation inside the Party. In the case of Party members who have committed mistakes, the Party should, in the spirit of "curing the illness to save the patient," allow them to remain in its ranks and receive education and help them to correct their mistakes, provided such mistakes can be corrected within the Party and the erring Party member himself is prepared to correct his mistakes. As for those who persist in their mistakes and carry on activities detrimental to the Party, it is essential to wage a determined struggle against them even to the point of expelling them from the Party.

The Communist Party of China requires all its members to place the Party's interests above their personal interests, to be diligent and unpretentious, to study and work hard, to unite the broad masses of the people, and to overcome all difficulties in order to build China into a great, mighty, prosperous, and advanced socialist state, and on this basis to advance toward the achievement of the loftiest ideal of mankind—communism.

CHAPTER I—MEMBERSHIP

Article 1: Membership of the Party is open to any Chinese citizen who works and does not exploit the labor of others, accepts the program and Constitution of the Party, joins and works in one of the Party organizations, carries out the Party's decisions, and pays membership dues as required.

Article 2: Party members have the following duties:

1. To strive to study Marxism-Leninism and unceasingly raise the level of their understanding;

2. To safeguard the Party's solidarity and consolidate its unity;

3. To faithfully carry out Party policy and decisions and energetically fulfill the tasks assigned them by the Party;

4. To observe strictly the Party Constitution and the laws of the state and behave in accordance with Communist ethics, no exception being made for any Party member, whatever his services and position;

5. To place the interests of the Party and the state, that is, the interests of the masses of the people, above their personal interests, and in the event of any conflict between the two, to submit unswervingly to the interests of the Party and the state, that is, the interests of the masses of the people;

6. To serve the masses of the people heart and soul, to strengthen their ties with the masses of the people, to learn from them, to listen with an open mind to their wishes and opinions

and report these without delay to the Party, to explain Party policy and decisions to the people;

7. To set a good example in their work and constantly raise their productive skill and professional ability;

8. To practice criticism and self-criticism, expose shortcomings and mistakes in work, and strive to overcome and correct them; to report such shortcomings and mistakes to the leading Party bodies, up to and including the Central Committee; and to fight both inside and outside the Party against everything which is detrimental to the interests of the Party and the people;

9. To be truthful and honest with the Party and not to conceal or distort the truth;

10. To be constantly on the alert against the intrigues of the enemy, and to guard the secrets of the Party and the state.

Party members who fail to fulfill any of the above-mentioned duties shall be criticized and educated. Any serious infraction of these duties, splitting of Party unity, breaking of the laws of the state, violation of Party decisions, damaging Party interests, or deception toward the Party constitutes a violation of Party discipline, and disciplinary action shall be taken against it.

Article 3: Party members enjoy the following rights:

1. To participate in free and practical discussion at Party meetings or in the Party press on theoretical and practical questions relating to Party policy;

2. To make proposals regarding the Party's work and give full play to their creative ability in their work;

3. To elect and be elected within the Party;

4. To criticize any Party organization or any functionary at Party meetings;

5. To ask to attend in person when a Party organization decides to take disciplinary action against them or to make an appraisal of their character and work;

6. To reserve their opinions or submit them to a leading body of the Party, in case they disagree with any Party decision, which, in the meanwhile, they must carry out unconditionally;

7. To address any statement, appeal, or complaint to any Party organization, up to and including the Central Committee.

Party members and responsible members of Party organizations who fail to respect these rights of a Party member shall be criticized and educated. Infringement of these rights constitutes a violation of Party discipline, and disciplinary action shall be taken against it.

Article 4: Only persons of 18 years and upward are eligible for Party membership.

Applicants for Party membership must each undergo the procedure of admission individually.

New members are admitted to the Party through a Party branch. An applicant must be recommended by two full Party members, and is admitted as a probationary member after being accepted by the general membership meeting of a Party branch and approved by the next higher Party committee; he may become a full Party member only after the completion of a probationary period of a year.

Under special conditions, Party committees at the county or municipal level and above have the power to admit new Party members to the Party directly.

Article 5: Party members who recommend an applicant for admission to the Party must be highly conscientious in furnishing the Party with truthful information about the applicant's ideology, character, and personal history and must explain the Party program and Constitution to the applicant.

Article 6: Before approving the admission of an applicant for Party membership, the Party committee concerned must assign a Party functionary to have a detailed conversation with the applicant and carefully examine his application form, the opinions of his recommenders, and the decision made by the Party branch on his admission.

Article 7: During the probationary period, the Party organizations concerned shall give the probationary member an elementary Party education and observe his political qualities.

Probationary members have the same duties as full members. They enjoy the same rights as full members except that they have no right to elect or be elected or to vote on any motion.

Article 8: When the probationary period of a probationary member has expired, the Party branch to which he belongs must discuss without delay whether he is qualified to be transferred to full membership. Such a transfer must be accepted by a general membership meeting of the said Party branch and approved by the next higher Party committee.

When the probationary period of a probationary member has expired, the Party organization concerned may prolong it for a period not exceeding a year if it finds it necessary to continue to observe him. If a probationary member is found to be unfit for transfer to full membership, his status as probationary member shall be annulled.

Any decision by a Party branch to prolong the probationary period of a probationary member or to deprive him of his status as probationary member must be approved by the next higher Party committee.

Article 9: The probationary period of a probationary member begins from the day when the general membership meeting of a Party branch accepts him as probationary member. The Party standing of a Party member dates from the day the general membership meeting of a Party branch accepts his transfer to full membership.

Article 10: Party members transferring from one Party organization to another become members of the latter organization.

Article 11: Party members are free to withdraw from the Party. When a Party member asks to withdraw, the Party branch to which he belongs shall, by decision of its general membership meeting, strike his name off the Party rolls and report the matter to the next higher Party committee for registration.

Article 12: A Party member who, over a period of six months and without proper reasons, fails to take part in Party life or to pay membership dues is regarded as having quitted the Party himself. The Party branch to which this member belongs shall, by decision of its general membership meeting, strike his name off the Party rolls and report the matter to the next higher Party committee for registration.

Article 13: Party organizations at all levels may, according to each individual case, take disciplinary measures against any Party member who violates Party discipline, such as warning, serious warning, removal from posts held in the Party, placing on probation within the Party, or expulsion from the Party.

The period in which a Party member is placed on probation shall not exceed two years. During this period, the rights and duties of the Party member concerned are the same as those of a probationary member. If after a Party member has been placed on probation the facts show that he has corrected his mistakes, his rights as full Party member shall be restored and the period in which he is placed on probation will be reckoned in his Party standing. If he is found to be unfit for Party membership, he shall be expelled from the Party.

Article 14: Any disciplinary measure taken against a Party member must be decided on by a general membership meeting of the Party branch to which he belongs and must be approved by a higher Party control commission or higher Party committee.

Under special conditions, a Party branch committee or a higher Party committee has the power to take disciplinary measures against a Party member, but it must be subject to approval by a higher Party control commission or higher Party committee.

Article 15: Any decision to remove a member or alternate member of the Party committee of a county, an autonomous county, a municipality, a province, an autonomous region, or a municipality directly under the central authority, or an autonomous *chou* from the said committee, to place him on probation, or to expel him from the Party must be taken by the Party congress that has elected the said member. In conditions of urgency, such decision may be taken by a two-thirds majority vote at a plenary session of the Party committee to which the member belongs, but it must be subject to approval by the next higher Party committee. A primary Party organization has no power to take decisions on the removal of a member or alternate member of a higher Party committee from the said committee, or placing him on probation or expelling him from the Party.

Article 16: Any decision to remove a member or alternate member of the Central Committee of the Party from the Central Committee, to place him on probation, or to expel him from the Party must be taken by the National Party Congress. In conditions of urgency, such decision may be taken by a two-thirds majority vote of the Central Committee at its plenary session, but it must be subject to subsequent confirmation by the next session of the National Party Congress.

Article 17: Expulsion from the Party is the most severe of all inner-Party disciplinary measures. In taking or approving such a decision, all Party organizations must exercise the utmost caution, thoroughly investigate and study the facts and material evidence of the case, and listen carefully to the statement made in his own defense by the Party member concerned.

Article 18: When a Party organization discusses or decides on disciplinary measures against a Party member, it must, barring special circumstances, notify the member concerned to attend the meeting to defend himself. When disciplinary action is decided on, the person against whom such action is taken must be told the reasons for it. If he disagrees, he may ask for a reconsideration of his case and address an appeal to higher Party committees, to Party control commissions, up to and including the Central Committee. Party organizations at all levels must deal with such appeals seriously or forward them promptly; no suppression is permitted.

CHAPTER II—ORGANIZATIONAL STRUCTURE AND ORGANIZATIONAL PRINCIPLES OF THE PARTY

Article 19: The Party is formed on the principles of democratic centralism.

Democratic centralism means centralism on the basis of democracy and democracy under centralized guidance. Its basic conditions are as follows:

1. The leading bodies of the Party at all levels are elected.

2. The highest leading body of the Party is the National Party Congress, and the highest leading body in each local organization of the Party is the local Party Congress. The National Party Congress elects the Central Committee, and the local Party congresses elect their respective local Party committees. The Central Committee and local Party committees are responsible to their respective Party congresses to which they should report on their work.

3. All leading bodies of the Party must pay constant heed to the views of their lower organizations and the rank-and-file Party members, study their experiences, and give prompt help in solving their problems.

4. Lower Party organizations must present periodical reports on their work to the Party organizations above them and ask in good time for instructions on questions which need decision by higher Party organizations.

5. All Party organizations operate on the principle of com-

bining collective leadership with individual responsibility. All important issues are to be decided on collectively, and at the same time, each individual is enabled to play his part to the fullest possible extent.

6. Party decisions must be carried out unconditionally. Individual Party members shall obey the Party organization, the minority shall obey the majority, the lower Party organizations shall obey the higher Party organizations, and all constituent Party organizations throughout the country shall obey the National Party Congress and the Central Committee.

Article 20: Party organizations are formed on a geographical or industrial basis.

The Party organization in charge of Party work in a defined area is regarded as the highest of all the constituent Party organizations in that area.

The Party organization in charge of Party work in a particular production or work unit is regarded as the highest of all the constituent Party organizations in that unit.

Article 21: The highest leading bodies of the Party organizations at various levels are as follows:

1. For the whole country, it is the National Party Congress. When the National Party Congress is not in session, it is the Central Committee elected by the National Party Congress;

2. For a province, autonomous region, or municipality directly under the central authority, it is the provincial, autonomous regional, or municipal Party congress. When the congress is not in session, it is the provincial, autonomous regional, or municipal Party committee elected by the congress.

For an autonomous *chou,* it is the autonomous *chou* Party congress. When the congress is not in session, it is the autonomous *chou* committee elected by the congress;

3. For a county, autonomous county, or municipality, it is the county, autonomous county, or municipal Party congress. When the congress is not in session, it is the county, autonomous county, or municipal committee elected by the congress;

4. For primary units (factories, mines, and other enterprises, *hsiang,* nationality *hsiang,* towns, and agricultural producers' cooperatives, offices, schools, streets, companies of the People's Liberation Army, and other primary units), it is the delegate meeting or the general membership meeting of the particular primary

unit. When the delegate meeting or general membership meeting of the primary unit is not in session, it is the primary Party committee, the committee of a general Party branch, or the committee of a Party branch elected by the delegate meeting or the general membership meeting.

Article 22: Party elections must fully reflect the will of the electors. The lists of candidates for election put forward by the Party organization or by electors must be discussed by the electors.

Election is by secret ballot. Electors shall be insured of the right to criticize or reject any candidate, or nominate a person who is not on the list.

In an election in a primary Party organization, voting may be by a show of hands if voting by ballot is impossible. In such cases, each candidate shall be voted upon separately, and voting on a whole list of candidates is forbidden.

Article 23: Party electing units have the power to replace any member they have elected to a Party congress or Party committee during his term of office.

When a local Party congress is not in session, a higher Party committee, if it deems it necessary, may transfer or appoint responsible members of a lower Party organization.

Article 24: In places where, because of special circumstances, it is impossible for the time being to call Party congresses or general membership meetings to elect Party committees, such Party committees may be elected at Party conferences or appointed by higher Party organizations.

Article 25: The functions and powers of the central Party organizations and those of the local Party organizations shall be appropriately divided. All questions of a national character or questions that require a uniform decision for the whole country shall be handled by the central Party organizations so as to contribute to the centralism and unity of the Party. All questions of a local character or questions that need to be decided locally shall be handled by the local Party organizations so as to find solutions appropriate to the local conditions. The functions and powers of higher local Party organizations and those of lower local Party organizations shall be appropriately divided according to the same principle.

Decisions taken by lower Party organizations must not run counter to those made by higher Party organizations.

Article 26: Before decisions on Party policy are made by leading bodies of the Party, lower Party organizations and members of the Party committees may hold free and practical discussions inside the Party organizations and at Party meetings and submit their proposals to the leading bodies of the Party. However, once a decision is taken by the leading bodies of the Party, it must be accepted. Should a lower Party organization find that a decision made by a higher Party organization does not suit the actual conditions in its locality or in its particular department, it should request the higher Party organization concerned to modify the decision. If the higher Party organization still upholds its decision, then the lower Party organization must carry it out unconditionally.

On policies of a national character, before the central leading bodies of the Party have made any statement or decision, departmental and local Party organizations and their responsible members are not permitted to make any public statement or make any decision at will, although they may discuss it among themselves and make suggestions to the central leading bodies.

Article 27: The newspapers issued by Party organizations at all levels must publicize the decisions and policy of the central Party organizations, of higher Party organizations, and of their own Party organizations.

Article 28: The formation of a new Party organization or the dissolution of an existing Party organization must be decided on by the next higher Party organization.

Article 29: To facilitate the direction of the work in various localities the Central Committee may, if it deems it necessary, establish a bureau of the Central Committee as its representative body for an area embracing several provinces, autonomous regions, and municipalities directly under the central authority. A provincial or autonomous regional committee may, if it deems it necessary, establish a regional committee or an organization of equal status as its representative body for an area embracing a number of counties, autonomous counties, and municipalities. The Party committee of a municipality directly under the central authority, or of a municipality, county, or autonomous county may, if it deems it necessary, establish a number of district committees as its representative bodies within its area.

Article 30: Party committees at all levels may, as the situation requires, set up a number of departments, commissions, or other bodies to carry on work under their own direction.

CHAPTER III—CENTRAL ORGANIZATIONS OF THE PARTY

Article 31: The National Party Congress is elected for a term of five years.

The number of delegates to the National Party Congress and the procedure governing their election and replacement and the filling of vacancies shall be determined by the Central Committee.

A session of the National Party Congress shall be convened once a year by the Central Committee. Under extraordinary conditions, it may be postponed or convened before its due date as the Central Committee may decide. The Central Committee must convene a session of the National Party Congress if one third of the delegates to the National Party Congress or one third of the Party organizations at the provincial level so request.

Article 32: The functions and powers of the National Party Congress are as follows:

1. To hear and examine the reports of the Central Committee and other central organs;

2. To determine the Party's line and policy;

3. To revise the Constitution of the Party;

4. To elect the Central Committee.

Article 33: The Central Committee of the Party is elected for a term of five years. The number of members and alternate members of the Central Committee shall be determined by the National Party Congress. Vacancies on the Central Committee shall be filled by alternate members in order of established precedence.

Article 34: When the National Party Congress is not in session the Central Committee directs the entire work of the Party, carries out the decisions of the National Party Congress, represents the Party in its relations with other parties and organizations, sets up various Party organs and directs their activities, takes charge of and allocates Party cadres.

The Central Committee guides the work of the central state organs and people's organizations of a national character through leading Party members' groups within them.

Article 35: The Party organizations in the Chinese People's Liberation Army carry on their work in accordance with the instructions of the Central Committee. The General Political Department of the People's Liberation Army, under the direction of the Central Committee, takes charge of the ideological and organizational work of the Party in the army.

Article 36: The Central Committee meets in plenary session at least twice a year, to be convened by the Political Bureau of the Central Committee.

Article 37: The Central Committee elects at its plenary session the Political Bureau, the Standing Committee of the Political Bureau and the Secretariat, as well as the chairman, vice chairmen, and secretary general of the Central Committee.

When the Central Committee is not in plenary session, the Political Bureau and its Standing Committee exercise the powers and functions of the Central Committee.

The Secretariat attends to the daily work of the Central Committee under the direction of the Political Bureau and its Standing Committee.

The chairman and vice chairmen of the Central Committee are concurrently chairman and vice chairmen of the Political Bureau.

The Central Committee may, when it deems it necessary, have an honorary chairman.

CHAPTER IV—PARTY ORGANIZATIONS IN PROVINCES, AUTONOMOUS REGIONS, MUNICIPALITIES DIRECTLY UNDER THE CENTRAL AUTHORITY, AND AUTONOMOUS CHOU

Article 38: The Party congress for a province, autonomous region, or municipality directly under the central authority is elected for a term of three years.

The number of delegates to such a Party congress and the procedure governing their election and replacement and the filling of vacancies shall be determined by the Party committee in the given area.

The Party congress for a province, autonomous region, or municipality directly under the central authority shall be convened once a year by the Party committee in the area.

Article 39: The Party congress for a province, autonomous region, or municipality directly under the central authority hears and examines the reports of the Party committee and other organs in the area, discusses and decides on questions relating to policy and work of a local character in its area, elects the Party committee for the area, and elects delegates to the National Party Congress.

Article 40: The Party committee of a province, autonomous region, or municipality directly under the central authority is elected for a term of three years. The number of members and alternate members of the committee shall be determined by the Central Committee. Vacancies on the committee shall be filled by alternate members of the committee in order of established precedence.

The Party committee of a province, autonomous region, or municipality directly under the central authority shall, when the Party congress for the given area is not in session, carry out the decisions and directives of the Party in its area, direct all work of a local character, set up various Party organs and direct their activities, take charge of and allocate Party cadres in accordance with the regulations laid down by the Central Committee, direct the work of leading Party members' groups in local state organs and people's organizations, and systematically report on its work to the Central Committee.

Article 41: The Party committee of a province, autonomous region, or municipality directly under the central authority shall meet in full session at least three times a year.

The Party committee of a province, autonomous region, or municipality directly under the central authority elects at its plenary session its standing committee and secretariat. The standing committee exercises the powers and functions of the Party committee when the latter is not in plenary session. The secretariat attends to the daily work under the direction of the standing committee.

The members of the secretariat and those of the standing committee of the Party committee of a province, autonomous region, or municipality directly under the central authority must be approved by the Central Committee. Members of the secretariat must be Party members of at least five years' standing.

Article 42: Party organizations in an autonomous *chou* carry on their work under the direction of a provincial or autonomous regional Party committee.

The Party congress and Party committee for an autonomous

chou are constituted in the same manner as those for a province, autonomous region, or municipality directly under the central authority.

The Party congress and Party committee for an autonomous *chou* are elected for a term of two years.

An autonomous *chou* Party congress elects delegates to the provincial or autonomous regional Party congress.

The members of the secretariat and those of the standing committee of an autonomous *chou* Party committee must be approved by the Central Committee. The secretaries must be Party members of at least three years' standing.

CHAPTER V—COUNTY, AUTONOMOUS COUNTY, AND MUNICIPAL PARTY ORGANIZATIONS

Article 43: The Party congress for a county, autonomous county, or municipality is elected for a term of two years.

The number of delegates to the congress and the procedure governing their election and replacement and the filling of vacancies shall be determined by the Party committee in the area.

The Party congress for a county, autonomous county, or municipality shall be convened once a year by the Party committee in the area.

Article 44: The Party congress for a county, autonomous county, or municipality hears and examines the reports of the Party committee and other organs in the area, discusses and decides on questions relating to the policy and work of a local character in its area, elects the Party committee for the area, and elects delegates to the provincial or autonomous regional Party congress.

The Party congress for a county, autonomous county, or municipality under the jurisdiction of an autonomous *chou* elects delegates only to the Party congress of the said autonomous *chou*.

Article 45: The Party committee of a county, autonomous county, or municipality is elected for a term of two years. The number of members and alternate members of the committee shall be determined by the provincial or autonomous regional Party committee concerned. Vacancies on the committee shall be filled by alternate members of the committee in order of established precedence.

When the Party congress for a county, autonomous county, or

municipality is not in session, the Party committee in the area carries out Party decisions and directives in its area, directs all work of a local character, sets up various Party organs and directs their activities, takes charge of and allocates Party cadres in accordance with the regulations laid down by the Central Committee, directs the work of leading Party members' groups in local government organs and people's organizations, and systematically reports on its work to higher Party committees.

Article 46: The Party committee of a county, autonomous county, or municipality shall meet in plenary session at least four times a year.

The county, autonomous county, or municipal Party committee elects at its plenary session its standing committee and secretary, and, if necessary, a secretariat. The standing committee exercises the powers and functions of the Party committee when the latter is not in plenary session. The secretary or the secretariat attends to the daily work under the direction of the standing committee.

The members of the secretariat and those of the standing committee must be approved by the provincial or autonomous regional Party committee. In the case of a city with a population of 500,000 or more or in the case of a key industrial city, such members must be approved by the Central Committee. The secretaries of the Party committee of a county, autonomous county, or municipality must be Party members of at least two years' standing. In the case of a city with a population of 500,000 or more or in the case of a key industrial city, the secretaries of the Party committee must be Party members of at least five years' standing.

CHAPTER VI—PRIMARY ORGANIZATIONS OF THE PARTY

Article 47: Primary Party organizations are formed in factories, mines, and other enterprises, in *hsiang* [now replaced by the commune level] and nationality *hsiang,* in towns, in agricultural producers' cooperatives [now combined into communes], in offices, schools, and streets, in companies of the People's Liberation Army, and in other primary units where there are three or more full Party members. When a primary unit contains less than three full Party members, no primary Party organization should be established, but these members together with the probationary members in their unit may either form a group or join the primary Party organization of a nearby unit.

Article 48: Primary Party organizations take the following organizational forms:

1. A primary Party organization with one hundred or more Party members may, by decision of the next higher Party committee, hold a delegate meeting or a general membership meeting to elect a primary Party committee. Under the primary Party committee a number of general branches or branches may be formed in accordance with divisions based on production, work, or residence. Under a general Party branch a number of Party branches may be formed. The committee of a general Party branch is elected by a general membership meeting or a delegate meeting of the said general branch. The committee of a Party branch is elected by the general membership meeting of the said branch. The committee of the primary Party organization or of the general Party branch has the power to approve decisions made by a branch on the admission of new members and on disciplinary measures against Party members.

Under special conditions, individual primary Party organizations with less than one hundred members each may, by decision of the next higher Party committee, establish a committee of the said primary organizations.

2. A primary Party organization with fifty or more Party members may, by decision of the next higher Party committee, set up a general branch committee to be elected by a general membership meeting or a delegate meeting. Under a general branch committee a number of branches may be formed in accordance with divisions based on production, work, or residence. The general branch committee has the power to approve decisions made by a branch on the admission of new members and on disciplinary measures against Party members.

Under special conditions, a general branch committee may, by decision of the next higher Party committee, be set up in a primary Party organization whose membership is less than fifty but whose work requires a general branch committee or in a primary Party organization whose membership numbers one hundred or more but whose work does not require a primary Party committee.

3. A primary Party organization with less than fifty members

may, by decision of the next higher Party committee, set up a branch committee to be elected by a general membership meeting, and has the power to make decisions on the admission of new members and on disciplinary measures against Party members.

4. Groups may be formed under a general Party branch or a Party branch.

Article 49: A primary Party organization which has set up its own primary committee shall convene a delegate meeting at least once a year. A general Party branch shall hold a general membership meeting or a delegate meeting at least twice a year. A party branch shall hold a general membership meeting at least once in three months.

The delegate meeting or general membership meeting of a primary Party organization hears and examines the reports of the primary Party committee, the general branch committees, or the branch committees, discusses and decides on questions relating to work in its own unit, elects the primary Party committee, the general Party branch committees, or the branch committees, and elects delegates to the higher Party congress.

The primary Party committee, the general Party branch committee, and the branch committee are elected for a term of one year. The number of members of these committees shall be determined by their respective next higher Party committees.

A primary Party committee shall elect a secretary and from one to four deputy secretaries. If necessary, it may elect a standing committee. The general branch committee and the branch committee shall elect a secretary, and, if necessary, one to three deputy secretaries.

A Party branch with less than ten members only elects a secretary or in addition a deputy secretary, but no branch committee needs to be formed.

A Party group shall elect a leader and, if necessary, a deputy leader.

Article 50: Primary Party organizations must cement the ties of the workers, peasants, intellectuals, and other patriotic people with the Party and its leading bodies. The general tasks of primary Party organizations are as follows:

1. To carry on propaganda and organizational work among the masses and put into practice what the Party advocates and

the decisions of higher Party organizations;

2. To pay constant heed to the sentiments and demands of the masses and report them to higher Party organizations, to pay constant attention to the material and cultural life of the masses and strive to improve it;

3. To recruit new Party members, to collect membership dues, to examine and appraise Party members, and to maintain Party discipline among the membership;

4. To organize Party members to study Marxism-Leninism and the Party's policy and experience and raise the levels of their ideology and political understanding;

5. To lead the masses of the people to take an active part in the political life of the country;

6. To lead the masses to give full play to their activity and creative ability, to strengthen labor discipline, and to insure the fulfillment of the production and work plans;

7. To promote criticism and self-criticism, to expose and eliminate shortcomings and mistakes in work, and to wage struggles against the violation of laws and discipline, against corruption and waste, and against bureaucracy;

8. To educate the Party members and the masses to sharpen their revolutionary vigilance and to be constantly on the alert to combat the disruptive activities of the class enemy.

Article 51: Primary Party organizations in the enterprises, villages, schools, and army units should guide and supervise the administrative bodies and mass organizations in their respective units in the energetic fulfillment of the decisions of higher Party organizations and higher state organs and in ceaselessly improving their work.

Since special conditions obtain in public institutions and organizations, the primary Party organizations therein are in no position to guide and supervise their work, but they should supervise ideologically and politically all Party members in the said institutions and organizations, including those who hold leading administrative posts. The primary Party organizations should also take a constant interest in improving the work in their respective units, strengthen labor discipline, combat bureaucracy, and report without delay any shortcomings in the work to the administrative chiefs of the given units and to higher Party organizations.

CHAPTER VII—CONTROL ORGANS OF THE PARTY

Article 52: The Party's Central Committee, the Party committees of the provinces, autonomous regions, municipalities directly under the central authority, and autonomous *chou,* and the Party committees of the counties, autonomous counties, and municipalities shall set up control commissions. The Central Control Commission shall be elected by the Central Committee at its plenary session. A local control commission shall be elected by a plenary session of the Party committee for that locality, subject to approval by the next higher Party committee.

Article 53: The tasks of the Central and local control commissions are as follows: regularly to examine and deal with cases of violation of the Party Constitution, Party discipline, Communist ethics, and the state laws and decrees on the part of Party members; to decide on or cancel disciplinary measures against Party members; and to deal with appeals and complaints from Party members.

Article 54: The control commissions at all levels function under the direction of the Party committees at corresponding levels.

Higher control commissions have the power to check up on the work of lower control commissions and to approve or modify their decisions on any case. Lower control commissions must report on their work to higher control commissions and present accurate reports on the violation of discipline by Party members.

CHAPTER VIII—RELATION BETWEEN THE PARTY AND THE COMMUNIST YOUTH LEAGUE

Article 55: The Communist Youth League of China [also called the Young Communist League] carries on its activities under the guidance of the Communist Party of China. The Central Committee of the Communist Youth League accepts the leadership of the Party's Central Committee. The Communist Youth League's local organizations are simultaneously under the leadership of the Party organizations at the corresponding levels and of higher League organizations.

Article 56: The Communist Youth League is the Party's assistant. In all spheres of socialist construction Communist Youth League organizations should play an active role in publicizing and carrying out Party policy and decisions. In the struggle to promote production, improve work, and expose and eliminate shortcomings and mistakes in work, the Communist Youth League organizations should render effective help to the Party and have the duty to make suggestions to the Party organizations concerned.

Article 57: Party organizations at all levels must take a deep interest in the Communist Youth League's ideological and organizational work, give guidance to the Communist Youth League in imbuing all its members with Communist spirit and educating them in Marxist-Leninist theory, see to it that close contact is maintained between the Communist Youth League and the broad masses of young people, and pay constant attention to selecting members for the leading core in the Communist Youth League.

Article 58: Members of the Communist Youth League shall withdraw from the League when they have been admitted to the Party and have become full Party members, provided they do not hold leading posts or engage in specific work in the League organizations.

CHAPTER IX—LEADING PARTY MEMBERS' GROUPS IN NON-PARTY ORGANIZATIONS

Article 59: In the leading body of a state organ or people's organization, where there are three or more Party members holding responsible posts, a leading Party members' group shall be formed. The tasks of such a group in the said organ or organization are: to assume the responsibility of carrying out Party policy and decisions, to fortify unity with non-Party cadres, to cement the ties with the masses, to strengthen Party and state discipline, and to combat bureaucracy.

Article 60: The composition of a leading Party members' group shall be decided by a competent Party committee. The group has a secretary and may, in case of need, also have a deputy secretary.

A leading Party members' group must in all matters accept the leadership of the competent Party committee.

Chapter 5

Life in the Party

IN THE EARLY YEARS of the Chinese Communist Party, organizational life stemmed from the fortunes of events and the exigencies of the revolutionary struggle and the faith behind it. As the events and the revolution passed and the basic reasons for the mood of struggle faded, the way of life became even more desperately important—if only to uphold the faith and prove to the new Party members that a lifetime of sacrifice had really been worth the cost. Yet for the Party newcomer after the victory of 1949, the mood and belief seemed strangely detached—as indeed they are—and hopelessly irrelevant, and it is this division between the old and new Party generations that characterizes the organizational life in the Communist Party of China today.

Under Mao Tse-tung, the initial humanitarianism in the Communist program has been adapted to the necessities of enforcement and implementation and to the momentum of the popular movement. Other experiences, habits, and irrationalities —national pride, traditional preference for scholar leaders, reverence for history, disdain for "outsiders," and memories of the deadly struggle and its humiliations—have been blended into the program, and out of a conglomeration of ideas and emotions have arisen Party organizations and institutions to nourish the revolutionary mood and a distinctive way of life. Furthermore, the natural attraction of an idea that rescues the individual from meaningless oblivion, solves his problems in the process, and explains and justifies his fate has been dramatically enhanced by a maximum of propaganda and the use of dedicated, though selective, violence.

Outside China, life in the Chinese Communist Party has attracted remarkably little attention or analysis. Many people who have given any thought to it have found little relation to fact in the Communist statements on struggle, personal tension, obedience to the group, unending meetings, study, and the public nature of an individual's personal life. How, they have asked, can any human being live in a state of mental turmoil under the glare of Party publicity? Isn't there something obviously hideous to all Chinese in the Party's demand that its cadres "mind other people's business"? What kind of people put outdated revolutionary doctrine ahead of rational programs and judicious leadership? Those who have never believed in a cause with their whole being, see in Communist China a grotesque Leviathan, an aberration beyond human comprehension, while others attempt to understand Chinese Communism by comparison with some specific religious sect. Yet, in the final analysis, life in the Chinese Communist Party must be examined without resort to analogy.

The molding and remolding of an active, dedicated leadership cell, which is the goal of Party life, involves the heart of revolutionary doctrine. Consequently, the study of this aspect of doctrine makes more vividly real the general atmosphere or climate of opinion that prevails in Communist China. Nothing else sheds clearer light on the present dilemmas in the Chinese Communist movement and the apparent irrationalities in its policies. Study of the organizational life of the Party sharply illuminates the weaknesses and appallingly simple concerns of the Chinese Communist leadership. In the midst of extraordinary crisis, the Party press, for example, pesters its readers about the proper form of address among "comrades" or the revision of ideological textbooks. Massive social engineering in post-1949 China has been almost exclusively grounded on the mobilization techniques devised in military revolution when most current objectives were vague hopes and idle dreams. In an atmosphere of struggle, ideological study, and personal tensions, the Party members—conceiving themselves to be heroic vanguards—have failed to conceive the whole range of questions and problems that in any discussion of industrialization and modernization elsewhere would be raised as a matter of priority.

But for all the difficulties it has apparently created, the Chinese approach cannot be dismissed lightly. At the end of its first ten years of existence, Communist China probably had become one of the ten leading industrial powers in the world (if production figures are not computed on a per-capita basis), and from 1949 to 1959 its rate of annual industrial growth approximated 20 per cent, a rate three to four times that of India. The revolutionary momentum generated within the Party organizations may have its irrational and even self-defeating aspects, but the net results thus far in industry have been impressive. If blame for the human costs in Chinese development is assigned to the Party because of its choice of methods and priorities, so must substantial credit for China's rapid industrialization redound to it.

Struggle, tension, meetings, study, and group scrutiny of the members' personal life relate not only to social goals and revolutionary memories but to the general social pressures of the Chinese environment as well. This brief discussion can merely direct the reader to the broader context of Chinese society; it cannot examine that context in detail. In traditional Chinese society, the local family and kin groups within villages formed tight, mutually exclusive units. These units monopolized social life by determining limits on personal expectations, career horizons, and the standards of achievement of individual Chinese. From the Communist viewpoint, this situation presented a two-fold problem. On the one hand, in order to create in the Party and later in the whole of China, a collectivity bound by national rather than local or kinship ties, the Communists had to transform values and disrupt traditional social patterns. On the other hand, Party leaders had at the same time to depend on local peasants for support and, in the exigencies of war, had to penetrate local life on the basis of mutual respect and common interest. Although this feat of linking political leadership to the general population uniquely distinguished the Party's operation and in large measure accounted for its successes, the "corruption" of Party members in the process of establishing local relationships followed as a natural by-product of truly effective penetration. In short, Chinese kinship patterns either excluded you or consumed you. To penetrate the general population and yet hold aloft leadership identity and the long-range aim of a national collective, Party leaders bolstered members with an intimate, but controlled, life of their own.

Life Is Struggle

Mao Tse-tung • We advocate an active ideological struggle, because it is the weapon for achieving solidarity within the Party and the revolutionary organizations and making them fit to fight. Every Communist and revolutionary should take up this weapon.

But liberalism negates ideological struggle and advocates unprincipled peace, with the result that a decadent, Philistine style in work has appeared, and certain units and individuals in the Party and the revolutionary organizations have begun to degenerate politically.

Liberalism manifests itself in various ways.

Although the person concerned is clearly known to be in the wrong, yet because he is an old acquaintance, a fellow townsman, a schoolmate, a bosom friend, a beloved one, an old colleague, or a former subordinate, one does not argue with him on the basis of principles but lets things slide in order to maintain peace and friendship. Or [liberalism is] to touch lightly upon the matter without finding a thorough solution in order to maintain harmony all around. As a result, harm is done to the organization as well as to the individual concerned. This is the first type.

To indulge in irresponsible criticisms in private without making positive suggestions to the organization. To say nothing to people's faces, but to gossip behind their backs; or to say nothing at a meeting, but gossip after it. Not to care for the principle of collective life but only for unrestrained self-indulgence. This is the second type.

Things of no personal concern are put on the shelf; the less said the better about things that are clearly known to be wrong; to be cautious in order to save one's own skin, and anxious only to avoid reprimands. This is the third type.

To disobey orders and place personal opinions above everything. To demand special dispensation from the organization but to reject its discipline. This is the fourth type.

To engage in struggles and disputes against incorrect views not for the sake of solidarity, progress, or improvement in work, but

---

Full text of Mao Tse-tung, Combat Liberalism [*September 7, 1937*] (*Peking: Foreign Languages Press, 1954*).

for the sake of making personal attacks, letting off steam, venting personal grievance, or seeking revenge. This is the fifth type.

Not to dispute incorrect opinions on hearing them, and even not to report counterrevolutionary opinions on hearing them, but to bear with them calmly as if nothing had happened. This is the sixth type.

Not to engage in propaganda and agitation, make speeches, or carry on investigations and inquiries among the masses, but to leave the masses alone, without any concern about their weal and woe; to forget that one is a Communist and to behave as if a Communist were just an ordinary person. This is the seventh type.

Not to feel indignant at actions detrimental to the interests of the masses, not to dissuade or to stop the person responsible for them or explain to him, but to allow him to continue. This is the eighth type.

To work halfheartedly without any definite plan or direction; to work perfunctorily and let things drift; "so long as I remain a bonze [Buddhist monk], I go on tolling the bell." This is the ninth type.

To regard oneself as having performed meritorious service in the revolution and to put on the airs of a veteran; to be incapable of doing great things, yet to disdain minor tasks; to be careless in work and slack in study. This is the tenth type.

To be aware of one's own mistakes yet to make no attempt to rectify them and adopt a liberal attitude toward oneself. This is the eleventh type.

We can name some more. But these eleven are the principal ones.

All these are manifestations of liberalism.

In revolutionary organizations liberalism is extremely harmful. It is a corrosive which disrupts unity, undermines solidarity, induces inactivity, and creates dissension. It deprives the revolutionary ranks of compact organization and strict discipline, prevents the policies from being thoroughly carried out, and divorces the organizations of the Party from the masses under their leadership. It is an extremely bad tendency.

Liberalism stems from the selfishness of the petty bourgeoisie which puts personal interests foremost and the interests of the revolution in the second place, thus giving rise to ideological, political, and organizational liberalism.

Liberals look upon the principles of Marxism as abstract dogmas. They approve of Marxism but are not prepared to practice it or to practice it in full; they are not prepared to replace their own liberalism with Marxism. Such people have got Marxism, but they have also got liberalism; they talk Marxism but practice liberalism; they apply Marxism to others but liberalism to themselves. Both kinds of goods are in stock, and either has its particular use. That is the way in which the mind of certain people works.

Liberalism is a manifestation of opportunism and fundamentally conflicts with Marxism. It is passive in character and objectively produces the effect of helping the enemy; thus the enemy welcomes its preservation in our midst. Such being its nature, there should be no place for it in the revolutionary ranks.

We must use the active spirit of Marxism to overcome the liberalism with its passivity. A Communist should be frank, faithful, and active, looking upon the interests of the revolution as his very life and subordinating his personal interests to those of the revolution; he should, always and everywhere, adhere to correct principles and wage a tireless struggle against all incorrect ideas and actions, so as to consolidate the collective life of the Party and strengthen the ties between the Party and the masses; and he should be more concerned about the Party and the masses than about the individual and more concerned about others than about himself. Only thus can he be considered a Communist.

All loyal, honest, active, and staunch Communists must unite to oppose the liberal tendencies shown by certain people among us, and turn them in the right direction. This is one of the tasks on our ideological front.

Liu Shao-ch'i • Comrades! Now the question is very clear. It is how to conduct inner-Party struggle correctly and appropriately.

On this question, the Communist Parties of the U.S.S.R. and many other countries have much experience and so has the Chinese Party. Lenin and Stalin have issued many instructions and so has the Central Committee of our Party. Our comrades must make a careful study of these experiences and instructions, which will also be discussed when we come to the question of Party-building. Today I will not touch upon them. I will bring

From Liu Shao-ch'i, On Inner-Party Struggle [July 2, 1941] (Peking: Foreign Languages Press, n.d.).

up for the reference of our comrades only the following points, on the basis of the experience of the inner-Party struggle of the Chinese Party.

First of all, comrades must understand that inner-Party struggle is a matter of the greatest seriousness and responsibility. We must conduct it with the strictest and most responsible attitude and should never conduct it carelessly. In carrying out inner-Party struggle we must first fully adopt the correct stand of the Party, the unselfish stand of serving the interests of the Party, of doing better work, and of helping other comrades to correct their mistakes and to gain a better understanding of the problems. We ourselves must be clear about the facts and problems by making a systematic investigation and study. At the same time, we must carry on systematic, well-prepared, and well-led inner-Party struggles.

Comrades must understand that only by first taking the correct stand oneself can one rectify the incorrect stand of others. Only by behaving properly oneself can one correct the misbehavior of others. The old saying has it: "One must first correct oneself before one can correct others." . . .

Our self-criticism and inner-Party struggle are not intended to weaken the Party's organization, solidarity, discipline, and prestige or to obstruct the progress of its work. On the contrary, they are intended to strengthen our Party's organization and solidarity, enhance its discipline and prestige, and accelerate the progress of its work. Thus, inner-Party struggle must not be allowed to follow its own course and lead to ultrademocracy. Inside the Party, neither patriarchy nor ultrademocracy is allowed. These are the two extremes of abnormal life within the Party.

Inner-Party struggle must be conducted with the greatest sense of responsibility to the Party and to the revolution.

Second, comrades must understand that inner-Party struggle is basically a struggle between different ideologies and principles inside the Party. It represents antagonism between different ideologies and principles inside the Party. It is imperatively necessary to draw a clear line with regard to ideology and principle. But with regard to organization, the form of struggle, the manner of speaking and criticizing, comrades must be as little antagonistic as possible, must try their best to discuss or to argue over matters in a calm way, and must try their best not to adopt organizational measures and not to draw organizational conclusions. . . .

Third, criticism directed against Party organizations or against comrades and their work must be appropriate and well regulated. Bolshevik self-criticism is conducted according to the Bolshevik yardstick. Excessive criticism, the exaggeration of others' errors, and indiscriminate name-calling are all incorrect. The case is not that the more bitter the inner-Party struggle, the better; but that inner-Party struggle should be conducted within proper limits and that appropriateness should be observed. Both over-shooting the target or falling short of it are undesirable. . . .

Fourth, the holding of struggle meetings, either inside or out-side the Party, should in general be stopped. The various defects and errors should be pointed out in the course of summing up and reviewing work. We should first deal with "the case" and then with "the person." We must first make clear the facts, the points at issue, the nature, the seriousness, and the cause of the errors and defects, and only then point out who are responsible for these defects and errors, and whose is the major responsibility and whose is the minor responsibility. . . .

Fifth, every opportunity to appeal must be given to com-rades who have been criticized or punished. As a rule, a comrade should be personally notified of all records or organizational con-clusions that may be made about him, and these should be made in his presence. If he does not agree, then after discussion, the case may be referred to a higher authority. (In the case of any-one who expresses dissatisfaction after having been punished, the Party organization concerned must refer the case to a higher authority even if the comrade himself does not want to make an appeal.) No Party organization can prevent any comrade who has been punished from appealing to a higher authority. No Party member can be deprived of his right to appeal. No Party organiza-tion can withhold any appeal. . . .

Sixth, a clear line should be drawn and a proper link should be established between struggles waged inside the Party and those waged outside the Party. A struggle waged outside the Party must not adopt the same forms as are used in inner-Party struggle, nor vice versa. Particular care should be exercised to avoid taking advantage of outside forces and conditions in waging struggles against the Party or of intimidating the Party. All Party members must take great care to maintain sharp vigi-lance lest the hidden Trotskyites and counterrevolutionary elements should take advantage of the conflicts and struggles inside the Party to carry on their subversive activities. In conducting inner-Party struggles Party members must not allow themselves to be utilized by these elements. This can be done by strictly observing Party discipline and by carrying on the inner-Party struggle correctly.

Inside the Party, only open struggles and ideological struggles are allowed. No form of struggle which violates the Party Constitution or Party discipline will be allowed.

Seventh, in order to prevent unprincipled disputes within the Party, it is necessary to lay down the following measures:

1. Party members who disagree with the Party's leading body or any Party organization should submit their views and criticisms to the appropriate Party organization and should not talk about it casually among the masses.

2. Party members who disagree with other Party members or certain responsible Party members may criticize them in their presence or in certain specific Party organizations and should not talk about it casually.

3. Party members or Party committees of a lower level who disagree with a Party committee of a higher level may bring the issue to the Party committee of a higher level or ask it to call a meeting to study the matter, or should refer the matter to a Party committee of a still higher level, but they should not talk about it casually or inform Party committees of a still lower level about the matter.

4. When Party members discover any other Party member doing something wrong and acting in a manner detrimental to the interests of the Party, they must report such activities to the appropriate Party organization and should not attempt to cover up the matter or attempt mutually to shield each other.

5. Party members should promote an upright style of work and oppose anything of a deceitful nature, oppose any kind of deceitful talk and actions, and should severely condemn all those who indulge in idle talk, gossiping, prying into other's secrets, and the spreading of rumors. The leading bodies of the Party must from time to time issue instructions forbidding Party members to talk about certain specific matters.

6. The leading bodies at all levels must from time to time summon those comrades who indulge in idle and unprincipled disputes and talk with them, correct them, and warn them, or

subject them to discipline in other ways.

7. Party committees at all levels must respect the opinions set forth by Party members. They should frequently convene meetings to discuss questions and review their work, and provide Party members with ample opportunity to express their opinions.

Unprincipled disputes should in general be forbidden and no judgment should be passed on them, because it is impossible to judge who is right and who is wrong in such unprincipled disputes.

A Tool of the Party

Liu Shao-ch'i • If a Communist Party member, in his ideology, thinks only of the interest and the goal of the Party and communism and is truly selfless, without harboring any independent individual goal and plan in his mind apart from the Party, and if he can continuously advance his own awareness in revolutionary practice and in the study of Marxism-Leninism, then he will be capable of the following:

1. He will be capable of possessing good Communist ethics. As he adheres clearly and firmly to the proletarian standpoint, he will be able to show sincerity and love toward all comrades, revolutionaries, and working people, help them unconditionally, treat them with equality, and refuse to harm any of them for his own interest. He will be able to "place himself in the other person's shoes," thinking for and sympathizing with others. On the other hand, he will be able to engage in a firm struggle against the injurious elements in mankind and pursue a sustained battle against the enemy in defense of the interests of the Party and the proletariat as well as for the defense of the nation and mankind. He will be able to "anticipate the worries of the people and postpone his own enjoyment." In the Party and among the people, he will be the first to suffer the hardships and the last to enjoy the fruits. He will not compare his enjoyment with others but will compare the amount of revolutionary work and the spirit of perseverance. He will be able to volunteer fearlessly in dangerous situations and discharge his greatest, most difficult duties. He will possess the revolutionary persistency and revolutionary integrity of being "incorruptible by wealth, immovable by poverty,

From Liu Shao-ch'i, How to Be a Good Communist [*July 1939*] *as revised and reissued in* Jen-min jih-pao [People's Daily], *August 1, 1962.*

and not intimidated by force."

2. He will be capable of possessing the greatest revolutionary courage. As he has no selfishness in him, he is fearless. As he has never done anything "against conscience," he is always frank about his errors and shortcomings, which are as evident as the "eclipse of the sun and the moon" for all to see, and courageous in correcting them. With righteousness on his side, he is never afraid of the truth, bravely supporting the truth, spreading the truth to others, and fighting for the truth. Even when his action brings him temporary disfavor, when he receives all kinds of attacks because of his support for the truth, when he suffers the opposition and criticism of the greater majority of the people so that he is temporarily isolated (but gloriously isolated), or even when he has to sacrifice his life, he will be able to support the truth against the current and refuse to drift with the tide.

3. He will be capable of learning the theory and method of Marxism-Leninism in the best way. He will be able to employ the theory and method to study problems intelligently and quickly and to understand and reform reality. Because of his clear and firm proletarian standpoint and his Marxist-Leninist cultivation, he has no personal consideration or desire, and therefore he will not conceal or distort his observation of matters and his comprehension of truth. He seeks truth through the facts and verifies the correctness of all theories in revolutionary practice. He does not treat Marxism-Leninism with the dogmatic or empiricist attitude, but combines the Marxist-Leninist universal truth with the concrete practice of the revolution. . . .

Our Party member is no ordinary person but the vanguard of the awakened proletariat. He must become the conscious representative of the proletarian interest and proletarian ideology. Therefore, his individual interest must never stand out from the interest of the Party and the proletariat. This is even more true with respect to Party cadres and Party leaders who should be the concrete representatives of the general interest of the Party and the proletariat. Their individual interest should be entirely absorbed within the total interest and goal of the Party and proletariat. In China's environment today, only the proletariat can best represent the interest of national emancipation. Hence, our Party members should be the best representatives of the interest of the entire nation. . . .

In short, on the one hand, the individual Party member must

obey the Party's interest entirely and sacrifice himself for the public. He must not harbor any individual goal or private plan contrary to the Party's interest. He must not think of himself in everything, shower the Party with his demands, and blame the Party for not promoting and encouraging him. He must under all conditions study industriously, improve diligently, struggle courageously, elevate his own awareness continuously, and intensify his comprehension of Marxism-Leninism ceaselessly in order to make greater contributions to the Party and the revolution. On the other hand, when handling the Party member's problems, the Party organization and the Party's responsible persons should give due consideration to the work, livelihood, and education of the Party member, so that the latter can do better work for the Party and develop and advance himself in the proletarian revolutionary cause. Greater attention should be given those comrades who truly deny themselves for the public. Only thus . . . will the Party be more benefited.

Wang Yü • Why must the Party have strict discipline? The reasons are as follows: First, because the Party desires to lead the working class and the laboring people to defeat the enemies of the revolution, overcome all difficulties, fulfill its lines and policies, and win victories in the work of revolution and construction, the will of the entire Party must be united and its action concerted. Party discipline is a manifestation and also a safeguard of such united will and concerted action. Without it, the Party cannot form a united militant organization or become the vanguard of the working class or leader of the revolution. Second, in the process of class struggle, all kinds of nonproletarian thought, especially bourgeois and petty-bourgeois thought, are sure to try incessantly to corrupt the Party's ranks, loosen its organization, and weaken its fighting power. A number of alien class elements may even cheat their way into the Party organization and try to sabotage the revolution from within. In order to consolidate and purify the Party organization and increase its fighting power incessantly, it is necessary—while stepping up the Party's ideological and political work—to strengthen Party discipline as a sharp weapon in the struggle against such corruption and sabotage.

From Jen-min jih-pao [People's Daily], *November 15, 1961.*

In the years of the revolutionary wars, Party discipline was clearly and directly connected with the issue of victory or defeat in the revolutionary struggle. Where it was undermined, the revolution sometimes had to pay for it in blood. In those days, therefore, it was easier for the Party member to appreciate the importance of Party discipline. After the nationwide liberation, and especially during the period of socialist construction, because of the condition of peace in the nation, some Party members do not find it so easy to appreciate the importance of Party discipline deeply. In fact, however, Party discipline is still extremely important under today's conditions. The reasons for this are as follows: First, class struggle is still present both inside and outside the nation and will continue to be present for a considerable length of time. Second, because the Chinese Communist Party has founded political power in the whole nation, the influence of the Party member's words and acts over the people is greater than ever. Third, the socialist cause is a united and integral cause and socialist construction must proceed according to a unified plan and under unified leadership. These facts make it all the more necessary for the will of the entire Party to be united and its action to be in concert so that the entire Party may enforce its lines and policies and win victories in the work of revolution. . . .

Party discipline is unified, iron discipline. All Party members irrespective of seniority, position, or merit must abide by it alike. If any should be allowed to act differently from the rest and to infringe on the rules of the Party, the Party would become loosely disciplined and damage would be done to the interests of the Party and the people. That is why every Party member must strictly abide by Party discipline.

Party discipline is founded on a conscious observance by Party members. Party members are warriors bent on struggling to the last for the Communist cause and are tame instruments of the party. They know that the Party must have discipline before it can fulfill its lines and policies and realize socialism and communism. Thus they are able—in thought and deed—to comply consciously and fully with the requirements of Party discipline, without feeling the least "restricted" or "unfree" while so doing. The more conscious Party members are, the more consolidated will Party discipline become. Party discipline is iron discipline precisely because it is founded on the conscious observance by Party members.

Consolidation of Party discipline is in complete harmony with the promotion of inner-Party democracy and the promotion of the activeness and creativity of Party members. In the first place, Party discipline is formed according to the interests and requirements of the revolution and by a concentration of the will of the entire Party. Thus, it is intrinsically democratic. Secondly, Party discipline is militant discipline. The Party wants every one of its members to bring to full form his revolutionary activeness and creativity and to struggle, even at the risk of his own life, for the Party's cause. If a Party member is excessively careful in his work and does not fulfill his tasks assigned by the Party actively and creatively and in accordance with concrete conditions but has scruples about this or that, he fails to abide by Party discipline and even vulgarizes it though he may appear to be "very observant of the rules."

While emphasizing centralized and unified leadership and stricter discipline, the Party always emphasizes promotion of inner-Party democracy and promotion of the Party members' activeness and creativity. According to the Party Constitution, Party members have the right to discuss, criticize, and make suggestions on Party policies, resolutions, and work. If a Party member does not agree with a decision which his Party organization has taken, he may—while unconditionally carrying it out—reserve his own opinion about it. The Party always encourages its members—while enforcing policies and carrying out their tasks—to use their intelligence and consolidate the wisdom of the masses so as to create boldly new methods and experiences suited to the concrete local conditions at the time. The Party Constitution clearly lists as acts which violate Party discipline any violation of the Party members' rights and any suppression of or attack on the Party members' activeness and creativity. For this reason, promotion of inner-Party democracy and promotion of the Party members' activeness and creativity form the basis for the consolidation of Party discipline, while Party discipline provides the essential condition for correct promotion of inner-Party democracy and of the Party members' activeness and creativity. The two mutually complement and support one another.

Meetings, Meetings, Meetings

People's Daily • Since last March, the Party branch of Wanshou brigade, Fengshih commune, Haining *hsien,* Chekiang Province, has persevered in calling general meetings of Party members at least once a month. Through the general meeting of Party members, the members have further increased their activism, and the Party branch has played an even better role as a fighting bulwark. . . .

In the past year or so, this Party branch learned that the committee members of the Party branch had to study the instructions of the Party committees at the upper levels and to carry out investigation and research first in order to hold a general meeting of the branch membership properly. Simultaneously, the Party committee had to define the business of the meeting and make the required preparations. It was also necessary for them to inform all Party members beforehand of the date and agenda of the meeting and the problems to be solved at the meeting so that Party members could make mental preparations and take part in the meeting as scheduled.

At the end of November last year, commune members of many brigades actively responded to the government's call for selling pigs to the state. Wanshou brigade did not take any action at that time. What was the reason for this inaction? The Party branch of the brigade decided to send three committee members separately to clarify the situation in the brigade. After the investigation and research, it was found that this brigade had a total of 142 pigs and that it was possible to fulfill the task of selling 17 pigs. Having studied the matter, the committee of the Party branch of this brigade was of the opinion that it would first be necessary to strengthen patriotic education among the Party members. At a general meeting of Party members of the Party branch, instructions from the upper levels were studied and accounts on the advantages of selling agricultural and sideline products to the state and on the support rendered by the state to agriculture were reckoned, thereby increasing the consciousness of the Party members. After the meeting the Party members could set examples for others. On the one hand, they took the

From Jen-min jih-pao [People's Daily], *February 25, 1962.*

lead in selling pigs to the state, and, on the other, they conducted propaganda and education among the masses. Consequently, the task of selling pigs to the state was fulfilled within three days. . . .

To guarantee the fulfillment of the resolution made at a general meeting of a Party branch constitutes the final target for the realization of the desires of the meeting. In this respect, the Party branch of Wanshou brigade has learned that it is first necessary to publicize seriously the resolution made at the meeting. With the aid of the administrative committee, the Young Communist League organization, the women's federation, militia units, and the other organizations of the brigade and through all Party members, the Party branch relays the Party's resolution to the masses and turns it into mass action. In the process of implementing the Party's resolution, the Party group should also develop its role. In the second place, the Party branch regularly examines how the Party members have enforced the resolution it has made. It commends those Party members who have produced favorable results and helps those who have produced poor results.

Huo Chü-lin • Communist Party member Sung Hsüeh-liang is leader of the No. 6 production team, Hsipaichu production brigade, Lunghua commune in Ich'eng *hsien*, Shansi. Ever since the land reform, he had been a cadre in his village and was perpetually enthusiastic in the fulfillment of whatever tasks were given him by the Party. However, in his work style he recently succumbed more or less seriously to "commandism" and spoke in a rigid and cold manner. The commune members called him "a man who does not turn around." This meant that when he decided to do something, other people could not raise any objection. When he had made a mistake, he would never publicly admit it, although he was aware of it. In the autumn of 1959, the No. 6 production team received a share of persimmons. On the day the persimmons were received, Sung Hsüeh-liang called a conference of commune members at which he declared that the persimmons were not to be sold. However, not long afterward, Wang Chin-ch'eng, his wife's nephew, took a picul of persimmons to the trade fair to be sold. Hsüeh-liang then went to see

From Jen-min jih-pao [People's Daily], *January 22, 1962.*

Chin-ch'eng * and severely criticized him for failing to observe discipline and for profiteering through speculative activities. But Chin-ch'eng did not accept his view and a quarrel ensued.

This incident was brought to the attention of the Party branch secretary, Kan Li-tuan. As he was aware that the numerous problems which had arisen recently in the No. 6 production team were connected with the working style of Hsüeh-liang, he was therefore determined to help Hsüeh-liang to rectify his shortcomings. He knew, however, that old Sung had a hot temper, so he did not point out his mistakes directly. Instead he invited old Sung to his home to have a meal with him and talk. After talking about many things, they turned to the subject of the sale of persimmons. Deliberately, Kan Li-tuan asked: "Why did you object to Chin-ch'eng's selling of persimmons?" Straightforwardly, Hsüeh-liang replied: "I had given the order first which must be obeyed by all." Smiling, old Kan said: "When commune members don't obey the orders of their team leader, it is their mistake. But is your order correct? Should the commune members obey it? The persimmons belong to the commune members; why shouldn't they sell them? Moreover, your order had not been approved either by the administrative committee of the production brigade or by the Party branch. It did not even conform to the organizational procedure." Hearing this, Hsüeh-liang did not speak but was angry in his heart.

In the evening the Party branch held a meeting to discuss the matter. The Party branch sincerely criticized the simple and crude methods of work adopted by old Sung. The branch held that it was wrong for old Sung to forbid the commune members to sell the fruits, for this was an infringement on the right of the commune members to sell their subsidiary foodstuffs. All the participants at the meeting asked Sung to make an examination of his working style and his relations with the commune members as a member of the Communist Party and a member of the Party branch. After hearing this, Hsüeh-liang thought that the whole blame was being thrown upon him. He could no longer control his temper and rising angrily said: "What I have done is not for my own sake. If you want to take my job, go ahead and do it." Having said this, he turned on his heels and went home.

After returning home, he calmed down a bit. He carefully re-

* Hsüeh-liang and Chin-ch'eng are given names. This familiar usage is common in the Party press articles on inner-Party life.

viewed the criticisms leveled at him, and he reminded himself of the state policy on the disposal of agricultural subsidiary food-stuffs. He now felt that he had made a mistake. He should not have turned down the criticisms and walked out of the meeting. He was sorry for what he had done, and he wanted to return to the meeting. Yet he was still reluctant to admit his mistake publicly, and so he comforted himself by saying: "Well, that is it. Everything will be all right if you correct your mistake. If you admit it publicly, people would look down on you." . . .

After some consideration, the Party branch sent Kan Li-tuan to No. 6 production team to help Sung Hsüeh-liang to see his mistakes. . . . That night old Kan and Hsüeh-liang slept together on a warm brick bed. As they talked, they turned from the land reform to mutual aid and cooperation and then to the people's communes. Kan Li-tuan asked Hsüeh-liang: "Can you recall how we struggled against Chang Wen-hai? Can you still remember the days when we first set up a mutual aid team?" "How could I forget such things in these years?" replied Hsüeh-liang. Kan Li-tuan continued: "What do you think? Was the work easier or more difficult in the past than it is now?" Hsüeh-liang replied with a sigh: "Of course, the work was easier to do in the past. . . ." Kan Li-tuan said: "You are right. . . . In the past the masses followed us because we treated them well and explained the Party's policies to them patiently. . . . In this way, our work was naturally easy to do." Hastily, Sung Hsüeh-liang said: "Do you mean that I think the present work more difficult to do because I do not perform the work carefully and don't consult the masses?" Smiling, Kan Li-tuan said: "Please, why did you forbid the commune members from selling their persimmons?" Sung Hsüeh-liang did not answer but was deep in thought. Eventually, he knew where his mistake lay. The night was far advanced. Sung Hsüeh-liang rose and steamed a pot of persimmons and ate them with Kan Li-tuan, while examining his mistakes. Further, Kan Li-tuan told him why it was necessary to follow the mass line and the harm that would come from refusing to do so. Sung Hsüeh-liang said to Kan Li-tuan: "Your words have enlightened me."

Early the next morning, Sung Hsüeh-liang and Kan Li-tuan went together to the house of Wang Chin-ch'eng and apologized to him. Since then, Sung Hsüeh-liang's working style of "commandism" has begun to change.

The Party Schoolhouse

People's Daily • How should the Party's basic-level organizations persist in the teaching of Party lessons? The Party branch of Hsisan village, Ch'engkuan commune, Huaijou *hsien,* Peking municipality, is well experienced in this matter.

Ever since its establishment, the Party branch of Hsisan village has paid attention to the teaching of Party lessons. Although the teaching of Party lessons was interrupted from time to time, it was resumed every time within a few months. Since 1959, this Party branch has paid closer attention to the teaching of Party lessons and adopted various concrete measures for persisting in this teaching and has thus secured the general support and approval of the Party members. . . .

Textbooks are necessary in the teaching of Party lessons in the rural Party branches so that Party members may learn their lessons step by step and with good results. Otherwise, the teachers will teach what they can think of or teach one lesson on one subject and another lesson on another subject without connections between lessons. They sometimes find nothing suitable for teaching and thus find it difficult to carry on the teaching of Party lessons with persistence. The contents of teaching the Party lessons given by the Party branch of Hsisan village are comparatively stable. The teachers of the branch had previously learned the Party Constitution thoroughly. They are now studying the *Reader on the Constitution of the Chinese Communist Party* (compiled by the Propaganda Department of the Hopeh Party Provincial Committee) and *News on Life in a Party Branch* (compiled by the Propaganda Department of the Peking Party Municipal Committee). The reports and writings on the current situation of production and thought contained in *News on Life in a Party Branch* are selected for their use as part of the Party lessons. Apart from this, all the Party's guidelines and policies, especially policies on the people's communes, are spelled out appropriately for teaching and explanation in the Party lessons. These are the contents of the Party lessons, but textbooks are still necessary. If there are textbooks, lessons can be given in an overall manner and the students will find the lessons compre-

From Jen-min jih-pao [People's Daily], *October 21, 1961.*

hensive. Ts'ao Shih-fa, a teacher of the Party branch, says: "Without a textbook, a teacher cannot give a lesson extemporaneously because a lesson so taught will be irrelevant. The substance will either be overdone or underdone." At present, almost all the lessons in the old textbook have been taught and new textbooks are required for teaching new things, especially things in connection with the realities of the rural people's communes.

How is teaching to be carried out once a new textbook is made available? That is an important question of perseverance in the teaching of Party lessons. The method which the Party branch of Hsisan village practices is to teach lessons with reference to reality. When the teaching of Party lessons was first carried out, its teachers also committed the mistake of teaching lessons only from a textbook without making any reference to reality. Some Party members thus said: "It is insufficient just to read the textbook." Later, when the teachers taught the lessons in conjunction with actual facts, the Party members said: "When actual facts are introduced in a lesson, we can understand things better with the teacher's guidance." With a view to combining the teaching of Party lessons properly with practice, the Party branch committee makes serious preparation for every Party lesson. Before a lesson begins, the committee members of the Party branch often meet to study the current situations of production and the thinking of the Party members and, on the basis of these situations, decide the way to teach Party lessons. If a meeting of the committee members of the Party branch is impossible, the secretary of the Party branch at the very least has to discuss things separately with the committee members of the Party branch and clarify the current actual situation so that Party lessons may be taught to the point.

T'ao Pai • Party schools have been established by all Party committees at the *hsien* and higher levels in Kiangsu Province this year for the purpose of training, on the basis of rotation, Party cadres, particularly those attached to rural people's communes. These schools educate cadres in the Party's policies concerning socialist construction, in the Marxist-Leninist style of work and methods of work, and in the basic knowledge of the Party.

The content of the teaching must be simple and concise.

From Jen-min jih-pao [People's Daily], *October 24, 1961.*

This means that the key points must be brought into focus, the center of gravity must be made clear, the principal problems must be explained unequivocally and clearly, and learning must be deep and profound; the practice of imposing excessive burdens on the students, demanding perfection from the students, requiring the students to read without understanding what they read, and ignoring practical results must be combated.

Yüan Ch'un-hua • In February 1960, when I was transferred to Tungfanghung commune, I participated in study. To tell the truth, I found study quite a headache at that time. First, because of my low cultural [literacy] standard, I was unable to understand clearly some common terms, much less the spirit and substance of the books. Second, I was very busy and was always afraid that my work might be delayed because of study. It struck me that rather than spend time on study, it would be better to have more work done.

In August last year, in resolute response to the great call of the Party Central Committee to take up agricultural and grain production in a big way, I applied for transfer to the basic level. The Party committee of the commune granted my request and sent me to the Sungshan production brigade to serve as brigade leader. Once I arrived at the basic level, I gradually sensed that because of my poor knowledge of theory and policies, I was unable to fulfill the tasks entrusted to me by the Party satisfactorily. For example, when the Party Central Committee suggested in November last year that, provided that collective production was not impeded, commune members should be allowed to cultivate private plots and to operate sideline businesses on a small scale, I was full of excessive fear when I put the new policy into operation because I had not conscientiously studied and delved into this Party policy. Thanks to the direction of the leadership, I discovered that this was the result of my insufficient study.

From then on I made up my mind to study policies and theories, and, apart from participating in study in the commune, I constantly found time to study the works of Chairman Mao and the documents of the Party. My way of study was to read more, think more, ask more questions, write more, and talk more.

From Jen-min jih-pao [People's Daily], *September 13, 1961.*

Whenever I read an article, I always mulled it over in my mind and tried to comprehend the spirit and substance of the article in the real sense. I wrote down the things which I did not understand and asked other people to explain them whenever there was a chance. After reading an article, I wrote down what I understood in accordance with the actual circumstances.

People's Daily • The admission of new members into the Party is only the first step in Party building. What is more important is to strengthen the management over probationary Party members and raise further their political consciousness. In the past, the Party organizations of Miaoch'ien commune lacked sufficient understanding on this point. The saying, "The master leads his disciple to the door, and the disciple must do the rest on his own," once prevailed among the Party members. Work was therefore carried out with emphasis on expansion of the Party membership while consolidation was neglected and some new Party members could not raise their consciousness rapidly.

In February this year, the Party committee of the commune called the cadres of all Party branches together to study and discuss the work with respect to probationary Party members. In the discussion, the cadres cited many examples: Because the Party branch of Wangkuk'ou production brigade had paid attention to this work, all nine probationary Party members received last year were good in thinking and work and had passed to regular Party membership in due course. Because the Party branch of Yangts'un production brigade had neglected this work, most of the seven probationary Party members admitted did not produce good results. As a result, three of them had their probationary period prolonged, and one was disqualified for Party membership. All cadres realized from practice that it was definitely necessary to strengthen the management over probationary Party members and criticized all incorrect ways of thinking and work methods. On this basis, they decided that from the level of Party committee to the level of Party branch, a deputy secretary or a member of the organization department had to be charged with this work. In addition, the work on probationary Party members was to be shared by the whole Party by adopting

From an article by the Organization Departments of the Chinnan Party District Committee and the Hsiahsien Party hsien Committee in Jen-min jih-pao [People's Daily], *December 12, 1961.*

the method of making every area take up full responsibility and assigning responsibility to every cadre. From the level of the Party committee to the level of the Party branch, the ideological condition of the probationary Party members was to be summed up monthly, fresh arrangements were to be made quarterly, and problems were to be solved promptly. In this way, probationary Party members were put under the strict management of the Party organizations, so that they might get regular help from the Party. . . .

[In this management, stress is laid on ideological education.] With regard to the method of teaching, the Party committee of the commune lays emphasis on intensive training. Training was carried out for two terms each lasting approximately five days. At the same time, the members of the Party committee in various areas occasionally organized the probationary Party members for intensive study. The Party branch of every brigade generally persists in the system of giving one Party lesson monthly. In everyday tasks, the Party branches also pay attention to teaching probationary Party members special lessons. Thus educated, all probationary Party members have raised their ideological understanding and made clearer the nature of the Party and their obligations as Party members.

One Big Family

Ch'en Yi-yen • There are differences of opinion as to whether Party members and cadres in the Party and public organs should call one another comrades and not by their official titles when they meet.

Those who are in favor of calling one another comrades say that calling one another comrades in the Party is a fine Party tradition because it shows that every member in our Party shares the same will and ideals under the Marxist-Leninist banner, gets organized voluntarily, and establishes close, inalienable revolutionary relationships which are incomparable in the world. This fine tradition should be carried on and extended to all public organs. Instead of calling one another comrade, the calling of one another by official titles—such as Secretary Ch'en, Director Li,

From Nan-fang jih-pao [Southern Daily], *March 14, 1962.*

Chairman Chang, and Accountant Huang, etc.—would result in man-made barriers which would affect the close comradely relations and also result in misunderstanding among the masses of the people with serious consequences.

Those who think that this is unnecessary say that under the socialist system various official posts represent a division of labor which is absolutely necessary in society. Although there are high and low official posts, politically all are equal since there are no class distinctions. What is more, our Party has always held that all Party members and cadres are only servants of the people, so that those who hold higher posts will only assume greater responsibilities in order to render more and better services to the people, and, apart from their functions, they have no special authority. If official posts are viewed in this light, calling one another by official titles would in no way do any harm, although calling one another comrades is, of course, a good practice.

While I agree with the latter people, I still think that it is better to call one another comrade instead of by official titles. . . . "Officialdom" and "bureaucracy" have long ago been sent to the historical museum. However, their influences still exist widely in our society. "Bureaucratic style" may still breed and grow among our Party members and cadres. That is why our Party has always maintained that all bureaucratic dust must be wiped off and has patiently exhorted and educated our Party members and cadres to treat the people as equals, appear as ordinary laborers among the masses, and rid themselves of "bureaucratic style." We should promote the practice of calling one another comrade instead of by our official titles; this is also one aspect of such exhortation and education.

People's Daily • Must the marital questions (including marriages and divorces) of Party members have the approval of the Party?

It should be explicitly stated that our Party has never laid down a blanket rule requiring Party approval for all marriages and divorces of Party members. There is no such rule in the Party discipline. Certain regulations concerning such marriages were adopted by local Party organizations in accordance with the needs of local conditions, but these have been rescinded since

From Jen-min jih-pao [People's Daily], *January 12, 1957.*

1949. Even now, however, the system of "approving" marriages of Party members still exists in a number of Party organizations. According to a report in the *People's Railway Journal*, the Party organization in the Paochi-Lanchow Railway Construction Office of the 6th Engineering Bureau of the Ministry of Railways has laid down such a rule: Any Party member who intends to marry must first pass through these stages: personal application for permission to marry; discussion by the Party branch of the application; investigation by the Party general branch; and approval from the Party committee of the office. Similar rules have been laid down by other local organizations.

During the period of intense and complicated political struggle in the country, it was necessary and correct for a Communist charged with an important political mission to ask the Party organization, when choosing a mate, to help the pair know each other's political make-up so as to avoid being politically deceived and made to suffer. The Party organizations concerned would not regard such help as their right, and the Party members concerned would not regard such help as an imposition. Is it still necessary for Party organizations to give Party members such help? We should say that so long as the political struggle between the revolution and counterrevolution goes on, such help and concern should also go on.

As the question of marriage is a matter of lifelong importance to a Party member as well as anybody else, a Party member is naturally often willing to consult his or her Party organization about other things that need be considered besides the political make-up of the prospective spouse. In the circumstances, it is also entirely proper and necessary for Party organizations to help Party members learn more about the other person and the make-up of his mind. Many Party organizations have done so in the past, and it should be admitted that their action has generally produced good results. It should not be considered an interference with the freedom of Party members to marry.

People's Daily • The system of organizational life in the Party branch of T'unghsin production brigade has always been healthy, and the content of organizational life has been relatively rich. This Party branch consists of a total of 33 Party members divided

From Jen-min jih-pao [People's Daily], *September 5, 1961.*

into 8 Party groups. The Party branch convenes at least one general meeting of Party members a month, while the Party groups hold two meetings separately each month. In ordinary times, Party lessons are taught, though irregularly. At meetings held both by the Party branch and by the Party groups, Party policies, guidelines, and directives are frequently studied, the state of the implementation of Party policies examined, and criticism and self-criticism launched in addition to the carrying out of ideological and political education for Party members and the discussion of the transfer of probationary Party members to full membership. . . .

The reason why the organizational life in the Party branch has always been relatively normal is principally that both the committee of the branch and the Party members have, by and large, attached great importance to the improvement of the organizational life. The secretary of the Party branch, Kung Ken-t'ao, said: "We feel that our organizational life is as indispensable as our food. Just as a man cannot live without food, so a Party member cannot raise his ideological and political consciousness and do his work well without participating in organizational life." Meanwhile, they have a set of systems to govern organizational life properly. If the dates for organizational life meetings coincide with the dates for the convening of other conferences, the former are postponed one or two days. If some individual Party members are absent from organizational life meetings without cause or do not attach sufficient importance to organizational life, they are appropriately criticized. The secretary of the Party branch as well as members of the committee of the branch and group leaders as a rule, take the lead in participating in organizational life and refrain from being absent without cause. The content of organizational life is also comparatively rich. Each time an organizational life meeting is held, its agenda are always made known in advance to the Party groups and Party members so that they may make preparations.

Chapter 6

The Communist Party in Operation

THE CHINESE COMMUNIST PARTY operates in accordance with three interrelated concepts. The first of these, "collective leadership combined with individual responsibility," is limited to Party cadres operating within a single unit. Cadres, as was explained on page 52, occupy the leading and working positions on committees, where they determine strategies, policies, and tasks. For the operation of a single unit, the concept of "collective leadership combined with individual responsibility" means that the cadres jointly study and discuss political topics and individually assume responsibility for implementing selected aspects of decisions and supervising and reporting on results. At each level in the Party hierarchy, from the branch to the Central Committee, central authority belongs to a single leading cadre—usually a first secretary.

In Party operations that involve more than a single unit, the concept of "democratic centralism" is applied, whereby the "minority" and lower echelons are subordinate to the "majority" and higher levels and give unflinching obedience after decisions have been reached. Although the term *democratic centralism* is also used to describe the general relationships among the members or the "people" in all "working-class" organizations, including the state itself, it is used in its most familiar sense when Party members apply the term to the inter-unit process of decision-making.

The third concept is the "mass line," perhaps the most familiar aspect of Chinese Communist operation, according to which the Party creates a correct balance of guidance, initiative, and support by the cadres and the general population. By definition, the mass-line concept rejects erroneous forms of cadre leadership that alienate the Chinese people from the Party or fail to achieve bold, successful advances of Party programs. Mao Tsetung has stipulated that decisions must be made after consultation with Chinese peasants and workers and that policy decisions should be presented to the population in a manner that encourages their genuine interest and active participation. According to the mass line principle, cadres at the lower levels have wide latitude to break general policies into specific tasks and to adapt policies to local conditions.

All three concepts for Party operation are meant to promote flexible, creative, collective participation, subject to disciplined, unified centralism. Each is relied upon to define the relationships between senior and junior elements and to encourage active participation of subordinate elements in support of the leadership mission of the senior elements. But despite the extraordinary amount of attention paid by the Party press to these three concepts, collective leadership, democratic centralism, and the mass line obviously are little more than textbook theories to most Party members. We know from Communist statements that violations of these concepts by Party cadres have become more frequent and severe in recent years. (Some of the vast material on the mass line in action is sampled in the selection on pages 182–186.)

The three operational concepts typify the pervasiveness of contradictions in the thinking of the Party. "Collective leadership *and* individual responsibility," "democracy *and* centralism," and "general mass interests *and* the specific Party line" constitute pairs of contradictions. The task of Party members and cadres is to resolve the contradictory aspects by properly acting on the policies set by the Central Committee. Failure to resolve these contradictions allegedly is revealed in more obvious failures to achieve goals or through repudiation by the Chinese people. Behind the overt manifestations of failure, however, lies a deeper ideological failure, specifically a deviation from prescribed thinking. "The correctness or incorrectness of a political, military, or organizational line fundamentally depends on whether it starts ideologically from the Marxist-Leninist theory of dialectical materialism and historical materialism and from the objective realities of the Chinese revolution and the objective needs of the Chinese people," Mao said in 1945. Thus conceived, correct operation depends on right thinking.

In addition to changing the character and focus of blame for failures, the three concepts provide a theoretical mechanism for maintaining the supposed infallibility of the leadership elite. When things go badly, Party leaders can reinterpret a policy in terms of the flexibility or rigidity of implementation without markedly changing the terminology of the policy itself. For example, in theory the commune line remains approximately as firm as it did in 1958; in practice, however, the people's commune has given way to a lower form of organization—the production team—which is similar in form to the rural organization common before 1955. Given the wide latitude of potential alternatives for the implementation of general policies, working-level Party cadres must not only convert into actual practice the illusive substance of official pronouncements but also assume the certain blame for the manner in which they have implemented a policy once it changes. If they have been unyielding, they should have been flexible. A "tailist" act today may become a "commandist" act tomorrow. Yet, the cadres must not investigate the "sleight of hand" involved in this conceptual confusion. On the contrary, they must immediately scrutinize their own ideological motives and the backward state of their political consciousness. Indeed, they must express their gratitude to the Party for rescuing them from ignorance and for revealing its superior wisdom to them.

The Party has many instruments—so-called "transmission belts"—for extending its operations within the Chinese population. Among these are the organs of the state, people's organizations including trade unions and women's federations, and the organs of the united front, particularly the "democratic" parties that "cooperate" with the Chinese Communist Party. Two subsidiary organizations, the Young Communist League and the Young Pioneers, not only extend Party operations to the Chinese youth but also provide the principal educational and recruitment channels for prospective Party members. Children from the age of nine may join the Young Pioneers, which supplements regular classroom training with political indoctrination and rudimentary experience in Communist practices and collective living. The Young Communist League supervises the Young

Pioneers and principally draws its own recruits from the children's organization. Open to young men and women between 14 and 25, the League is in turn supervised by the Party and comprises the Party's main pool from which it selects new members.

Highly organized and concrete, Communist methods of operation served the Party well in its quest for military victory prior to 1949 and during the initial period of national consolidation. By selectively stressing "investigation and research," personal contacts between cadres and the people, and careful pretesting of planned moves—all principles that Mao Tse-tung popularized before 1949—the Party leaders expected to sustain the revolutionary operation in the periods of transition to socialism and communism. But the ambiguous nature of the major concepts related to operation and the failure to carry out key economic policies have caused dissatisfaction among the cadres and the loss of confidence among the Chinese people. The Party elite thus has yet to prove that the revolutionary code of operation continues to have genuine utility in the period of social and economic development.

Blueprint for Operation

Mao Tse-tung • I would like to say something about our Party's style in work.

Why should there be a revolutionary party? There should be a revolutionary party because there are in the world enemies of the people who oppress them, and the people want to shake off their oppression. In the era of capitalism and imperialism we need such a revolutionary party as the Communist Party. Without such a revolutionary party as the Communist Party it is simply impossible for the people to shake off the oppression of their enemies. As Communists who are to lead the people to overthrow the enemy, we must keep our ranks in good order, march in step, train our troops well, and secure well-made weapons. Without these conditions, the enemy cannot possibly be overthrown.

Now what are the problems that still confront our Party? The general line of our Party is undoubtedly correct and our Party

From Mao Tse-tung, Rectify the Party's Style in Work [*February 1, 1942*] (*Peking: Foreign Languages Press, 1955*).

has also made achievements in its work. The Party has a membership of several hundred thousands who are leading the people to fight the enemy amid untold difficulties and with surpassing bravery. This is what we all see and nobody can doubt.

Then is there any problem that confronts our Party? There is, I should say, and what is more, the problem is in a certain sense quite serious.

What is it? It is the fact that a number of our comrades have certain ideas which strike one as not quite correct, not quite desirable.

That is to say, there is still something incorrect in the approach in our study, in the style in our Party work, and in the tendency in our literary work. The incorrect approach in study refers to the evil of subjectivism. The incorrect style in Party work refers to the evil of sectarianism. The incorrect tendency in our literary work refers to the evil of the Party "eight-legged essay" [excessive formalism]. These are like ill winds, but they do not sweep the sky like [the] north wind in winter. Subjectivism, sectarianism, and the Party "eight-legged essay" are no longer dominant in our style in work; they are but a gust of contrary wind, a foul draught escaped from the air-raid shelter. (*Laughter.*) But, it is bad that such winds should still be blowing in the Party. We must stop the passage of the foul draught. Our whole Party should take up this job, and the Party School should do the same. These three ill winds, subjectivism, sectarianism, and the Party "eight-legged essay," have their historical origins; though no longer dominant in the whole Party, they still do constant mischief and make assaults on us, and we must stop them and study, analyze, and explain them.

It is our task to oppose subjectivism in order to rectify the incorrect approach in our study, to oppose sectarianism in order to rectify the incorrect style in Party work, and to oppose the Party "eight-legged essay" in order to rectify the incorrect tendency in our literary work.

In order to accomplish the task of overthrowing our enemy, we must accomplish the task of rectifying our Party's unsound style in work. The approach in study and the tendency in literary work form part of the Party's style in work or Party style. Once our Party's style in work becomes completely right, the people of the whole country will follow us. Those outside the Party who are tainted with such bad style in work will, in so far as they are good people, also follow our example and rectify their own errors and we shall then be able to exercise an influence upon the whole nation. So long as the ranks of us Communists are in good order, our steps in perfect coordination, our troops well trained, and our weapons well made, we can overthrow any enemy, no matter how powerful.

Mao Tse-tung • 1. The two methods which we Communists should employ in carrying out any task are, first, the linking of the general with the specific and, second, the linking of the leadership with the masses.

2. We cannot mobilize the broad masses for a particular task unless we publicize those general directives which are applicable to all. But there is no possibility of testing the correctness of such general directives and of making them more specific and concrete, and there is a danger of their coming to nothing, unless the leaders, instead of contenting themselves with issuing directives, personally carry out the tasks on hand in a concrete and thorough manner in some of their organizations until initial success is achieved in one place, and then use the experience so gained to direct the work in the rest of the organizations. For example, in the course of the 1942 campaign to rectify the style in work, success was achieved wherever the method of linking general directives with specific guidance was used and failure occurred wherever it was ignored. In the rectification campaign of 1943 all bureaus and subbureaus of the Central Committee of the Party, all regional and district Party committees should, in addition to issuing general directives (*i.e.*, the year's plan for the campaign), endeavor to gain experience in the following way: Select two or three units (but not too many) in their own organizations or other nearby organizations, schools, or troops, and thoroughly investigate them to get acquainted in detail with the way they are carrying on the campaign; pick a few of their typical members (again, not too many), and make a detailed study of their political records, their outlook, their attitude to study, and the records of their work and, furthermore, give direct personal guidance to the leaders of the selected units to help them effectively solve the practical problems which crop up in their respective units. As an office, a school, or an army unit is

Full text of Mao Tse-tung, On Methods of Leadership [*June 1, 1943*] (*Peking: Foreign Languages Press, 1955*).

also composed of a number of subunits, its leaders should do the same. This is also the method of giving leadership while learning how to lead. No leading worker can possibly give general guidance to all the units under his direction if he does not get actual experience in working on specific tasks with individual workers in particular units. This method should be widely popularized so that leading workers at all levels can learn to apply it.

3. The experience gained in the rectification campaign of 1942 also proves that, to achieve success in the campaign, it is essential that within each unit a leading group should be formed comprising a small number of active workers united around the head of the given unit and that this group should maintain close contact with the masses taking part in the campaign. The activity of this leading group, unless combined with that of the masses, will dissipate itself in the fruitless efforts of a handful of people. On the other hand, mass activity, unless well organized by a strong leading group, can be neither sustained long nor be developed in the right direction and raised to a higher level. The masses in all cases are by and large composed of three groups of people: the active, the relatively passive, and those who are betwixt and between. The leadership must therefore be skilled in drawing the small number of active individuals into the leading group and in relying on them to enhance the activity of the betwixt and between and draw the passive into the work. A leading group that is genuinely united and firmly linked with the masses can be gradually formed only in the course of a mass campaign, not apart from it. In most cases, the composition of the leading group should not and cannot remain entirely unchanged throughout the initial, intermediate, and final stages of a great campaign. The active people who emerge in the course of the struggle should be constantly promoted to replace those members of the leading group who cannot keep up the pace or have become demoralized. The fundamental reason for failure to advance our work in various places and organizations is precisely the absence of such a permanently healthy leading group firmly united and linked with the masses. A school with about a hundred students cannot be run properly unless it has a leading group comprising a few or a dozen or more people, which has emerged naturally (and not been formed artificially) from among the most active, staunch, and capable members of its faculty, staff, and student body.

The principles concerning the creation of a basic leading group which J. V. Stalin set forth in the ninth of his twelve conditions for building up a Bolshevik Party should be applied in every office, school, military unit, factory, or village, whether large or small.* In creating such a leading group the criteria should be those four for choosing cadres given in Georgi Dimitrov's discussion on cadres policy (namely, absolute devotion to the cause, close contact with the masses, ability to find one's orientation independently, and strict observance of discipline).** In any case, whatever the task, whether a central task connected with the war, production, or education (including the rectification campaign) or such a task as checking up work or examining cadres, etc., we must not only link general directives with specific guidance, but also link the leading group with the broad masses.

4. In all practical work of our Party, correct leadership can only be developed on the principle of "from the masses, to the masses." This means summing up (*i.e.*, coordinating and systematizing after careful study) the views of the masses (*i.e.*, views scattered and unsystematic), then taking the resulting ideas back to the masses, explaining and popularizing them until the masses embrace the ideas as their own, stand up for them, and translate them into action by way of testing their correctness. Then it is necessary once more to sum up the views of the masses, and once again take the resulting ideas back to the masses so that the masses give them their wholehearted support. . . . And so on, over and over again, so that each time these ideas emerge with greater correctness and become more vital and meaningful. This is what the Marxist theory of knowledge teaches us.

5. In order to correct the wrong views obtaining among our cadres, we should, during the present campaign to rectify the style in work, widely publicize the idea that, whether in an organization or in a campaign, proper relations must be established between the leading group and the broad masses; that the leadership can work out correct ideas only if it sums up the views of the masses and takes the resulting ideas back to the masses so that they can gain firm mass support; and that, in putting the

---

* See J. V. Stalin, "The Prospects of the Communist Party of Germany and the Question of Bolshevisation" [February 1925], *Works*, Vol. VII (Moscow: Foreign Languages Publishing House, 1954).
** See Georgi Dimitrov, "Unity of the Working Class Against Fascism" [August 1935], *Selected Articles and Speeches* (London: Lawrence and Wishart, 1951).

ideas of the leadership into practice, general directives must be linked with specific guidance. Many comrades neither care nor know how to rally active people to form a leading group, nor do they care or know how to link such a leading group closely with the broad masses; as a result, their leadership becomes bureaucratic and divorced from the masses. Many other comrades neither care nor know how to sum up the experience of a mass struggle, but are fond of proclaiming their own subjective opinions with an air of great profundity, as a result of which their judgments become empty talk divorced from reality. Still others content themselves with giving out general directives on various questions and, having done that, do not bother and, in fact, do not know how to go on immediately to give specific guidance on the tasks on hand; as a result, their directives remain mere words, directives only put down on paper or issued at the conference table, and their leadership becomes bureaucratic. During the present campaign to rectify the style in work, we must get rid of these defects; in the course of rectifying our style in work, checking up our work and examining our cadres, we must learn how to maintain close contact between the leadership and the masses and also how to link general directives with specific guidance, and we must apply these methods consistently in all our future work.

6. The basic method of leadership is to sum up the views of the masses, take the results back to the masses so that the masses give them their firm support and so work out sound ideas for leading the work on hand. In summing up the opinions of the masses and mobilizing them to uphold the ideas so adopted, the leadership should use the method of combining general directives with specific guidance, which is an organic part of the method "from the masses, to the masses." On the basis of numerous cases of giving specific guidance we work out general ideas (general directives) for action, then put these general ideas to the test in many individual units (not only by ourselves, but by others acting on our advice), and finally generalize (*i.e.*, sum up) the new experience so gained so as to work out new directives for the general guidance of the masses. This is the way all comrades should carry on their work, not only in the present rectification campaign, but also in every other kind of work. The better one grasps this method, the better his leadership proves.

7. In assigning a task (such as prosecution of the revolution-

ary war, production, education, the rectification campaign, checking up work, examining cadres, propaganda, organizational, or antiespionage work, etc.) to a subordinate unit, the higher leading organization and its departments should act through the leader who has overall responsibility for the lower organization concerned, so that he can undertake the assignment with a full sense of responsibility, thereby achieving a division of duties under unified leadership (centralized authority). It is inadvisable for one department of a higher organization to have contacts only with its counterpart in lower organizations (for example, the organizational, propaganda, or antiespionage departments of a higher organization to have contacts only with the corresponding departments of lower organizations), leaving the responsible head of a lower organization (for example, the secretary, chairman, director, or school principle, etc.) uninformed and unable to answer for the work assigned. It is essential that the leader of a lower organization concerned as well as the heads of its particular departments should be informed of the assigned task and held answerable for its fulfillment. Such a centralized authority, *i.e.,* division of duties under unified leadership, permits the leader at the top to mobilize a large number of people—on occasion even the entire personnel of an organization—to carry out a particular task; in this way, shortage of workers in particular units can be remedied and a large number of people can be drawn in as active participants in a given task. This is also a form of linking up the leadership with the masses. If, for example, a checkup on personnel is carried out by only a few members of such a leading body as the Organization Department, there is little doubt that it will not be done successfully; if on the other hand, through the head of an institution or school principal we can secure the participation of a considerable number of the personnel of that institution or of the students, or, perhaps, even the entire staff or the whole student body, while the leadership of the organizational department concerned gives adequate guidance and actually applies the principle of linking the leadership with the masses, then it is certain that the objectives of the checkup can be fully achieved.

8. Not more than one main task should be assigned at any one time to any one locality; at any given time there can be only one central task, though it may be supplemented by tasks of secondary and third-rate importance. Thus the leader of a locality

should put each kind of work in its proper place according to the history and the circumstances of the struggle in that locality rather than act without plan and rush from task to task as higher organizations assign them, thereby causing havoc and confusion with a bewildering number of "central tasks." Nor should a higher organization on its part simultaneously hand down a lot of assignments to organizations at a lower level, irrespective of their relative importance and urgency and without specifying which is the main task, because this will disorganize the work of the lower organizations and prevent them from achieving the desired end. The art of leadership is for a leader to take into account the situation as a whole in accordance with the historical conditions and immediate circumstances of each specific locality, correctly determine the central task and program of work in a given period, then steadfastly carry out this decision, and see to it that results are achieved. This also is a question of methods of leadership which must be carefully solved in applying the principles of linking the leadership with the masses and combining the general with the specific.

9. We have not gone into the details of the question of methods of leadership, and we hope that comrades everywhere can, in the light of the principles and directives here set forth, think over the details carefully and use their own initiative. The harder the struggle, the greater is the necessity of closely linking Communist leadership with the demands of the masses, of closely combining general Communist directives with specific guidance and thus completely ending subjective and bureaucratic methods of leadership. All the leading comrades of the Party must at all times oppose and overcome subjective and bureaucratic methods of leadership with scientific, Marxist methods of leadership. The development of Party work is greatly impeded by subjectivists and bureaucrats who ignore the principles of linking the leadership with the masses and of combining the general with the specific. In order to combat subjective and bureaucratic methods of leadership, we must extensively and thoroughly promote scientific, Marxist methods of leadership.

Collective Leadership in the
Guidance of Operation

Mao Tse-tung • 1. The secretary of a Party committee must be good at being a "squad leader." A Party committee has ten to twenty members; it is like a squad in the army, and the secretary is like the "squad leader." It is indeed not easy to lead this squad well. Each bureau or subbureau of the Central Committee now leads a vast area and shoulders very heavy responsibilities. To lead means not only to decide general and specific policies but also to devise correct methods of work. Even with correct general and specific policies, troubles may still arise if methods of work are neglected. To fulfill its task of exercising leadership, a Party committee must rely on its "squad members" and enable them to play their parts to the full. To be a good "squad leader," the secretary should study hard and investigate thoroughly. A secretary or deputy secretary will find it difficult to direct his "squad" well if he does not take care to do propaganda and organizational work among his own "squad members," is not good at handling his relations with committee members, or does not study how to run meetings successfully. If the "squad members" do not march in step, they can never expect to lead tens of millions of people in fighting and construction. Of course, the relation between the secretary and the committee members is one in which the minority must obey the majority, so it is different from the relation between a squad leader and his men. Here we speak only by way of analogy.

2. Place problems on the table. This should be done not only by the "squad leader" but by the committee members too. Do not talk behind people's backs. Whenever problems arise, call a meeting, place the problems on the table for discussion, take some decisions, and the problems will be solved. If problems exist and are not placed on the table, they will remain unsolved for a long time and even drag on for years. The "squad leader" and the committee members should be tolerant and understanding in their relations with each other. Nothing is more important than mutual tolerance, understanding, support, and friendship

Full text of Mao Tse-tung, "Methods of Work of Party Committees" [March 13, 1949] in Selected Works, *Vol. IV (Peking: Foreign Languages Press, 1961).*

between the secretary and the committee members, between the Central Committee and its bureaus, and between the bureaus and the area Party committees. In the past this point received little attention, but since the Seventh Party Congress [in 1945] much progress has been made in this respect and the ties of friendship and unity have been greatly strengthened. We should continue to pay constant attention to this point in the future.

3. "Exchange information." This means that members of a Party committee should keep each other informed and exchange views on matters that have come to their attention. This is of great importance in achieving a common language. Some fail to do so and, like the people described by Lao Tzu, "do not visit each other all their lives, though the crowing of their cocks and the barking of their dogs are within hearing of each other." The result is that they lack a common language. In the past some of our high-ranking cadres did not have a common language even on basic theoretical problems of Marxism-Leninism, because they had not studied enough. There is more of a common language in the Party today, but the problem has not yet been fully solved. For instance, in the land reform there is still some difference in the understanding of what is meant by "middle peasants" and "rich peasants."

4. Ask your subordinates about matters you don't understand or don't know, and do not lightly express your approval or disapproval. Some documents, after having been drafted, are withheld from circulation for a time because certain questions in them need to be clarified and it is necessary to consult the lower levels first. We should never pretend to know what we don't know, we should "not feel ashamed to ask and learn from people below," and we should listen carefully to the views of the cadres at the lower levels. Be a pupil before you become a teacher; learn from the cadres at the lower levels before you issue orders. In handling problems, this should be the practice of all bureaus of the Central Committee and Party committees of the fronts, except in military emergencies or when the facts of the matter are already clear. To do this will not lower one's prestige, but can only raise it. Since our decisions incorporate the correct views of the cadres at the lower levels, the latter will naturally support them. What the cadres at the lower levels say may or may not be correct; we must analyze it. We must heed the correct views and act upon

them. The reason why the leadership of the Central Committee is correct is chiefly that it synthesizes the material, reports, and correct views coming from different localities. It would be difficult for the Central Committee to issue correct orders if the localities did not provide material and put forward opinions. Listen also to the mistaken views from below; it is wrong not to listen to them at all. Such views, however, are not to be acted upon but to be criticized.

5. Learn to "play the piano." In playing the piano all ten fingers are in motion; it won't do to move some fingers only and not others. But if all ten fingers press down at once, there is no melody. To produce good music, the ten fingers should move rhythmically and in coordination. A Party committee should keep a firm grasp on its central task and at the same time, around the central task, it should unfold the work in other fields. At present, we have to take care of many fields; we must look after the work in all the areas, armed units, and departments, and not give all our attention to a few problems, to the exclusion of others. Wherever there is a problem, we must put our finger on it, and this is a method we must master. Some play the piano well and some badly, and there is a great difference in the melodies they produce. Members of Party committees must learn to "play the piano" well.

6. "Grasp firmly." That is to say, the Party committee must not merely "grasp," but must "grasp firmly," its main tasks. One can get a grip on something only when it is grasped firmly, without the slightest slackening. Not to grasp firmly is not to grasp at all. Naturally, one cannot get a grip on something with an open hand. When the hand is clenched as if grasping something but is not clenched tightly, there is still no grip. Some of our comrades do grasp the main tasks, but their grasp is not firm and so they cannot make a success of their work. It will not do to have no grasp at all, nor will it do if the grasp is not firm.

7. "Have a head for figures." That is to say, we must attend to the quantitative aspect of a situation or problem and make a basic quantitative analysis. Every quality manifests itself in a certain quantity, and without quantity there can be no quality. To this day many of our comrades still do not understand that they must attend to the quantitative aspect of things—the basic statistics, the main percentages, and the quantitative limits that

determine the qualities of things. They have no "figures" in their heads and as a result cannot help making mistakes. For instance, in carrying out the land reform it is essential to have such figures as the percentages of landlords, rich peasants, middle peasants, and poor peasants among the population and the amount of land owned by each group, because only on this basis can we formulate correct policies. Whom to call a rich peasant, whom a well-to-do middle peasant, and how much income derived from exploitation makes a person a rich peasant as distinct from a well-to-do middle peasant—in all these cases too, the quantitative limits must be ascertained. In all mass movements we must make a basic investigation and analysis of the number of active supporters, opponents, and neutrals and must not decide problems subjectively and without basis.

8. "Notice to Reassure the Public." Notice of meetings should be given beforehand; this is like issuing a "Notice to Reassure the Public," so that everybody will know what is going to be discussed and what problems are to be solved and can make timely preparations. In some places, meetings of cadres are called without first preparing reports and draft resolutions, and only when people have arrived for the meeting are makeshifts improvised; this is just like the saying, "Troops and horses have arrived, but food and fodder are not ready," and that is no good. Don't call a meeting in a hurry if the preparations are not completed.

9. "Fewer and better troops and simpler administration." Talks, speeches, articles, and resolutions should all be concise and to the point. Meetings also should not go on too long.

10. Pay attention to uniting and working with comrades who differ with you. This should be borne in mind both in the localities and in the army. It also applies to relations with people outside the Party. We have come together from every corner of the country and should be good at uniting in our work not only with comrades who hold the same views as we but also with those who hold different views. There are some among us who have made very serious mistakes; we should not be prejudiced against them but should be ready to work with them.

11. Guard against arrogance. For anyone in a leading position, this is a matter of principle and an important condition for maintaining unity. Even those who have made no serious mistakes and have achieved very great success in their work should not be

arrogant. Celebration of the birthdays of Party leaders is forbidden. Naming places, streets, and enterprises after Party leaders is likewise forbidden. We must keep to our style of plain living and hard work and put a stop to flattery and exaggerated praise.

12. Draw two lines of distinction. First, between revolution and counterrevolution, between Yenan [headquarters of the Chinese Communist Party, 1937–1947] and Sian [a major Kuomintang-held city in the same province as Yenan]. Some do not understand that they must draw this line of distinction. For example, when they combat bureaucracy, they speak of Yenan as though "nothing is right" there and fail to make a comparison and distinguish between the bureaucracy in Yenan and the bureaucracy in Sian. This is fundamentally wrong. Secondly, within the revolutionary ranks, it is necessary to make a clear distinction between right and wrong, between achievements and shortcomings and to make clear which of the two is primary and which secondary. For instance, do the achievements amount to 30 per cent or to 70 per cent of the whole? It will not do either to understate or to overstate. We must have a fundamental evaluation of a person's work and establish whether his achievements amount to 30 per cent and his mistakes to 70 per cent, or vice versa. If his achievements amount to 70 per cent of the whole, then his work should in the main be approved. It would be entirely wrong to describe work in which the achievements are primary as work in which the mistakes are primary. In our approach to problems we must not forget to draw these two lines of distinction, between revolution and counterrevolution and between achievements and shortcomings. We shall be able to handle things well if we bear these two distinctions in mind; otherwise we shall confuse the nature of the problems. To draw these distinctions well, careful study and analysis are of course necessary. Our attitude toward every person and every matter should be one of analysis and study.

The members of the Political Bureau and I personally feel that only by using the above methods can Party committees do their work well. In addition to conducting Party congresses well, it is most important for the Party committees at all levels to perform their work of leadership well. We must make efforts to study and perfect the methods of work so as to raise further the Party committee's level of leadership.

Teng Hsiao-p'ing • Another fundamental question with regard to democratic centralism in the Party is the question of collective leadership in Party organizations at all levels. Leninism demands of the Party that all important questions should be decided by an appropriate collective body, and not by any individual. The 20th Congress of the Communist Party of the Soviet Union [in 1956, at which Khrushchev denounced Stalin] has thrown a searching light on the profound significance of adhering to the principle of collective leadership and combating the cult of the individual, and this illuminating lesson has produced a tremendous effect not only on the Communist Party of the Soviet Union but also on the Communist Parties of all other countries throughout the world. It is obvious that the making of decisions on important questions by individuals runs counter to the Party-building principles of the political parties dedicated to the cause of communism, and is bound to lead to errors. Only collective leadership, in close touch with the masses, conforms to the Party's principle of democratic centralism and can reduce the possibility of errors to the minimum.

From Teng Hsiao-p'ing, *"Report on the Revision of the Constitution of the Communist Party of China"* [September 16, 1956], Eighth National Congress of the Communist Party of China, *Vol. I (Peking: Foreign Languages Press, 1956).*

The Mass Line in Action

Chao P'eng-fei and Li Ching-jung • In the middle of October this year, Secretary Liu Shou-mo of the Party branch of the 8th Company of a certain People's Liberation Army unit called a meeting of the Party branch to discuss the problem of how to strengthen the weak links in winter military training. In the discussion, it was unanimously held that the fact that the company was elected a "four-good" company and the Party branch elected an advanced branch in the first half of this year was an honor for all concerned. To maintain this honor, however, it was necessary to look for the weak points and grasp the weak links and seek continuous improvement. However, as to what the weak links were in the company, nobody was quite clear. As a result, the

From Jen-min jih-pao [People's Daily], *December 14, 1961.*

Party branch members separately held forums with the Party members and the company commander to find out the true conditions and canvass opinions. The wisdom of the masses was thus gathered together from the bottom to the top, and a groundwork was laid for holding an enlarged meeting of the Party branch.

At the enlarged meeting, the present weak links were quickly discovered. In military training, it was found, signs of momentary strain and relaxation appeared alternately, and the results were not as good as those obtained in the first half of the year. However, when it came to the analysis of the causes, different views were voiced. Some branch members believed that one cause was that the plan was improperly set and the key points were not brought to the fore. But the principal cause was that the soldiers did not sufficiently understand the aim and significance of everyday training. Other branch members believed that unsatisfactory planning was the main cause and that the initiative and consciousness of the soldiers gave no cause for concern. Still others believed that insufficient attention had been paid to the study of the good points of other fraternal companies, which only reduced the effect of everyday training. The secretary, seeing that uniformity of views could not be achieved at once, and that therefore a conclusion would not be reached quickly, adjourned the meeting temporarily and carried on discussions outside the meeting.

The next day, members of the branch went separately to the squads of the company to ask for opinions. Through their friendly talks with the soldiers, they eventually discovered the crux of the problem. It was that after this company had been elected a "four-good" company, a number of the cadres and soldiers gave way to self-complacency. They had no idea that the building of a "four-good" company was a long-term construction task. Unsatisfactory planning and arrangements and failure to learn from fraternal companies sufficiently were also contributing causes.

After unifying their understanding, the several company cadres then reconvened the enlarged meeting at which the feeling of self-complacency was opposed and the work of the cadres examined. On this basis, they devised measures for the improvement of work and adopted a suitable resolution. The resolution was then made known to the rank and file, and discussions were organized among them.

People's Daily • By reporting actual conditions, putting forth criticism, and making suggestions in their letters or during their calls on Party or government functionaries, the masses of the people have helped the Party organizations and government offices at various levels in Kansu Province to improve their work effectively.

Last year, the Party organizations and government offices at various levels in Kansu Province handled more letters and received more calls from the people than they did in 1960. According to incomplete statistics, in the 16 *hsien* and municipalities including Lanchow, Changyeh, and P'ingliang, more than 28,900 letters and calls were received from the people between January and October 1961, which number was 70 per cent greater than that received in the whole of 1960.

The Party organizations and government offices seriously handled the letters from the people and received visitors from among the people, with a view to improving their work and drawing closer their relationship with the popular masses. In the spring last year, Wang Ch'eng-wen, a commune member of Yüchia production team, Wuchai commune, T'ienshui municipality, reported in a letter to the local Party organization that the production team in which he was working did not assess work and record wage points strictly and had not implemented the principle of distribution according to work and that he had been credited with fewer wage points than he should have gained. After making an investigation, the local Party organization discovered that the system of assessing work and recording wage points adopted by this production team was really unsound. It therefore organized the cadres to study the socialist principle of distribution according to work and publicized and explained clearly this principle among the commune members so that certain faulty practices existing in the assessment of work and recording of wage points might be rectified and the masses' activism in production might be further mobilized. In the spring last year, some people wrote to the leadership organization of the province and suggested that more vegetables should be planted so that the masses might also have enough vegetables for consumption in the winter. The leadership organization accepted this

From Jen-min jih-pao [People's Daily], *January 9, 1962.*

suggestion and instructed that vacant lots and land around houses should be utilized for growing vegetables. As a result, good harvests of vegetables were reaped in all areas last year, and the masses were assured of vegetables for consumption in the winter. . . .

The Party organizations and government offices at various levels in Kansu Province have led cadres to pay close attention to the letters and calls from the people. From January to November last year, Wang Feng, first secretary of the CCP Kansu Provincial Committee, and Kao Chien-chün, second secretary of the CCP Kansu Provincial Committee, handled a total of over 300 letters from the people and replied to every letter. When important problems were revealed by the people in their letters or during their calls, these two secretaries asked the leadership cadres of relevant departments to hold informal meetings together with the people who had sent in letters or who had called, listen humbly to their views, and take prompt action accordingly.

Sun Shou-chih • After considering these problems [concerning my method of work], I discovered that, although I had formerly done a great deal of work, I was not good at grasping important problems and had dealt with some problems too loosely. Thereupon, I decided to improve my leadership style and work method. After that, on the one hand, I often went to the neighboring brigade (Fanlou brigade) and chatted with Chang Shih-tsun, secretary of the Party branch who was experienced in doing leadership work, and asked his advice; on the other hand, I studied documents concerning methods for carrying out the Party's assignments. After paying visits and doing some study, I further realized that, to rid myself of administrative work and to carry out all tasks actively instead of passively, I must define clearly the boundary line between the work of the Party branch and that of the administrative committee. I also realized that I must fully develop the role played by the administrative committee while I arranged farm jobs and dealt with everyday administrative work. The Party branch should concentrate forces on the implementation of the Party's policies, ideological and political work, and important problems. When I found this good method of work, I tried to enforce it. In this year's busy summer harvest-

From Jen-min jih-pao [People's Daily], *December 21, 1961.*

ing and plowing, we successively called meetings of the Party branch committee and of the Party members, at which we studied ways to carry out summer harvesting and plowing properly. After discussion, all participants suggested that the Party branch should lay emphasis on the propaganda and implementation of the Party's policy on distribution and give the cadres and masses an education in collectivism, and that the administrative committee should take up major responsibility for the organization of such concrete farm jobs as harvesting, transportation, threshing, and plowing. When the spheres of work were clearly defined, all participants at the meetings had their doubts dispelled. For the purpose of properly organizing summer harvesting and summer plowing, the administrative committee divided all tasks clearly among its members, who tried their best to carry out these tasks. When I came to the fields, I saw that people were enthusiastically harvesting and threshing wheat and plowing the land. The work was busy but not chaotic and was carried out at high speed and with good results. Consequently, our brigade was elected one of the advanced brigades in the whole commune.

From the General to the Specific

Liu Shao-ch'i • In the light of the practical experience gained in the people's struggle and of the development of Comrade Mao Tse-tung's thinking in the past few years, the Central Committee of the Party is of the opinion that the following are the basic points of our general line [of socialist construction], which is to build socialism by exerting our utmost efforts, and pressing ahead consistently to achieve greater, faster, better, and more economical results:

To mobilize all positive factors and correctly handle contradictions among the people;

To consolidate and develop socialist ownership, *i.e.*, ownership by the whole people and collective ownership, and consolidate the proletarian dictatorship and proletarian international solidarity;

From Liu Shao-ch'i, *"Report on the Work of the Central Committee of the Communist Party of China"* [*May 5, 1958*], Second Session of the Eighth National Congress of the Communist Party of China (*Peking: Foreign Languages Press, 1958*).

To carry out the technical revolution and cultural revolution step by step, while completing the socialist revolution on the economic, political, and ideological fronts;

To develop industry and agriculture simultaneously while giving priority to heavy industry;

With centralized leadership, overall planning, proper division of labor, and coordination, to develop national and local industries, and large, small, and medium-sized enterprises simultaneously; and

By means of all this to build our country, in the shortest possible time, into a great socialist country with a modern industry, modern agriculture, and modern science and culture.

T'ao Chu • In addition to a correct general line, there must be a correct method of work. Without a correct method of work, the general line cannot be correctly carried out, and the correct general line will become meaningless. Thus the general line for socialist construction having been correctly proposed, the question seriously confronting us is how to concretely carry it out.

The general line . . . is a Marxist summing up and generalization of our experiences in building socialism and is undoubtedly correct. The general line expressed in these words was chartered by the Central Committee according to the strong aspiration of the whole nation for, and with the practical possibility of, rapidly changing the "white and poor" outlook of our country.

The correctness of the general line might be explained in two ways. First, let us look at the characteristics of the socialist society. With the elimination of class exploitation and oppression, the working people become masters of the society and perform labor for the sake of building a happy society and constantly raising their living standard. Anarchy in production, competition, and crises are replaced by the planned development of social production and the rational use of the means of production and labor power. As the productive forces are basically adapted to the relationship of production and as antagonistic social forces are nonexistent, contradictions arising from development may be constantly resolved through internal adjustment. For this reason, socialist construction is bound to develop at a fast tempo. This is the law of objectivity. It is in accordance with this law of ob-

From Jen-min jih-pao [People's Daily], *June 18, 1959.*

jectivity that the Party charted the general line. . . .

However, a correct general line does not amount to a solution of all problems. There is also involved here the question of how to carry it out, *i.e.*, the question of whether the work is good or bad. True, the general line is of decisive significance for our acceleration of socialist construction, but the existence of the general line does not amount to the acceleration of socialist construction. Therefore, the crux of the matter is whether there is a good method of work to realize this general line. How to exert efforts to the utmost, how to press ahead consistently, to what extent should more, faster, better, and more economical results be obtained—all these matters should be determined in concrete terms according to different times, localities, and conditions.

Liu P'ei-ying • The Young Communist League * group is an assistant to the Party group [and adapts its methods of work to the Party's guidance in production teams]. The League's chief task is to rally the youth of the whole team around the Party so that they can share the same will and same goal in promoting well the production and livelihood of the team. Over the past year and more, the League groups have performed many tasks [in organizational work and ideological education].

Our experiences in organizational work are as follows:

1. To improve organized life, we make it our general practice to "live an organized life" every ten days, when circumstances permit. Prior to such an occasion, the League group heads first hold discussions on the crucial problems existing among the League members. Then they ask the Party groups for instructions, and a meeting is called to work out timely solutions.

2. To enable every League member to play an exemplary role, we have appointed 13 of the 15 League members in different offices in the team. We constantly educate them in the necessity of completing first the tasks at their own posts and playing an exemplary role in work and labor. We make it our practice to laud achievements promptly and criticize defects. As a result, the 15 League members were all cited as "five-good" League members last year.

* The Young Communist League comprises approximately 25 million youth between the ages of 14 and 25.

From Chung-kuo ch'ing-nien pao [China Youth News], *February 8, 1961.*

3. Leadership is exercised at all levels. Every League member undertakes to get in touch with three young activists and guide them in production and livelihood as their bosom friends. In the whole brigade, 34 young activists emerged last year. They were all given citations or awards by the teams or the brigade. They have actually formed the backbone of the brigade and, through them, over 90 per cent of the youth of the whole brigade have been united.

Our experiences in ideological work are as follows:

1. We must educate the League members and the young people in the Party's guidelines and policies regularly and in good time and enable them to master the spirit of the policies in concrete correlation with practice. Immediately after the Party groups formulate concrete measures for a campaign, we must call a League group meeting to discuss and carry them out. We must have a definite idea of the task to be done and the way of doing it and also understand the reasons for so doing. During the harvesting and distribution last spring, last summer, and last autumn, we discussed and studied accordingly the "three guarantees and one reward" system, the basic man-day system, and other basic policies doing so in correlation with the prevailing state of production of the brigade. We then took the lead in carrying these systems out.

2. We always find out the crucial problems related to the thinking of the League members and the young people and give them timely ideological education helpful to the elimination of erroneous thinking. In the second half of the past year, a small number of youths cherished an erroneous idea about the situation. Thereupon, we organized a discussion and invited the old peasants to tell stories in which the past was compared with the present. In addition, we educated them in the principle of regarding the whole country as a chess game and the necessity of building it industriously and thriftily.

The ideological education is of a varied pattern. Apart from calling the usual meetings of League members and youths through the personal contacts of League members, we often organize the people to do ideological work. As ideological education was firmly grasped, 59 of the youth of our team earned basic work points last year in excess of what they were required to earn.

T'ung Yün • Persuasive education [which is our basic method of work among the people] is penetrating, painstaking, concrete, and vivid ideological work. First, one must go into the midst of the masses to discover their worries, analyze them concretely, and deal with them separately. The contradictions within the ranks of the people are varied and numerous, and the ideological problems of the masses are complicated. The first step in conducting persuasive education is to discern correctly the substance of such problems and to explain clearly what is right and what is wrong in this connection. Persuasive education cannot be carried out correctly before the substance of the concrete problem concerned has been clearly discerned.

To extend ideological education into the minds of others, to persuade others really, and to heighten their ideological consciousness with true success, one must adopt the "one key for one lock" method and carry out work carefully and not roughly. The object of persuasive education has life, for it is man himself. Because of their differences in origin, age, work, environment, income, educational level, experience of life, and mental development, two people may differ also in thought and in the level of their ideological consciousness. Even thoughts and feelings of the same person may vary according to the time, the environment, the kind of work he is doing, and the knowledge he has. The advanced state, the mediocre state, and the backward state also change constantly. Because of this, one must, when conducting ideological education, analyze concretely the specific person, thing, problem, and thought concerned, and discern the substance and the facts of the problem; that is, find out whether the problem involves a contradiction between the people and the enemy or one within the ranks of the people, whether it is a political or an ideological problem, whether it is due to failure to take the proletarian stand firmly or due to one-sidedness in understanding, whether it is a historical problem or a present problem, whether it is a moral problem or a problem of one's habitual way of living, whether it involves any principle or is merely an accident, and so on. One should then deal with the object of persuasive education and the problem concerned in a specific suitable manner, such as by arranging for individual talks, holding forums,

From Jen-min jih-pao [People's Daily], *January 13, 1962.*

or commending the advanced—that is, conducting education with advanced cases as examples. The holding of individual talks is the most important of these methods, because it provides the greatest facility for the consideration of the concrete conditions of the individual. This is essential to the success of persuasive education.

When we say that we should employ "one key for one lock" as a method, we do not mean that centralized, unified education may be dispensed with. The masses have many common problems in thinking and understanding. All these can and must be solved through such methods of more centralized, more unified education such as the making of reports, the organization of discussions, and the calling of conferences. Similarly, when we say that ideological work must be carried out carefully, we do not mean that large-scale mass movements should be left out. The two form a dialectical union. Large-scale mass movements are to be based on penetrating and painstaking work. Without regular, careful work, no true large-scale mass movement in which the broad masses take part consciously can be formed.

Chapter 7

State Power

D URING the late 1930's the Communist Party elite adapted its concepts of leadership to the operation of state institutions, emerging with two fundamental purposes of state. The first purpose held that the state should have the monopoly of legitimate force to suppress "enemies" and threaten any who might side with the enemy; the second, that the state should give expression to the "united will" of the working classes.

In the light of impending victory, shortly before the establishment of the Chinese People's Republic on October 1, 1949, Mao Tse-tung reexamined the first purpose of the state in his *On People's Democratic Dictatorship*. In it he advocated an alliance of two cooperative elements of the Chinese middle class— the so-called "petty bourgeoisie" and "national bourgeoisie"— with the working class and the peasantry under the leadership of the Chinese Communist Party. These four allied classes would constitute the "people" who would be organized and led by the "democratic" methods of persuasion rather than compulsion. In turn, the people's state would exercise a dictatorship "for the oppression of antagonistic classes." Leaving nothing to doubt on the coercive nature of the new Chinese state, Mao added:

> Our present task is to strengthen the people's state apparatus —mainly the people's army, the people's police, and the people's courts. . . . Our policy of benevolence is applied only within the ranks of the people, not beyond them to the reactionaries or the reactionary activities of reactionary classes.

The authoritative status of the democratic dictatorship was affirmed in the 1949 Organic Law for the Chinese People's Political Consultative Conference (CPPCC), and at its first session the

CPPCC adopted a Common Program, which rationalized the maximization of state power within the framework of the "united-front" alliance of the four classes of the people.

Communist leaders, however, have long argued that this state structure based on selective applications of force and on a limited united-front alliance was a temporary expedient. The second—and more fundamental—purpose of a "people's state," they insisted, was the expression of the "united will" of the working classes for whom the Party acted as "director and faithful instrument," and they pointed out that a government "of the people" must correspond to the genuine interests of the working classes—interests that could best be comprehended by their leading element, the Chinese Communist Party. When applied to Communist-led government, this line of argument precluded the notion of limited or "constitutional" government, which was condemned as a "fraudulent attempt to restrict the will of the masses." Thus in its dealings with the working-class and peasant population, the people's government theoretically had unlimited power to carry out the "popular will" and to manipulate that will in accordance with the policies of the Party. In the mobilization of the Chinese people for Party purposes, regulations require cadres in the state administration to use mass-line methods.

The shift to persuasion and the mass line, signifying a positive role for state operation, occurred in 1954 with the establishment of the people's congresses and the adoption of the Constitution of the People's Republic of China. Somewhat optimistically, the new Constitution postulated a condition of unity and cooperation in Chinese social relations and formulated the "positive" principle of state operation in terms of democratic centralism. (Formerly, both the mass line and democratic centralism were concepts reserved for the organization and operation of the Party.) The 1954 Constitution, however, retained the CPPCC—and hence democratic dictatorship within the overall state system—in order to deal with remaining domestic and foreign enemies. Thus rationalized, force was retained as an integral aspect of the new "administrative state." The Communist leaders, however, assumed that the elimination of antagonistic classes by collectivization of the means of production and systematic impoverishment of former "wealthy groups" would gradually permit all state institutions to become direct instruments of the working classes, whereupon force, presumably, would then be retained for external aggressors. With no antagonistic classes present internally, democratic dictatorship would disappear completely.

Effective elimination of antagonistic classes appeared imminent in 1955–1956, when the Party cadres substantially concluded the socialization of industries and business enterprises and the collectivization of agriculture. Shortly thereafter, Mao Tsetung examined the new "nonantagonistic" relations among the people brought about by the developments in 1955–1956 and their effect on the organization and operation of the state. Since Article 4, the main article of the Chinese Constitution, had stipulated that the principal goal of the People's Republic is the "building of a socialist society," some writers suggested that socialization and collectivization necessitated the creation of state organs for the "building of communism." From the spate of writings in 1956–1957 dealing with state structure, it appeared that at that time the Chinese Communists indeed believed that the so-called "central task" for accomplishing the transition to socialism had been largely completed and were giving their attention to the "next form" of the state structure. It was this discussion that in 1958 helped to shape the rural people's communes as agencies of local government.

Initially, the Party conceived the commune to be the most effective governmental instrument for the transition from socialism to communism (see Chapter 9, pp. 292–293), intending that the commune replace local-level people's congresses and people's councils at the *hsiang* (subcounty) level. But, as the Party has had to admit, the amalgamation of state and commune apparatus is still incomplete. The post-1958 production crisis in agriculture not only undermined the amalgamation but brought about a revision of the commune to account for variations among villages and for lack of incentives. By 1961, the production team, the lowest institutional level of the commune and the equivalent of lower-level agricultural unit in the older collectivization organization, had assumed the dominant role in ownership, production, distribution, and accounting, and the role of the commune as an agency of the state was in serious doubt. The commune had failed to launch the next transitional stage—transition to communism—and Communist leaders were left in the awkward position of having backed an unsuccessful state form.

In Marxist theory, a failure of this order can only result from a fundamental misunderstanding of the productive forces and the social relations that together comprise the "economic base." The implications of such a misunderstanding have proved so serious that the Chinese Communist Party has found it necessary to overemphasize the "mistakes" of individual cadres and the "unavoidable natural catastrophes" to explain the retarding of the proper development of the "objective" economic base.

In Part I of this chapter, the selections on the state reveal the extent to which the state is conceived as an instrument of the Party. The Chinese Communists do not equivocate on this point and are even more precise when they discuss their concepts of law and foreign policy (see Parts II and III of this chapter). Only Party cadres may determine principles, objectives, and policy. Implementation—and thus the blame for failure—belongs to the state. Nevertheless, policy-making is difficult to separate from implementation and administration, and Party cadres, who often hold leading posts in the state as well as the Party, may both determine specific policies and supervise their execution in the state administration.

The overlapping of Party and state personnel is particularly evident at the national level, where members of the Political Bureau hold major positions in the government. For example, the chief administrative organ, the State Council, is composed of Premier Chou En-lai and sixteen vice premiers, 12 of whom are members or alternate members of the Political Bureau. Chu Teh heads the Standing Committee of the National People's Congress, and Lin Piao controls the military arm of the state, the Ministry of National Defense. The highest state official, the Chairman of the Chinese People's Republic, is Liu Shao-ch'i, the No. 2 man in the Standing Committee of the Political Bureau.

The Party has devoted unusual attention to the function of law in the socialist state. Annual compendiums of laws include major speeches and reports of Party leaders, Central Committee and State Council directives, and bills formally enacted by the National People's Congress and promulgated by Chairman Liu Shao-ch'i. Since there are no restrictions, the Party can announce the new "will of the people" at any time without recourse to constitutional procedures. With respect to criminal law, legal writers in mainland China have specifically rejected the principles that the accused should be presumed innocent until proved guilty and that judges should have discretion when determining guilt or passing sentence. Law is a weapon of the people against the enemy, and the people's representatives or "people's assessors" sit on the court to insure that the will of the people is done. Since the Party's unlimited role in lawmaking precludes any significant consideration of popular rights, this section of the Constitution is virtually meaningless and has been omitted. Doctrine asserts that "rights" belong only to the "people," and that the Party has the duty to eliminate the "enemies" who lurk among the people. But, anyone who violates the law may be redesignated as an "enemy," and his rights thus vanish at the one time they would be applicable.

In addition to the hierarchy of courts, the Constitution provides for people's procuratorates that investigate criminal violations, supervise the courts, and execute the sentences of the courts. The procuratorates maintain the penal apparatus in China, which includes "reform through labor" camps as well as prisons and jails.

The principles of foreign policy given in Part III of this chapter should not be confused with individual policies, which are very fluid in nature. The selections here stress the doctrinal rather than the substantive content of Chinese foreign policy and demonstrate some of the consistencies of approach and outlook and the continuities that have existed between domestic and foreign questions. The present "general line" of foreign relations is based on a set of judgments on the world's people, "marginal" people, and enemies that have been derived from similar judgments on the domestic level. During the three post-1949 periods—the 1949–1952 period of reconstruction and ruthless elimination of landlords and other inimical elements by force and terror; the 1953–1957 period of economic development for the transition to socialism; and since 1958 the period of the rise and decline of the "great leap"—a striking consistency can be found between internal and external decisions. For example, the militant tone evident in the measures that led to the extermination of the Kuomintang and the landlords carried into the Korean War and the open Chinese support for violent revolutions throughout Asia. This hostile stance gave way to the more moderate and conciliatory line that lasted from 1954 through 1957 and was sloganized as the "Bandung spirit." Supposedly derived from the 1955 meeting of Asian and African states at Bandung, Indonesia, that spirit rapidly faded after 1958, when China stepped up its propaganda offensive on "American aggression in

Taiwan," made armed forays into Indian territory, casually toss-
ing away its good will in that country, and actively attempted
to take the place of pro-Russian Communists in the politics of
the Middle East, Africa, and Latin America. The most sensational aspect of the post-1958 Chinese political posture abroad
has been the widening rift between Peking and Moscow. At no
time has the complex interaction of domestic and international
attitudes been more clearly demonstrated than in the mounting
antagonism between the Communist bloc's two great powers. The
last selection in Part III of this chapter, dealing with Chinese
foreign policy, highlights basic Chinese Communist outlooks that
have aggravated the tensions and led to increasingly provocative
Chinese statements toward the Soviet Union. The reader may
then compare the Party's general attitudes and policies toward
foreign relations with the lengthy statement on the Sino-Soviet
dispute in Chapter 8.

I. PARTY AND STATE

The Administration of Things
on the Way to Utopia

Constitution of the People's Republic of China

PREAMBLE

In the year 1949, after more than a century of heroic struggle,
the Chinese people, led by the Communist Party of China, finally
achieved their great victory in the people's revolution against imperialism, feudalism, and bureaucratic capitalism and so brought
to an end a long history of oppression and enslavement and
founded the People's Republic of China, a people's democratic
dictatorship. The system of people's democracy—new democracy
—of the People's Republic of China guarantees that China can
in a peaceful way banish exploitation and poverty and build a
prosperous and happy socialist society.

---

*From the text of the Constitution of the People's Republic of China, adopted
September 20, 1954, by the First National People's Congress of the People's
Republic of China.*

From the founding of the People's Republic of China to the attainment of a socialist society is a period of transition. During the transition the fundamental task of the state is, step by step, to bring about the socialist industrialization of the country and, step by step, to accomplish the socialist transformation of agriculture, handicrafts, and capitalist industry and commerce. In the last few years our people have successfully carried out a series of large-scale struggles: the reform of the agrarian system, resistance to American aggression and aid to Korea, the suppression of counterrevolutionaries, and the rehabilitation of the national economy. As a result, the necessary conditions have been created for planned economic construction and gradual transition to socialism.

The First National People's Congress of the People's Republic of China, at its first session held in Peking, the capital, solemnly adopted the Constitution of the People's Republic of China on September 20, 1954. This Constitution is based on the Common Program of the Chinese People's Political Consultative Conference of 1949, and is an advance on it. It consolidates the gains of the Chinese people's revolution and the political and economic victories won since the founding of the People's Republic of China; and, moreover, it reflects the basic needs of the state in the period of transition, as well as the general desire of the people as a whole to build a socialist society.

In the course of the great struggle to establish the People's Republic of China, the people of our country forged a broad people's democratic united front, composed of all democratic classes, democratic parties and groups, and popular organizations, and led by the Communist Party of China. This people's democratic united front will continue to play its part in mobilizing and rallying the whole people in common struggle to fulfill the fundamental task of the state during the transition and to oppose enemies within and without.

All nationalities of our country are united in one great family of free and equal nations. This unity of China's nationalities will continue to gain in strength, founded as it is on ever-growing friendship and mutual aid among themselves, and on the struggle against imperialism, against public enemies of the people within the nationalities, and against both dominant-nation chauvinism and local nationalism. In the course of economic and cultural development, the state will concern itself with the needs of the different nationalities, and, in the matter of socialist transformation, pay full attention to the special characteristics in the development of each.

China has already built an indestructible friendship with the great Union of Soviet Socialist Republics and the people's democracies; and the friendship between our people and peace-loving people in all other countries is growing day by day. Such friendship will be constantly strengthened and broadened. China's policy of establishing and extending diplomatic relations with all countries on the principle of equality, mutual benefit, and mutual respect for each other's sovereignty and territorial integrity, which has already yielded success, will continue to be carried out. In international affairs our firm and consistent policy is to strive for the noble cause of world peace and the progress of humanity.

CHAPTER ONE—GENERAL PRINCIPLES

Article 1: The People's Republic of China is a people's democratic state led by the working class and based on the alliance of workers and peasants.

Article 2: All power in the People's Republic of China belongs to the people. The organs through which the people exercise power are the National People's Congress and the local people's congresses.

The National People's Congress, the local people's congresses, and other organs of state practice democratic centralism.

Article 3: The People's Republic of China is a single multi-national state.

All the nationalities are equal. Discrimination against, or oppression of, any nationality, and acts which undermine the unity of the nationalities are prohibited.

All the nationalities have freedom to use and foster the growth of their spoken and written languages, and to preserve or reform their own customs or ways.

Regional autonomy applies in areas where people of national minorities live in compact communities. National autonomous areas are inalienable parts of the People's Republic of China.

Article 4: The People's Republic of China, by relying on the organs of state and the social forces, and by means of socialist industrialization and socialist transformation, insures the gradual abolition of systems of exploitation and the building of a socialist society.

Article 5: At present, the following basic forms of ownership of means of production exist in the People's Republic of China: state ownership, that is, ownership by the whole people; co-operative ownership, that is, collective ownership by the working masses, ownership by individual working people; and capitalist ownership.

Article 6: The state sector of the economy is a socialist sector, owned by the whole people. It is the leading force in the national economy and the material basis on which the state carries out socialist transformation. The state insures priority for the development of the state sector of the economy.

All mineral resources and waters, as well as forests, undeveloped land, and other resources which the state owns by law, arc the property of the whole people.

Article 7: The cooperative sector of the economy is either socialist, when collectively owned by the working masses, or semi-socialist, when in part collectively owned by the working masses. Partial collective ownership by the working masses is a transitional form by means of which individual peasants, individual handicraftsmen, and other individual working people organize themselves in their advance toward collective ownership by the working masses.

The state protects the property of the cooperatives, encourages, guides, and helps the development of the cooperative sector of the economy. It regards the promotion of producer's cooperatives as the chief means for the transformation of individual farming and individual handicrafts.

Article 8: The state protects the right of peasants to own land and other means of production according to law.

The state guides and helps individual peasants to increase production and encourages them to organize producers', supply and marketing, and credit cooperatives voluntarily.

The policy of the state toward rich-peasant economy is to restrict and gradually eliminate it.

Article 9: The state protects the right of handicraftsmen and other nonagricultural individual working people to own means of production according to law.

The state guides and helps individual handicraftsmen and other nonagricultural individual working people to improve their enterprise and encourages them to organize producers' and supply and marketing cooperatives voluntarily.

Article 10: The state protects the right of capitalists to own means of production and other capital according to law.

The policy of the state toward capitalist industry and commerce is to use, restrict, and transform them. The state makes use of the positive sides of capitalist industry and commerce which are beneficial to national welfare and the people's livelihood, restricts their negative sides which are not beneficial to national welfare and the people's livelihood, encourages and guides their transformation into various forms of state-capitalist economy, gradually replacing capitalist ownership with ownership by the whole people; and this it does by means of control exercised by administrative organs of state, the leadership given by the state sector of the economy, and supervision by the workers.

The state forbids capitalists to engage in unlawful activities which injure the public interest, disrupt the social-economic order, or undermine the economic plan of the state.

Article 11: The state protects the right of citizens to own lawfully earned incomes, savings, houses, and other means of life.

Article 12: The state protects the right of citizens to inherit private property according to law.

Article 13: The state may, in the public interest, buy, requisition, or nationalize land and other means of production both in cities and countryside according to provisions of law.

Article 14: The state forbids any person to use his private property to the detriment of the public interest.

Article 15: By economic planning, the state directs the growth and transformation of the national economy to bring about the constant increase of productive forces, in this way enriching the material and cultural life of the people and consolidating the independence and security of the country.

Article 16: Work is a matter of honor for every citizen of the People's Republic of China who is able to work. The state encourages citizens to take an active and creative part in their work.

Article 17: All organs of state must rely on the masses of the people, constantly maintain close contact with them, heed their opinions, and accept their supervision.

Article 18: All servants of the state must be loyal to the people's democratic system, observe the Constitution and the law, and strive to serve the people.

Article 19: The People's Republic of China safeguards the people's democratic system, suppresses all treasonable and counterrevolutionary activities, and punishes all traitors and counterrevolutionaries.

The state deprives feudal landlords and bureaucrat-capitalists of political rights for a specific period of time according to law; at the same time it provides them with a way to earn a living, in order to enable them to reform through work and become citizens who earn their livelihood by their own labor.

Article 20: The armed forces of the People's Republic of China belong to the people; their duty is to safeguard the gains of the people's revolution and the achievements of national construction, and to defend the sovereignty, territorial integrity, and security of the country.

CHAPTER TWO—THE STATE STRUCTURE

SECTION I—*The National People's Congress*

Article 21: The National People's Congress is the highest organ of state authority in the People's Republic of China.

Article 22: The National People's Congress is the only legislative authority in the country.

Article 23: The National People's Congress is composed of deputies elected by provinces, autonomous regions, municipalities directly under the central authority, the armed forces, and Chinese resident abroad.

The number of deputies to the National People's Congress, including those representing national minorities, and the manner of their election are prescribed by electoral law.

Article 24: The National People's Congress is elected for a term of four years.

Two months before the term of office of the National People's Congress expires, its Standing Committee must complete the election of deputies to the succeeding National People's Congress. Should exceptional circumstances arise preventing such an election, the term of office of the sitting National People's Congress may be prolonged until the first session of the succeeding National People's Congress.

Article 25: The National People's Congress meets once a year, convened by its Standing Committee. It may also be convened whenever its Standing Committee deems this necessary or one fifth of the deputies so propose.

Article 26: When the National People's Congress meets, it elects a presidium to conduct its sittings.

Article 27: The National People's Congress exercises the following functions and powers:

1. to amend the Constitution;
2. to enact laws;
3. to supervise the enforcement of the Constitution;
4. to elect the Chairman and the Vice Chairman of the People's Republic of China;
5. to decide on the choice of the Premier of the State Council upon recommendation by the Chairman of the People's Republic of China, and of the component members of the State Council upon recommendation by the Premier;
6. to decide on the choice of the Vice Chairmen and other members of the Council of National Defense upon recommendation by the Chairman of the People's Republic of China;
7. to elect the President of the Supreme People's Court;
8. to elect the Chief Procurator of the Supreme People's Procuratorate;
9. to decide on the national economic plans;
10. to examine and approve the state budget and the financial report;
11. to ratify the status and boundaries of provinces, autonomous regions, and municipalities directly under the central authority;
12. to decide on general amnesties;
13. to decide on questions of war and peace; and
14. to exercise such other functions and powers as the National People's Congress considers necessary.

Article 28: The National People's Congress has power to remove from office:

1. the Chairman and the Vice Chairman of the People's Republic of China;
2. the Premier and Vice Premiers, Ministers, heads of Commissions, and the Secretary General of the State Council;
3. the Vice Chairmen and other members of the Council of National Defense;
4. the President of the Supreme People's Court; and
5. the Chief Procurator of the Supreme People's Procuratorate.

Article 29: Amendments to the Constitution require a two-thirds majority vote of all the deputies to the National People's Congress.

Laws and other bills require a simple majority vote of all the deputies to the National People's Congress.

Article 30: The Standing Committee of the National People's Congress is a permanently acting body of the National People's Congress.

The Standing Committee is composed of the following members, elected by the National People's Congress:

the Chairman;
the Vice Chairman;
the Secretary General; and
other members.

Article 31: The Standing Committee of the National People's Congress exercises the following functions and powers:

1. to conduct the election of deputies to the National People's Congress;
2. to convene the National People's Congress;
3. to interpret the laws;
4. to adopt decrees;
5. to supervise the work of the State Council, the Supreme People's Court, and the Supreme People's Procuratorate;
6. to annul decisions and orders of the State Council which contravene the Constitution, laws, or decrees;
7. to revise or annul inappropriate decisions issued by the government authorities of provinces, autonomous regions, and municipalities directly under the central authority;

8. to decide on the appointment or removal of any Vice Premier, Minister, head of Commission, or the Secretary General of the State Council when the National People's Congress is not in session;

9. to appoint or remove the Vice Presidents, judges, and other members of the Judicial Committee of the Supreme People's Court;

10. to appoint or remove the Deputy Chief Procurators, procurators, and other members of the Procuratorial Committee of the Supreme People's Procuratorate;

11. to decide on the appointment or recall of plenipotentiary representatives to foreign states;

12. to decide on the ratification or abrogation of treaties concluded with foreign states;

13. to institute military, diplomatic, and other special titles and ranks;

14. to institute and decide on the award of state orders, medals, and titles of honor;

15. to decide on the granting of pardons;

16. to decide, when the National People's Congress is not in session, on the proclamation of a state of war in the event of armed attack on the country or in fulfillment of international treaty obligations concerning common defense against aggression;

17. to decide on general or partial mobilization;

18. to decide on the enforcement of martial law throughout the country or in certain areas; and

19. to exercise such other functions and powers as are vested in it by the National People's Congress.

Article 32: The Standing Committee of the National People's Congress exercises its functions and powers until a new Standing Committee is elected by the succeeding National People's Congress.

Article 33: The Standing Committee of the National People's Congress is responsible to the National People's Congress and reports to it.

The National People's Congress has power to recall members of its Standing Committee.

Article 34: The National People's Congress establishes a Nationalities Committee, a Bills Committee, a Budget Committee, a Credentials Committee, and other necessary committees.

The Nationalities Committee and the Bills Committee are under the direction of the Standing Committee of the National People's Congress when the National People's Congress is not in session.

Article 35: The National People's Congress, or its Standing Committee if the National People's Congress is not in session, may, if necessary, appoint commissions of inquiry for the investigation of specific questions.

All organs of state, people's organizations, and citizens concerned are obliged to supply necessary information to these commissions when they conduct investigations.

Article 36: Deputies to the National People's Congress have the right to address questions to the State Council, or to the Ministries and Commissions of the State Council, which are under obligation to answer.

Article 37: No deputy to the National People's Congress may be arrested or placed on trial without the consent of the National People's Congress or, when the National People's Congress is not in session, of its Standing Committee.

Article 38: Deputies to the National People's Congress are subject to the supervision of the units which elect them. These electoral units have power to replace at any time the deputies they elect, according to the procedure prescribed by law.

SECTION II—*The Chairman of the People's Republic of China*

Article 39: The Chairman of the People's Republic of China is elected by the National People's Congress. Any citizen of the People's Republic of China who has the right to vote and stand for election and has reached the age of thirty-five is eligible for election as Chairman of the People's Republic of China.

The term of office of the Chairman of the People's Republic of China is four years.

Article 40: The Chairman of the People's Republic of China, in pursuance of decisions of the National People's Congress or the Standing Committee of the National People's Congress, promulgates laws and decrees; appoints or removes the Premier, Vice Premiers, Ministers, heads of Commissions, and the Secretary General of the State Council; appoints or removes the Vice Chairmen and other members of the Council of National Defense; confers state orders, medals, and titles of honor; proclaims general amnesties and grants pardons; proclaims martial law; proclaims a state of war; and orders mobilization.

Article 41: The Chairman of the People's Republic of China represents the People's Republic of China in its relations with foreign states, receives foreign diplomatic representatives, and, in pursuance of decisions of the Standing Committee of the National People's Congress, appoints or recalls plenipotentiary representatives to foreign states and ratifies treaties concluded with foreign states.

Article 42: The Chairman of the People's Republic of China commands the armed forces of the country, and is Chairman of the Council of National Defense.

Article 43: The Chairman of the People's Republic of China, whenever necessary, convenes a Supreme State Conference and acts as its chairman.

The Vice Chairman of the People's Republic of China, the Chairman of the Standing Committee of the National People's Congress, the Premier of the State Council, and other persons concerned take part in the Supreme State Conference.

The Chairman of the People's Republic of China submits the views of the Supreme State Conference on important affairs of state to the National People's Congress, its Standing Committee, the State Council, or other bodies concerned for their consideration and decision. . . .

SECTION III—*The State Council*

Article 47: The State Council of the People's Republic of China, that is, the Central People's Government, is the executive organ of the highest state authority; it is the highest administrative organ of state.

Article 48: The State Council is composed of the following members:

> the Premier;
> the Vice Premiers;
> the Ministers;
> the heads of Commissions; and
> the Secretary General.

The organization of the State Council is determined by law.

Article 49: The State Council exercises the following functions and powers:

1. to formulate administrative measures, issue decisions and orders, and verify their execution, in accordance with the Constitution, laws, and decrees;

2. to submit bills to the National People's Congress or its Standing Committee;

3. to coordinate and lead the work of Ministries and Commissions;

4. to coordinate and lead the work of local administrative organs of state throughout the country;

5. to revise or annul inappropriate orders and directives issued by Ministers or by heads of Commissions;

6. to revise or annul inappropriate decisions and orders issued by local administrative organs of state;

7. to put into effect the national economic plans and provisions of the state budget;

8. to control foreign and domestic trade;

9. to direct cultural, educational, and public health work;

10. to administer affairs concerning the nationalities;

11. to administer affairs concerning Chinese resident abroad;

12. to protect the interests of the state, to maintain public order, and to safeguard the rights of citizens;

13. to direct the conduct of external affairs;

14. to guide the building up of the defense forces;

15. to ratify the status and boundaries of autonomous *chou,* counties, autonomous counties, and municipalities;

16. to appoint or remove administrative personnel according to provisions of law; and

17. to exercise such other functions and powers as are vested in it by the National People's Congress or its Standing Committee.

Article 50: The Premier directs the work of the State Council and presides over its meetings.

The Vice Premiers assist the Premier in his work.

Article 51: The Ministers and heads of Commissions direct the work of their respective departments. They may issue orders and directives within the jurisdiction of their respective departments and in accordance with laws and decrees, and decisions and orders of the State Council.

Article 52: The State Council is responsible to the National People's Congress and reports to it; or, when the National People's Congress is not in session, to its Standing Committee.

SECTION IV—*The Local People's Congresses and Local People's Councils*

Article 53: The administrative division of the People's Republic of China is as follows:

1. The country is divided into provinces, autonomous regions, and municipalities directly under the central authority;
2. Provinces and autonomous regions are divided into autonomous *chou,* counties, autonomous counties, and municipalities; and
3. Counties and autonomous counties are divided into *hsiang,* nationality *hsiang,* and towns.

Municipalities directly under the central authority and other large municipalities are divided into districts. Autonomous *chou* are divided into counties, autonomous counties, and municipalities.

Autonomous regions, autonomous *chou,* and autonomous counties are all national autonomous areas.

Article 54: People's congresses and people's councils are established in provinces, municipalities directly under the central authority, counties, municipalities, municipal districts, *hsiang,* nationality *hsiang,* and towns.

Organs of self-government are established in autonomous regions, autonomous *chou,* and autonomous counties. The organization and work of organs of self-government are specified in Section V of Chapter Two of the Constitution.

Article 55: Local people's congresses at all levels are the organs of government authority in their respective localities. . . .

SECTION V—*The Organs of Self-government of National Autonomous Areas*

Article 67: The organs of self-government of all autonomous regions, autonomous *chou,* and autonomous counties are formed in accordance with the basic principles governing the organization of local organs of state as specified in Section IV of Chapter Two of the Constitution. The form of each organ of self-government may be determined in accordance with the wishes of the majority of the people of the nationality or nationalities enjoying regional autonomy in a given area. . . .

SECTION VI—*The People's Courts and the People's Procuratorate*

Article 73: In the People's Republic of China judicial authority is exercised by the Supreme People's Court, local people's courts, and special people's courts.

Article 74: The term of office of the President of the Supreme People's Court and presidents of local people's courts is four years.

The organization of people's courts is determined by law.

Article 75: The system of people's assessors applies, in accordance with law, to judicial proceedings in the people's courts.

Article 76: Cases in the people's courts are heard in public unless otherwise provided for by law. The accused has the right to defense.

Article 77: Citizens of all nationalities have the right to use their own spoken and written languages in court proceedings. The people's courts are to provide interpretation for any party unacquainted with the spoken or written language commonly used in the locality.

In an area where people of national minorities live in compact communities or where a number of nationalities live together, hearings in people's courts are conducted in the language commonly used in the locality, and judgments, notices, and all other documents of the people's courts are made public in such language.

Article 78: In administering justice the people's courts are independent, subject only to the law.

Article 79: The Supreme People's Court is the highest judicial organ.

The Supreme People's Court supervises the judicial work of local people's courts and special people's courts; people's courts at higher levels supervise the judicial work of people's courts at lower levels.

Article 80: The Supreme People's Court is responsible to the National People's Congress and reports to it; or, when the National People's Congress is not in session, to its Standing Committee. Local people's courts are responsible to the local people's congresses at corresponding levels and report to them.

Article 81: The Supreme People's Procuratorate of the People's Republic of China exercises procuratorial authority over all departments of the State Council, all local organs of state, persons working in organs of state, and citizens, to insure observance of the law. Local organs of the people's procuratorate and special people's procuratorates exercise procuratorial authority within the limits prescribed by law.

Local organs of the people's procuratorate and the special people's procuratorates work under the leadership of the people's procuratorates at higher levels, and all work under the coordinating direction of the Supreme People's Procuratorate.

Article 82: The term of office of the Chief Procurator of the Supreme People's Procuratorate is four years.

The organization of people's procuratorates is determined by law.

Article 83: In the exercise of their authority local organs of the people's procuratorate are independent and are not subject to interference by local organs of state.

Article 84: The Supreme People's Procuratorate is responsible to the National People's Congress and reports to it; or, when the National People's Congress is not in session, to its Standing Committee.

[Chapter Three (fundamental rights and duties of citizens) and Chapter Four (national flag, national emblem, capital) are omitted.]

Liu Shao-ch'i • Now I should like to give some explanation of the basic content of the Draft Constitution under four headings:

1. The Character of Our State

Article 1 of the Draft Constitution lays down that "the People's Republic of China is a people's democratic state led by the working class and based on the alliance of workers and peasants." The Preamble and many other articles of the Draft Constitution clearly indicate that a broad people's democratic united

From Liu Shao-ch'i, *"Report on the Draft Constitution of the People's Republic of China"* [*September 15, 1954*], Documents of the First Session of the First National People's Congress of the People's Republic of China (*Peking: Foreign Languages Press, 1955*).

front still exists under our country's system of people's democracy.

The truth that only by relying on the leadership of the working class is it possible for the Chinese people to win liberation from the oppression of imperialism, feudalism, and bureaucrat-capitalism has long since been proved by historical facts over a long period. After the people had won victory, a new problem cropped up, that is: Would the working class continue to be as capable and confident in leading national construction as it had been in the past? Some people may have adopted a wait-and-see attitude on this question in the beginning, but facts in the past five years have fully proved what unusual talent the working class possesses in leading the country. To secure the fruits of victory already won by the Chinese people, it is necessary to further consolidate and strengthen the working-class leadership of the state. Without such leadership, success in our cause of socialist construction and socialist transformation would be unthinkable. . . .

2. *Steps to Be Taken in the Transition to a Socialist Society*

Article 4 of the Draft Constitution states: "The People's Republic of China, by relying on the organs of state and the social forces, and by means of socialist industrialization and socialist transformation, insures the gradual abolition of systems of exploitation and the building of a socialist society."

To insure the thorough implementation of the policy laid down in Article 4, many provisions are made in other articles under the heading of General Principles. These provisions define both the general objective of building a socialist society and the concrete steps to be taken to build such a society.

In the transition period of our country there are still many different economic sectors. Ownership of the means of production in our country at present falls mainly into the following categories: state ownership, that is, ownership by the whole people; cooperative ownership, that is, collective ownership by the working masses; ownership by individual working people; and capitalist ownership. The task of the state is to strive to strengthen and extend the first two categories, that is, the socialist sector of our economy, and to bring about step by step the socialist transformation of the latter two categories, that is, the nonsocialist sector of our economy. Consequently, the state "insures priority for the development of the state sector of the economy" and pays special attention to the step-by-step building of heavy industry, the main economic foundation of socialism. The state "encourages, guides, and helps the development of the cooperative sector of the economy" and encourages and guides the transformation of capitalist industry and commerce "into various forms of state-capitalist economy, gradually replacing capitalist ownership with ownership by the whole people."

These provisions in the Draft Constitution are of course not based on imagination but on changes in social and economic relations that have actually taken place since the founding of the People's Republic of China, and on the experience of the masses. All of them are therefore practicable. With regard to these provisions, I should like to deal with the following questions.

The first is the question of forms of transition. As we are aware, the socialist transformation of agriculture, handicrafts, and capitalist industry and commerce is a very arduous task. We cannot hope to accomplish this transformation overnight. We must proceed step by step in the light of the experience and political consciousness of the masses and in accordance with what is possible in the actual situation. Our experience has proved that socialist transformation, either of agriculture and handicrafts or of capitalist industry and commerce, may have its transitional forms and that it is of primary necessity that the transitional forms we adopt be flexible and varied. . . .

3. Our Political System of People's Democracy and the People's Rights and Duties

Article 2 of the Draft Constitution lays it down that: "All power in the People's Republic of China belongs to the people. The organs through which the people exercise power are the National People's Congress and the local people's congresses." This provision and those contained in other articles specify that the political system of our country is that of people's congresses. In the light of long experience of political construction in our people's revolutionary bases and with the experience of the Soviet Union and other people's democracies as reference, our Common Program five years ago decided on this kind of political system for our country. Now, summing up the experience of the work of our organs of state and the experience of all levels of the people's representative conferences of all circles in the past five years, the Draft Constitution makes more complete provision for the political system of our country. This political system which we have adopted is bound up with the fundamental nature of our state. It is this political system which we, the Chinese people, are adopting to insure our country's advance toward socialism.

The system of people's congresses is the proper political system for our country, because it helps the people to exercise their own power and participate constantly in running the state through this political system, thereby bringing into full play their initiative and creativeness. Clearly, if there is no suitable political system that enables the masses to use their abilities in running the state, it is impossible to mobilize and organize them effectively for the building of socialism. . . .

Paragraph 2 of Article 2 of the Draft Constitution declares: "The National People's Congress, the local people's congresses, and other organs of state practice democratic centralism." Our system of democratic centralism is explained by the fact that the exercise of state power is unified and concentrated in the system of people's congresses. A reactionary publication issued in Hong Kong asserted that our "system of people's congresses is a system of concentration of power by the central authority." These reactionaries seem to think they have found something to attack us with. However, we Marxist-Leninists have long since publicly declared that we stand for centralism. The question is, what kind of centralism—the despotic centralism of a handful of big feudal lords and capitalists, or the democratic centralism of the masses of the people led by the working class? These two systems of centralism are poles apart. In the Draft Constitution, we have combined a high degree of centralism with a high degree of democracy. Our political system has a high degree of centralism but it is based on a high degree of democracy.

While people are themselves still subjected to oppression, they cannot fully concentrate their will and strength. It is precisely for this reason that the Chinese people in the past were ridiculed as being like "loose sand." The revolution concentrated the people's will and strength and, having liberated themselves and set up their own state, the people naturally concentrated their whole will and strength on building up their state apparatus, making it a powerful weapon. The stronger the people's state apparatus, the more powerfully it can defend the people's interests, protect the people's democratic rights, and assure the building of socialism.

When Comrade Mao Tse-tung discussed the political system

of our country in his work *On Coalition Government,* he stated clearly: "It is at once democratic and centralized, that is, centralized on the basis of democracy and democratic under centralized guidance" [Mao, *Selected Works,* IV, 272]. That is our principle.

Not a few people often mistakenly assume democracy and centralism to be two absolutely antagonistic things which cannot be combined. They think that where there is centralism there cannot be democracy. When they see the political unanimity of the people in our organs of state and find a highly unified leadership throughout the country, they try to show that "there is no democracy" here. The trouble with them is that they simply do not understand people's democracy, and consequently have no idea what centralism on the basis of people's democracy means.

The common interests of the people and their unity of will are the starting point of the work of the people's congresses and all other organs of state. Therefore, it is possible in all these organs of state to arrive at political unanimity of the people based on democracy. But political unanimity does not mean a lessening or elimination of criticism and self-criticism. On the contrary, criticism and self-criticism are most important expressions of our democratic life. In the work of all organs of state in our country there are bound to be defects and mistakes. Therefore, full scope must be given to criticism and self-criticism, at the sessions of the National People's Congress, at the sessions of the local people's congresses, and at meetings of all organs of state, and in their daily activities. We must use the weapon of criticism and self-criticism to drive forward the work of the organs of state, constantly correcting defects and mistakes and fighting against bureaucratism, which spells departure from the masses, so that the organs of state can maintain regular and close contact with the masses and correctly reflect their will. If there is not full criticism and self-criticism, political unanimity of the people can neither be achieved nor maintained. Suppression of criticism in our organs of state is a legal offense. . . .

4. The Question of National Regional Autonomy

The Preamble to the Draft Constitution and many of its articles define the relations of equality, friendship, and mutual help between all nationalities within the country and safeguard the right of all national minorities to autonomy.

Hsiung Hsi-yüan • All the activities of our state organs are directed to consolidating the people's democratic dictatorship, translating the central task of the state during the period of transition [to socialism] into reality, and building socialism. These tasks determine the principles or organization and activity of the state organs. These principles are as follows:

1. The Chinese Communist Party Is the Leadership Core of Our State Organs

Party leadership is the basis for the organization and operation of state organs; without Party leadership, it is impossible to have correctness and unity too in the organization and operation of state organs. The Chinese Communist Party, as the organized and advanced detachment of the Chinese working class, represents the interests of the whole nation and of all national minorities; the Party adopts the interests of the working people as its point of departure in dealing with all problems. History shows that the Chinese people's revolution can be victorious only under the leadership of the Chinese Communist Party, and that the people's democratic system of our country can be established and consolidated only under the leadership of the Chinese Communist Party. The Chinese Communist Party is the core of the system of the people's democratic dictatorship, whose constituent parts can be clearly related and whose tasks can be achieved only under the leadership of the Party. At the present stage, the mission of the Party consists of guiding its class and the entire people to one single objective, *i.e.*, socialist construction. The Party is the leading force to insure the realization of this central task of the state during the transitional period.

This leadership force derives from the fact that the Party is armed with the invincible theories of Marxism-Leninism and that it provides a strictly centralized leadership, maintaining close contact with the masses and growing constantly stronger through the processes of criticism and self-criticism. The Party formulates its policies and carries on its activities in accordance with the objective laws of development. Hence, the Party is able to solve correctly the concrete tasks of any given period of revolutionary development.

The Party's role in leading state organs finds its highest ex-

From Jen-min jih-pao [People's Daily], *November 18, 1954.*

pression in the fact that state organs decide all important problems according to the initiative and directives of the Party. Of
course, Party organs are not state organs, and they cannot take
the place of state organs. A long time ago [November 1928], Mao
Tse-tung instructed us: "The Party's recommendations and measures must, apart from the agitation undertaken for them, be
carried out through government organizations" [Mao, "Struggle
in the Chingkang Mountains," *Selected Works*, I, 93]. By methods of persuasion, the Party causes Party cadres in state organs
to express their political leadership deliberately. The leading
role of the Party finds expressions in such ways as these: (1) The
Party gives exact directives to the organs of state power on the
nature and direction of their work; (2) the Party enforces Party
policies through organs of state power and other work departments and exercises supervision over their activities; and (3)
the Party selects and promotes loyal and capable cadres (Party
and non-Party) for work in the organs of state power.

The Party now appeals for the strengthening of Party unity
because only thus can Party leadership be united and disciplined,
and the political leadership can be exerted more successfully and
powerfully. The unity of the Chinese Communist Party is a
heavy blow to imperialists and reactionaries and is the fundamental guarantee for translating the central task of the transition
period into reality and building our country into a great socialist
country.

2. *The Principle That the Working People Take Part in*
Running the State and Exercise Supervision Over State Organs

More than once, Lenin, the founder of the Soviet socialist
state, gave instructions to the effect that for the realization of
true democracy the people must be enabled to take part not only
in independent voting and elections, but also in day-to-day state
administration. Lenin regarded the participation of the masses
in state administration as one of the important factors in building
socialism.

The character of our state determines the popular and democratic character of our state administration. "The system of
people's congresses is the proper political system for our country,
because it helps the people to exercise their own power and
participate constantly in running the state through this political
system . . ." [quoted above in Liu Shao-ch'i report, p. 214].
Through democratic elections, the people of our country elect

deputies to constitute representative organs for the exercise of their power. These deputies are the best elements among the people, and many of them are of worker and peasant origin; moreover, national minorities, women, and military personnel, who could not take part in running the state in the past, now also elect deputies to organs of state power.

The people of the country participate in running the state in many fields and in many different ways. In addition to the fundamental duty mentioned above, that is, of electing deputies to the organs of state power, the people also (1) assume duties in different state organs, (2) participate in the subsidiary work of organs of state power and other organs, and (3) join people's organs, such as trade unions, youth organizations, women's organizations, cooperatives, democratic parties and groups, and so on—organizations, that is, which rally the broad masses of the people around state organs and give indispensable assistance to the state organs in their daily work. Discussion of the Draft Constitution by the people was another important expression of their participation in running the state. People's supervision over the activities of state organs is one of the rights prescribed by the Constitution. Voters and electoral units may recall their deputies at any time in accordance with legal procedures. This is the highest expression of the people's effective supervision over the activities of state organs. In addition, the people may also expose faults in the work of state organs and advance suggestions for improvement through social bodies, conferences, and the press.

Experience of the last five years proves that the people of our country, led by the working class, can create a new system as well as destroy the old. This refutes the absurd view of the bourgeoisie and Kuomintang that "commoners of the lower strata" are not qualified to run the state and that "citizens have to be trained to exercise state power." Our state organs have infinite vitality because they are inseparably connected with the working people, have the most extensive mass foundation, and are consequently the greatest agitational and organizational forces with the highest prestige. Such a democratic system is infinitely superior to the bourgeois system which prevents working people from running the state.

3. The Principle of Equal Rights for All National Minorities

Our country is a unified, multinational country. Like the Soviet Union, we have not only proclaimed the principle of equality of nationalities but have also insured the exercise of their rights, primarily the right to equal participation in running the state by all nationalities. The basic principles defined in the Constitution for dealing with nationality questions [see above, Arts. 3, 67] open a broad path for all the nationalities of our country to run the state equally and are strikingly reflected in the organization and activities of our state organs. Our democratic system of election does not place any restrictions on nationality and race; on the contrary it gives special consideration to the rights of national minorities. Thus it is assured that deputies from the national minorities participate in the organs of state power and become real masters. A number of national minority cadres have also assumed duties in connection with central and local state organs. . . .

4. The Principle of Democratic Centralism

Democratic centralism is the most fundamental principle of state organization and activity and is written into the Constitution (Art. 2). . . .

The principle of democratic centralism, applied to the organization and activities of state organs, finds expression in the following ways: (1) All powers of the state belong to the people; the people elect deputies to constitute the organs of state power. . . . (2) The Chairman of the state is elected by the supreme organ of state power [the National People's Congress], which has the power to recall him; administrative organs of state, courts, and procuratorates are responsible to the organs of state power which appoint them, report to them on their work, and are subject to supervision by organs of state power and the people. (3) State organs maintain close contact with the people. (4) The National People's Congress is a united legislative-executive organ, possessing legislative power and exercising direct control of the administrative organ (the State Council). . . . (5) Within state organs, and between state organs, the principles of minority subordinating to majority, lower level subordinating to higher level, and localities subordinating to the center are observed. (6) Decisions, directives, and orders of state organs of higher levels must be carried out by state organs of the lower level; state organs of the higher level may, in accordance with the law, suspend, change, or annul unlawful or improper decisions, directives, and orders of state organs of lower levels. (7) Local administrative organs of the state (people's councils) under the State Council enforce dual subordination—that is, local people's councils are responsible to people's congresses of the corresponding level and also to the administrative organs of the state of the higher level and report to them on their work [see also Chapter 9, pp. 289–290 for changes in local government after the communes]. (8) Democratic centralism insures the combination of unified and centralized leadership at the center with the initiative and creativeness of localities and insures the reconciliation of national responsibilities and different local conditions.

Obviously, our state organs—as is the case of those of the Soviet Union and the people's democracies—based on democratic centralism are of the socialist democratic type and are diametrically opposed to the "separation of three powers" and bureaucratic centralism of the bourgeoisie.

5. *The Principle of People's Democratic Legal System*

Strict observance of the people's democratic legal system is one of the basic principles of organization and operation of all state organs. The people's democratic legal system is an effective means for achieving the people's democratic dictatorship and is the necessary condition for building socialism. The people's democratic legal system falls in the category of superstructure and serves the economy according to the acts and standards prescribed by the state. With the founding of the Chinese People's Republic, our country established a revolutionary legal system and, by means of the legal system, suppressed counterrevolutionaries, effected social reforms, educated the people, and consolidated the people's democratic dictatorship. We must now go a step farther to strengthen and apply the people's democratic legal system so as to insure smooth progress in economic construction and socialist transformation. With the Constitution, we have raised the people's democratic legal system to a higher level. The Constitution is the base of the people's democratic legal system, and on this base our revolutionary legal system will be more highly perfected.

The demand and substance of the people's democratic legal system consist of the strict and resolute observance of laws and of the ordinances of the administrative organs of the state by all state organs and their personnel, as well as by social bodies and the masses of people. Administrative organs of state must place their operations on a strictly legal basis and must insure that all their activities conform to the law—that is, they must conduct their work according to the procedures and within the limits of the functions and powers prescribed by the organs of state power.

Why must we observe the law? Why should we take the consolidation of the people's democratic legal system as an important task? Here are the reasons: (1) Our laws reflect the will of the working people led by the working class, and nonobservance of the legal system would mean the destruction of the people's will and obstruction to the fulfillment of the public will in which event the people's democratic dictatorship would be weakened. (2) Our laws are enacted according to our knowledge of the laws of social development, and violation of the laws would inevitably hinder the cause of socialist construction. (3) Laws are instruments to carry out policies; the people's democratic legal system is connected with the development of the national economy and directly guarantees the attainment of state plans. (4) The legal system is an important condition for consolidating and developing the people's democracy; to guarantee the people's political, economic, and cultural rights, all laws must be observed.

In the past, it was inevitable and understandable that our people, long subjected to reactionary rule, would attach no importance to the legal system of the exploiting class. Now the people of our country, as masters, must observe the laws created by the people themselves and the legal system established by the people themselves. To strengthen the spirit of law observance by state organs and citizens is one of the important factors guaranteeing the founding of the socialist society.

Under contemporary conditions of growing development of socialist construction, the Party and government attach special importance to the work of strengthening the people's democratic legal system. The broader the range of socialist transformation, the more acute the class struggle becomes and consequently the significance of the revolutionary legal system becomes more pronounced. "The more powerful our Constitution and laws, the more powerful our public security, procurators', and judicial organs, the greater the safeguard for the people's rights and interests, the heavier the blows that fall on the people's enemies."

(Chou En-lai, "Report on the Work of the Government," September 23, 1954.*)

6. The Principle of Socialist Planning

Our aim is to build socialism, and our economy develops basically in accordance with plans. Naturally, since private economy still exists in our country [this situation changed radically in 1954–1955; see Chapter 3, pp. 98–105], our planning still differs in scope and extent from the planning of the national economy in the Soviet Union. But along with the development of socialist economy and socialist industrialization [on the economy, see Chapter 9, pp. 283–288], and the gradual transformation of the nonsocialist sector, there can be no doubt that the scope and extent of our national economic planning will increasingly expand.

At the beginning, the people's democratic state power of our country expropriated enterprises of bureaucratic capitalism and transformed them into a socialist sector, with means of production owned by the public, thus giving rise to the rule of planned and balanced development of the national economy. This rule makes it necessary and possible for the state to proceed with planned socialist construction. This principle is similarly expressed in the Constitution: "By economic planning, the state directs the growth and transformation of the national economy . . ." (Art. 15).

Our state organs are subjective forces for developing the national economy according to plan. Obviously, the character and historical mission of our country determine their role in organizing the national economy and conducting cultural and educational work. The state organs are instruments for creating the foundations for socialist economy. Article 4 of the Constitution states: "The People's Republic of China, by relying on the organs of state and the social forces, and by means of socialist industrialization and socialist transformation, insures the gradual abolition of systems of exploitation and the building of a socialist society." Relying on state organs and social forces during the past five years, we have restored the national economy, carried out socialist transformation of the national economy, and, as of 1953, commenced the First Five-Year Plan and achieved important

* In *Documents of the First Session of the First National People's Congress of the People's Republic of China* (Peking: Foreign Languages Press, 1955), p. 115.

results. In conducting such activities, the state should rely on its understanding and utilization of the objective laws of economy.

Inasmuch as the state organs play the role of building up a socialist economic foundation, their organization and operation must also conform to the principle of socialist planning. The substance of this principle consists in directing the development of the national economy and achieving socialist industrialization and socialist transformation by state organs. The Constitution provides that the supreme organ of state power decides on the national economic plan (Art. 27.9) and that local organs of state power also have the power to draw up plans for local economic development. . . . The supreme administrative organ of the state and the administrative organs of the different departments are to organize and insure the execution of the plans. The courts are to punish those who wreck national economic plans. The organs of state power, procuratorates, and state planning organs are to supervise the execution of national economic plans. The central task of the state during the transition period toward socialism is legally defined as a principle of the Constitution; and national economic plans will also become law once they have been decided upon. Therefore, the operation of state organs must be in accordance with state plans, the violation of which is a violation of the law. This we must emphasize.

The translation of the central task of the transition period into reality is a revolution more penetrating and extensive than the revolution against imperialism, feudalism, and bureaucratic capitalism. This revolution is led by the state organs from above and is directly supported and carried out by the masses from below. The political and legal systems and state organs have pronounced significance because, although they belong to the superstructure, they are closer to the foundations than other superstructures. The state organs of our country are instruments for eliminating the old system and building the new system: they will actively help to form and consolidate the socialist economic foundation of our country, stimulate the growth and development of productive forces, and ensure the transition of our country to a socialist society by peaceful means. Consequently, in accordance with Chairman Mao's instructions we must strive to strengthen the people's state machinery.* And, the primary factor in

* See above, pages 34-35, 192.

strengthening the people's state machinery is for all the state organs to organize and conduct their operations in accordance with the above-mentioned democratic principles.

II. LAW

On the Uses of Law

Lo Jui-ch'ing • The proclamation of the headquarters of the Chinese People's Liberation Army signed by Chairman Mao Tse-tung on April 25, 1949, announced that, apart from incorrigible war criminals and counterrevolutionaries with heinous crimes, we would not capture, arrest, or subject to indignities the personnel of the reactionary Kuomintang ruling clique—unless they carried out armed resistance or committed sabotage. The proclamation also said that the People's Government would employ, according to their individual circumstances, persons with any ability who had not engaged in serious reactionary activities, or whose personal record was not seriously stained. In *On People's Democratic Dictatorship,* written in July 1949, Chairman Mao said:

> So long as they do not rebel, sabotage, or create disturbance after their political power has been overthrown, members of the reactionary classes and the reactionaries will also be given land and work and allowed to live and remold themselves through labor into new men.

This policy is the greatest humanitarian policy ever found in history.

This most benevolent policy of the Party and the people's government awakened many members of the reactionary classes, and many reactionaries, to the fact that they had a future—provided they obeyed the people's power, admitted and repented of their crimes before the people, worked honestly, and turned over a new leaf. Thus the disintegration among the counter-revolutionaries was greatly accelerated, some surrendering to the people and some beginning to waver. But there were also a number of obstinate counterrevolutionaries who refused to accept our policy and insisted on sabotaging the revolution. . . .

From Lo Jui-ch'ing, *"The Struggle Between Revolution and Counterrevolution in the Past Ten Years"* [September 28, 1959] in Ten Glorious Years (Peking: Foreign Languages Press, 1960).

The struggle between revolution and counterrevolution in China has been carried out most resolutely, correctly, and thoroughly. In the short space of ten years, we have successfully accomplished the following tasks pertaining to it: (1) We have purged the country fairly thoroughly of counterrevolutionaries and crushed enemy intrigues for a comeback; (2) we have thoroughly wiped out the remnants of the Kuomintang reactionary forces in some backward areas and consolidated the people's democratic rule; (3) we have achieved the further political emancipation of the people, and thus given impetus to the great liberation of the productive forces, raised the political consciousness of the broad mass of people and their enthusiasm in production, in the course of the struggle; (4) we have got rid of the scum left by the old society, thus creating increasingly secure order in our socialist society. All this has guaranteed the successful conclusion of the country's socialist revolution and its gigantic strides forward in socialist construction.

What we call thorough suppression of the counterrevolutionaries means the uncovering of all counterrevolutionaries and the meting out to them of such punishment as they deserve; it does not mean that the counterrevolutionaries whom it was necessary to punish were all put to death. The imperialists have slandered us maliciously on this point, and the bourgeois rightists inside the country have also raised a hostile clamor. This only shows that they have been trying to frighten us and tie our hands in the struggle so that the counterrevolutionaries can be saved to facilitate their activities for staging a comeback in China. The struggle between revolution and counterrevolution is a life-and-death struggle, an irreconcilable, sharp class struggle. Any class struggle inevitably involves bloodshed. This is true of the dictatorship of the proletariat, as it is even more so with the dictatorship of the bourgeoisie and of all exploiting classes. The difference is that in the dictatorship of the proletariat it is the revolution that suppresses counterrevolution, the majority of the people who suppress the few reactionaries, while the reverse is true of the exploiting-class dictatorships. To preserve their dictatorship, the bourgcoisie and all the exploiting classes have shed an enormous amount of the people's blood. . . . In suppressing the resistance of the counterrevolutionaries, the dictatorship of the proletariat also cannot, of course, avoid the shedding of blood. But the nature of such bloodshed is entirely different from the bloodshed under the dictatorship of the exploiting classes; here the blood that is shed is not the people's but that of counterrevolutionaries. As far as the amount of bloodshed is concerned, it is much less than that under the cruel dictatorships of the exploiting classes and of Chiang Kai-shek's Kuomintang. So all the slanders of the imperialists and bourgeois rightists are barefaced lies. It was precisely because the struggle between revolution and counterrevolution in China was carried out most resolutely, correctly, and thoroughly that it involved the least possible bloodshed.

Complying with the instructions of the Central Committee of the Chinese Communist Party and Chairman Mao Tse-tung, we meted out the death penalty only to a small number of counterrevolutionaries who had committed heinous crimes and had to be put to death. For most criminals who had to be punished and even those who deserved the death penalty for their crimes but were not yet in the category of criminals who must definitely be executed, the method of reform through labor was adopted. One of the ways of punishing criminals in our country is "the death sentence with reprieve for two years, and with reform through compulsory labor to see what effect is produced." The imperialists slander this as the cruelest thing imaginable; but we say it is the most humane. Even the criminals concerned understand that the death sentence with reprieve, saving them as it does from execution, is the last opportunity the people's government gives them to reform themselves into new men. In fact, the criminals who were so treated were, in practically every case, saved. We may ask: Has there ever been any such great creation, at home or abroad, in ancient or modern times? Can such a humane law be found in the capitalist world? In practicing our policy of the reform of counterrevolutionaries and other criminals through labor, we aim not only to completely deprive counterrevolutionaries of the conditions in which they can carry out disruptive activities, but, above all, to eliminate the class and ideological roots of counterrevolutionary and other crimes, so that the counterrevolutionaries will not commit crimes again after serving their terms.

In the past ten years, through participation in labor and production and through the ideological education given them, most of the criminals have reformed to varying degrees, and a number of them have actually changed from evil to good. Not only have a certain part of the former bandits, local despots, secret agents, key members of reactionary parties and organizations, chieftains of reactionary secret societies, and other criminals reformed their reactionary ideas; many have acquired the habit of manual work. Some who had not the slightest knowledge of production in the past have become relatively skilled technicians or engineers. Those who were illiterate have learned to read ordinary books, newspapers, and magazines. These wonders seem almost incredible but they are a well-attested fact. And they are not isolated cases in our new society.

III. FOREIGN POLICY

The Universals of Mao's Foreign Policy

Lu Ting-yi • The present time is still a period when the world reaction can be cocky, baring its fangs and extending its talons. This is primarily because struggles of the peoples in the various countries have not entered a higher stage and at the same time this is also because the American economic crisis has not yet arrived. But even in this kind of period, the reactionary forces have already revealed that they are hollow within and outwardly strong. When struggles of the peoples of all countries reach a higher development and the American economic crisis has broken out, that will be the time when the grand arrogance of the reactionaries will collapse. This is already not far distant. Before the arrival of this time, the people of each country will meet with difficulties, and in individual countries and regions, may even meet with very serious difficulties. Difficulties of this kind, however, can and must be conquered. The present task is for everyone to exert all efforts and to overcome these difficulties.

Following the development of three factors—world progress, Soviet successes, and American crises—the democratic forces will become even stronger and the relative strength of the democratic and antidemocratic forces will become more beneficial to the people. But it is not to be imagined that the reactionary forces

From Lu Ting-yi, "Explanations of Several Basic Questions Concerning the Postwar International Situation" [Emancipation Daily, *January 4 and 5, 1947*], *translated in U. S. Department of State,* United States Relations with China; *with Special Reference to the Period* 1944–1949 (*Washington: Government Printing Office, 1949*).

will voluntarily abdicate to the democratic forces. Therefore before we have attained what Comrade Mao Tse-tung calls "broadest victory of the people" and the "insurance of stable and en-
during peace," there is still a long and tortuous struggle ahead.
The Chinese Communists and the Chinese people will fear no
difficulties. They will fight on till the complete victory of the
democratic cause and winning of the peace and independence of
their nation. We have the strongest confidence in this brilliant
future, but the world bourgeoisie on the other hand have completely lost confidence in their future. The terrorism whipped up
by the antidemocratic forces in various countries after the war
against the forces of people, their terror at the strength of the
Soviet Union, their fanatical oppression of the peoples, their
horror of the truth, their complete reliance on lies for a living—
these all are manifestations of their complete loss of confidence.
It is certainly not accidental that all newspapers of the Chinese
bourgeoisie express an unprecedented pessimism and disappoint-
ment with regard to their future.

In general, everything has changed after the Second World
War, and is still continuing to change. How strong the people
have become—how conscious, how organized, determined, and
full of confidence! How maniacally savage the reactionaries have
become—outwardly strong yet inwardly feeble, turned against by
the masses and deserted by their allies, devoid of all confidence in
their future! It may be forecast categorically that the face of
China and the world will be vastly different after three to five
more years. All comrades of our party and all people of China
must resolutely fight for a new China and a new world.

Mao Tse-tung • "You are leaning to one side." Exactly. The
forty years' experience of Sun Yat-sen and the twenty-eight years'
experience of the Chinese Communist Party have taught us to
lean to one side, and we are firmly convinced that in order to
achieve victory and consolidate it we must lean to one side. To
sit on the fence is impossible. A third road does not exist. Not
only in China but also in the world, without exception, one either
leans to the side of imperialism or to the side of socialism. Neu-
trality is a camouflage, and a third road does not exist.

---

*From Mao Tse-tung, On People's Democratic Dictatorship [June 30, 1949]
(Peking: Foreign Languages Press, 1959). Translation in parts is based on
original.*

"You are too provocative." We are talking about how to deal with domestic and foreign reactionaries, *i.e.,* the imperialists and their jackals, and not about dealing with any other people. With regard to the reactionaries, the question of being provocative or not does not arise; provocation or no provocation, they will remain the same, because they are reactionaries. Only by drawing a sharp line between reactionaries and revolutionaries, by exposing the intrigues and plots of the reactionaries and arousing the vigilance and attention of the revolutionaries, and by raising our own morale while deflating the enemy's prestige, can we isolate the reactionaries, defeat them, or oust them. We must not show the slightest fear before a wild beast, and must learn from the example of Wu Sung on the Chingyang Ridge. As Wu Sung [one of the 108 heroes in the historical novel, *All Men Are Brothers*] saw it, the tiger on the Chingyang Ridge would fall on a man and eat him up, provocation or no provocation. There are only two alternatives: either kill the tiger or be eaten by it.

"We want to do business." All right; business must be done anyway. We oppose only the domestic and foreign reactionaries who hamper our business transactions and not anyone else. We should all realize that it is none other than the imperialists and their jackals, Chiang Kai-shek's reactionary clique, who are hindering us from doing business as well as establishing diplomatic relations with foreign countries. When, by uniting all domestic and international forces, we have beaten the reactionaries inside and outside the country, we can do business, and we shall find it possible to establish diplomatic relations with all foreign countries on the basis of equality, mutual benefit, and mutual respect for territorial integrity and sovereignty.*

"We can win victory even without international assistance." This is an erroneous idea. In an era when imperialism still exists, it is impossible for a genuine people's revolution in any country to win victory without various forms of help from the international revolutionary forces. Even should victory be won, it could not be consolidated. This was true of the victory of the October Revolution and its consolidation, as Stalin long ago told us. This was also the case in the establishment of the new democracies after three imperialist countries were overthrown in the Second

* These last phrases later were incorporated in the 1954 Sino-Indian treaty on Tibet and made famous as the basic elements in the "five principles" of peaceful coexistence at the 1955 Bandung Conference.

World War. This is also true of the present and the future of the people's China. Just think, if the Soviet Union did not exist, if there had been no victory over fascism in the Second World War, if Japanese imperialism had not been defeated, if the various new democracies had not arisen, if the oppressed nations of the East had not risen to fight, and if there were no struggle between the masses of the people and the reactionary rulers inside the United States, Great Britain, France, Germany, Italy, Japan, and other capitalist countries—if there were no combination of all these things, the international reactionary forces bearing down upon us would certainly be immeasurably greater then they are now. Could we have won victory in such circumstances? Obviously not. And even should victory be won, it could not be consolidated. The Chinese people have already had more than enough experience in such matters. The experience was reflected long ago in Sun Yat-sen's deathbed injunction on the necessity of uniting with the international revolutionary forces.

"We need assistance from the British and U.S. governments." At present, this is a naïve way of thinking. Would the present rulers of Britain and the United States, who are imperialists, give aid to a people's state? Yet, why is business done between these countries and ourselves? And why eventually would these countries, as it can be assumed, grant us loans on terms of mutual benefit? The reason is that their capitalists want to make money and their bankers want to earn interest in order to avert their own crisis; they certainly do not mean to help the Chinese people. The Communist Parties and the progressive parties and groups in Britain and the United States are at this moment campaigning for the establishment of trade and even diplomatic relations with us. This is well intentioned, this is aid, and this has nothing in common with the actions of the bourgeoisie in these countries. During his lifetime Sun Yat-sen appealed countless times to the capitalist countries for help, but all in vain; he met with cruel rebuffs. Only once did Sun Yat-sen receive foreign aid, which came from the Soviet Union. Let the readers refer to Dr. Sun Yat-sen's Testament; there he earnestly enjoins people not to look for help from the imperialist countries but to "unite . . . with those nations of the world who treat us on the basis of equality." Dr. Sun had the experience; he had been taken in and given a raw deal. We should remember his words and not allow ourselves to be taken in again. Internationally we belong to the side of the anti-imperialist front headed by the Soviet Union, and so we can only turn to this side for genuine and friendly help, not to the side of the imperialist front.

Mao Tse-tung • 1. The forces of world reaction are definitely preparing a Third World War, and the danger of war exists. But the democratic forces of the people of the world have surpassed the reactionary forces and are forging ahead; they must and certainly can overcome the danger of war. Therefore, the question in the relations between the United States, Britain, and France and the Soviet Union is not a question of compromise or break, but a question of compromise earlier or compromise later. "Compromise" means reaching agreement through peaceful negotiation. "Earlier or later" means several years, or more than ten years, or even longer.

2. The kind of compromise mentioned above does not mean compromise on all international issues. That is impossible so long as the United States, Britain, and France continue to be ruled by reactionaries. This kind of compromise means compromise on some issues, including certain important ones. But there will not be many such compromises in the near future. There is, however, a possibility that the trade relations of the United States, Britain, and France with the Soviet Union will expand.

3. Such compromise between the United States, Britain, and France and the Soviet Union can be the outcome only of resolute, effective struggles by all the democratic forces of the world against the reactionary forces of the United States, Britain, and France. Such compromise does not require the people in the countries of the capitalist world to follow suit and make compromises at home. The people in those countries will continue to wage different struggles in accordance with their different conditions. The principle of the reactionary forces in dealing with the democratic forces of the people is definitely to destroy all they can and to prepare to destroy later whatever they cannot destroy now. Face to face with this situation, the democratic forces of the people should likewise apply the same principle to the reactionary forces.

From Mao Tse-tung, *"Some Points in Appraisal of the Present International Situation"* [*April 1946*], Selected Works, *Vol. IV (Peking: Foreign Languages Press, 1961).*

Liu Shao-ch'i • All that which was said above [in Liu's discussion on "The Two Great Camps in the World Today and the Path of the National Liberation Movement," which is part 4 of the essay] explains one fundamental question; that is: the oppressed nations, the proletariat, and the people's democratic forces in all countries must unite with each other, unite with the Soviet Union, and unite with the new democracies of Eastern Europe before they can defeat the plans of American imperialism for the enslavement of the world and the rule of other imperialists over their colonies, before they can solve the national question of the world today, *i.e.,* to liberate all oppressed nations and consequently to abolish the rule of the monopoly capitalists in their home countries, which is the cause of imperialist aggression.

That is to say: the Communists and the peoples of all countries must base themselves on proletarian internationalism, on the proletarian-internationalist programs and policies with regard to the question of the nation, unite with the laboring people and the anti-imperialist revolutionary forces in all countries of the world, and unite with the Soviet Union and the new democracies of Eastern Europe, in a common struggle through mutual assistance and mutual support in order to liberate all oppressed nations and solve the national question of the world today.

That is to say: if one follows the bourgeois-nationalist concept of the nation, and adopts its programs and policies with regard to the national question, opposes the Soviet Union instead of uniting with it, opposes the new democracies of Eastern Europe instead of uniting with them, opposes the Communists, the proletariat, and the people's democratic forces in all countries instead of uniting with them, opposes the national liberation movements in colonial and semicolonial countries instead of uniting with them, does the same as the Tito clique is doing in Yugoslavia, then one will of course unite with the American and other imperialists, will of course line up with the imperialist camp, will of course unite with the reactionary forces in all countries, will of course fail to achieve national liberation, will never accomplish anything in the cause of socialism, will of course make one's own nation prey to the deception and aggression of American and other imperialism, with the result that one's own nation will

From Liu Shao-ch'i, Internationalism and Nationalism [*November 1, 1948*] (*Peking: Foreign Languages Press, 1951*).

lose its independence and turn into a colony of the imperialists. Therefore, just as the Central Committee of the Chinese Communist Party has said: The resolution of the Information Bureau of the Communist Parties, in pointing out this dangerous future to the whole world and the people of Yugoslavia so that the people of Yugoslavia may become vigilant and correct the mistakes of the Tito clique, "is fulfilling its obligations to the cause of preserving world peace and democracy, and of defending the people of Yugoslavia from the deception and aggression of American imperialism."

That is to say: in directing the national liberation movements and proletarian socialist movements of the world today, the Communists and the peoples of all countries must base themselves on proletarian internationalism and not oppose proletarian internationalism, must discard bourgeois nationalism and not base themselves on bourgeois nationalism, and must closely link together the national democratic revolution of the oppressed nations and the socialist revolution of the proletariat, before these two kinds of revolution can both win victory, before we can liberate every nation of the world, and before we can solve all national questions of the world today. Otherwise, not only will we be unable to win any socialist victory, we will also not be able to win real victory in any national liberation movement.

That is to say: the national question of the present-day world must be viewed in connection with the question of world revolution as a whole, in connection with history as a whole, and the world as a whole; it should not be viewed in isolation and from a narrow viewpoint, or from any unrealistic and abstract viewpoint. Just as Lenin and Stalin have said: the national question must not be appraised in isolation, but must be appraised on a worldwide scale.

Chapter 8

Chinese Doctrine and the Communist Bloc Dispute

THE Chinese Communist Party in 1963 chose to epitomize its doctrine, developed during the years of revolution within China, in a "proposal concerning the general line of the international Communist movement." Essentially, that proposal of June 14, 1963, became the fundamental statement of the Chinese case in the Sino-Soviet controversy.

At the time of its publication, the proposal intensified the existing antagonism between the two countries. Its distribution by Chinese in the Soviet Union precipitated *inter alia* the expulsions of several Chinese from Russia and the staging of anti-Chinese demonstrations throughout the Soviet bloc. A month after the June 14 proposal, while embroiled in discussions with a high-level Chinese delegation, the Russians responded with an "open letter to all Party organizations and Party members" and then, on the heels of the abortive discussions with China, signed the nuclear test ban treaty with the United States and Great Britain. In their fury, the Chinese called for a world conference to discuss "the question of complete, thorough, total, and resolute prohibition and destruction of nuclear weapons," and added "betrayal of socialism" to their former charges that the Russian leaders had been party to a "Munich" at the time of the 1962 Cuban crisis and to a "holy alliance" against the "specter of true Marxism-Leninism." The Soviet open letter in reply accused the Chinese of deliberately aggravating the dispute since 1960, of interfering in Russian domestic affairs, and of "openly imposing their erroneous views" on bloc parties. The heart of the dispute, the Russians held, lay in the alleged Chinese interpretation of the revolutionary struggle and its implications for certain nuclear war as well as for de-Stalinization and internal Russian development and for the selection of specific tactics vis-à-vis the non-aligned and the West. The Russian letter and the nuclear test ban touched off a series of even more bitter exchanges that set the tone for an anticipated showdown at a later world meeting of Communist leaders.

From the bulky documentation on Russian-Chinese relations, it has long been possible to distinguish divisive and integrative elements. Soviet and Chinese leaders in the early 1950's were not blind to potential sources of conflict between them and at that time made a highly publicized effort to accentuate cooperation as a way to eliminate tension and dispute. Thus, after a prolonged series of talks in Moscow, Mao Tse-tung and Stalin, on Valentine's Day 1950, signed the Treaty of Friendship, Alliance, and Mutual Assistance. The terms of this and subsequent agreements stressed three main pillars of unity and cooperation: a common revolutionary outlook and ideology, an alliance for military security, and a joint program for mutual economic development and trade. Marxism-Leninism provided the common language as well as the outline of a program of action and a set of tactical priorities and methodological principles. Meanwhile, Chinese and Russian propaganda agencies attempted to erase the sources of potential conflict: memories of Russian betrayal of the Communists in 1927 and misconduct in Manchuria in 1945, irredentist aspirations among nationalistic Chinese, divergent outlooks among the two elites because of different levels of national socio-economic development and because of vastly different experiences in rise to power, and contradictory racial and cultural patterns that evoked xenophobia and feelings of superiority.

Thus structured, disagreement between Peking and Moscow became focused on the terms of cooperation and on the consequences of their unity. Undoubtedly, Chinese dissatisfaction with their status in and rewards from the alliance can be traced to Stalin's reluctance to recognize the Maoist "contribution" to Marxism-Leninism and to support generously the economic construction of China. Nevertheless, common bonds remained relatively firm until January 1956, when, at the 20th Congress of the Soviet Communist Party, Khrushchev dramatically reopened the question of the central purposes and priorities within the Communist bloc. At first, Russian policies—toward Stalin, Tito, and Eastern Europe—rather than vaguely understood doctrinal shifts signaled danger to the Chinese, a danger that required their "comradely criticism and assistance." Significantly, moreover, the Chinese agreed with some of Khrushchev's assumptions in the policy of "peaceful coexistence." They acknowledged, for example, that Western collapse need not depend on a nuclear holocaust; that the newly independent nations could add force to the "rising wave" of communism; and that nationalist aspirations in Asia, Africa, and Latin America could be exploited and manipulated with great advantage for the Communist movement. But the Chinese contested the policy inferences drawn by Khrushchev from these and other assumptions and demanded a new, more comprehensive statement of the terms of bloc cooperation. In this way, the Chinese questioned the very foundations of international Communist unity and thereby unleashed the underlying—and long bottled up—sources of conflict, as outlined above.

The fundamental shift from preoccupation with the terms of cooperation to containment of conflict gradually gained momentum after 1956 and became fully evident in October 1962 at the time of the Cuban missile crisis and the Chinese invasion of the Indian frontier. In general, the shift began with a Chinese insistence on "clarification" of these three aspects of "peaceful coexistence": unity, diversity, and struggle. First, the Chinese denied that a "natural unity" of intrabloc or Communist-nationalist interests could be assumed. Communist unity, they said, required formal explication and clear direction; periodic conferences of bloc leaders must hammer out the details of agreement. To Mao Tse-tung, de-Stalinization, which came as a surprise, and overtures to Tito, who had become an "imperialist stooge," violated real unity. Since 1959–1960, when the Russians withdrew technicians and aid and tore up the agreement to provide China with nuclear weapons, the Chinese have not lacked fresh and ever more provocative examples of genuine disunity. Second, distinctions would have to be drawn between intrabloc diversity and the diversity displayed by nonaligned nations. Bloc diversity could not violate the rigid necessity for Communist Party leadership, while the wooing of the nonaligned must not dangerously disperse Communist resources or aid avowed anti-Communists. Finally, the Chinese insisted that "peaceful coexistence" must not deprive the "oppressed" of the right to throw off "imperialism" and must not make Communists shy away from the risks of war in order to obliterate imperialism. To preserve their identity, Mao stated, Communists must struggle. Those who would not struggle are "social democrats," not Communists, and thus they denigrate communism and the Party and become "revisionists" and "splitters." According to the Maoist version of Leninism, unity with "revisionists and splitters" is unthinkable; they must be opposed.

Conferences were called in Moscow in 1957, 1960, 1961, and 1963 to restore cooperation as the focus of bloc discussion and to ward off a possible split. Though no longer at the heart of the dialogue, the elements of cooperation—ideology, security, and economic development—continued to have a compelling logic in the minds of Chinese and Russian officials, but each conference seemed to exacerbate further the tensions and to introduce new elements of conflict. Basic hostilities had by 1960 distorted the content of the ideas and interests that had once united the two Communist powers. While the revolutionary dogma seemed relatively superficial and irrelevant to Moscow, it became important as never before to the crisis-ridden Chinese. In 1963, Mao and Khrushchev clearly recognized that shattered loyalties could not be made whole by an act of will, but neither man was quite sure where to go from there.

Tactical problems further complicated this uncertainty. Other bloc leaders placed severe constraints on the dispute, which held great local advantages as long as a complete split could be avoided. The dispute played havoc, however, with Communist Parties outside the bloc which previously could hold out Communist solidarity and discipline as their greatest selling points but which now could not authoritatively silence even their own bitter factionalism. Should a split come, Mao and Khrushchev would like to have a maximum number of supporters, and therefore each must juggle contradictory or ambiguous policies toward Communists inside and outside the bloc. Neither leader wishes to be held responsible for a final breach, and each seeks to wear the mantle of orthodox communism. In this uncertain game— which could, of course, change with the deaths of significant members of either leadership—Peking attempts to appear less belligerent, while Moscow initiates dangerous disputes with Washington and thereby undermines its plans for better relations with the West.

The Chinese Communist proposal of June 14, 1963, establishes a useful baseline to differentiate firm objectives from tactical maneuvers. Reproduced in full in this chapter, the proposal constitutes the most complete statement of the principal issues as understood by the Chinese and, by inference, attacks some of the key positions held by the Communist Party of the Soviet Union (C.P.S.U.). In the last point, No. 25, of the proposal, the Chinese list some of the other significant Soviet and Chinese statements in the early 1963 phase of the dispute.

Mao's Case: China's Revolution Upgraded

Central Committee Proposal •

The Central Committee of the Communist
   Party of the Soviet Union
Dear Comrades,

The Central Committee of the Communist Party of China has studied the letter of the Central Committee of the Communist Party of the Soviet Union of March 30, 1963 [in which the Russion Communists argued for their policy of peaceful coexistence].

All who have the unity of the socialist camp and the international Communist movement at heart are deeply concerned about the talks between the Chinese and Soviet Parties and hope that our talks will help to eliminate differences, strengthen unity, and create favorable conditions for convening a meeting of representatives of all the Communist and Workers' Parties.

It is the common and sacred duty of the Communist and Workers' Parties of all countries to uphold and strengthen the unity of the international Communist movement. The Chinese and Soviet Parties bear a heavier responsibility for the unity of the entire socialist camp and international Communist movement and should of course make commensurately greater efforts.

A number of major differences of principle now exist in the international Communist movement. But however serious these differences, we should exercise sufficient patience and find ways to eliminate them so that we can unite our forces and strengthen the struggle against our common enemy.

Full text of Chinese Communist Party Central Committee, A Proposal Concerning the General Line of the International Communist Movement [*June 14, 1963*] (*Peking: Foreign Languages Press, 1963*).

It is with this sincere desire that the Central Committee of the Communist Party of China approaches the forthcoming talks between the Chinese and Soviet Parties [to be held in Moscow from July 5–20, 1963].

In its letter of March 30, the Central Committee of the C.P.S.U. systematically presents its views on questions that need to be discussed in the talks between the Chinese and Soviet Parties, and in particular raises the question of the general line of the international Communist movement. In this letter we too would like to express our views, which constitute our proposal on the general line of the international Communist movement and on some related questions of principle.

We hope that this exposition of views will be conducive to mutual understanding by our two Parties and to a detailed, point-by-point discussion in the talks.

We also hope that this will be conducive to the understanding of our views by the fraternal Parties and to a full exchange of ideas at an international meeting of fraternal Parties.

1. The general line of the international Communist movement must take as its guiding principle the Marxist-Leninist revolutionary theory concerning the historical mission of the proletariat and must not depart from it.

The Moscow Meetings of 1957 and 1960 adopted the Declaration and the Statement respectively after a full exchange of views and in accordance with the principle of reaching unanimity through consultation. The two documents point out the characteristics of our epoch and the common laws of socialist revolution and socialist construction, and lay down the common line of all the Communist and Workers' Parties. They are the common program of the international Communist movement.

It is true that for several years there have been differences within the international Communist movement in the understanding of, and the attitude toward, the Declaration of 1957 and the Statement of 1960. The central issue here is whether or not to accept the revolutionary principles of the Declaration and the Statement. In the last analysis, it is a question of whether or not to accept the universal truth of Marxism-Leninism, whether or not to recognize the universal significance of the road of the October Revolution [see above, pp. 35–36], whether or not to accept the fact that the people still living under the imperialist and capitalist system, who comprise two thirds of the world's population, need to make revolution, and whether or not to accept the fact that the people already on the socialist road, who comprise one third of the world's population, need to carry their revolution forward to the end.

It has become an urgent and vital task of the international Communist movement resolutely to defend the revolutionary principles of the 1957 Declaration and the 1960 Statement.

Only by strictly following the revolutionary teachings of Marxism-Leninism and the general road of the October Revolution is it possible to have a correct understanding of the revolutionary principles of the Declaration and the Statement and a correct attitude toward them.

2. What are the revolutionary principles of the Declaration and the Statement? They may be summarized as follows:

Workers of all countries, unite; workers of the world, unite with the oppressed peoples and oppressed nations; oppose imperialism and reaction in all countries; strive for world peace, national liberation, people's democracy, and socialism; consolidate and expand the socialist camp; bring the proletarian world revolution step by step to complete victory; and establish a new world without imperialism, without capitalism, and without the exploitation of man by man.

This, in our view, is the general line of the international Communist movement at the present stage.

3. This general line proceeds from the actual world situation taken as a whole and from a class analysis of the fundamental contradictions in the contemporary world, and is directed against the counterrevolutionary global strategy of U. S. imperialism.

This general line is one of forming a broad united front, with the socialist camp and the international proletariat as its nucleus, to oppose the imperialists and reactionaries headed by the United States; it is a line of boldly arousing the masses, expanding the revolutionary forces, winning over the middle forces, and isolating the reactionary forces.

This general line is one of resolute revolutionary struggle by the people of all countries and of carrying the proletarian world revolution forward to the end; it is the line that most effectively combats imperialism and defends world peace.

If the general line of the international Communist movement is one-sidedly reduced to "peaceful coexistence," "peaceful competition," and "peaceful transition," this is to violate the revolutionary principles of the 1957 Declaration and the 1960 Statement, to discard the historical mission of proletarian world revolution, and to depart from the revolutionary teachings of Marxism-Leninism.

The general line of the international Communist movement should reflect the general law of development of world history. The revolutionary struggles of the proletariat and the people in various countries go through different stages and they all have their own characteristics, but they will not transcend the general law of development of world history. The general line should point out the basic direction for the revolutionary struggles of the proletariat and people of all countries.

While working out its specific line and policies, it is most important for each Communist or Workers' Party to adhere to the principle of integrating the universal truth of Marxism-Leninism with the concrete practice of revolution and construction in its own country.

4. In defining the general line of the international Communist movement, the starting point is the concrete class analysis of world politics and economics as a whole and of actual world conditions, that is to say, of the fundamental contradictions in the contemporary world.

If one avoids a concrete class analysis, seizes at random on certain superficial phenomena, and draws subjective and groundless conclusions, one cannot possibly reach correct conclusions with regard to the general line of the international Communist movement but will inevitably slide on to a track entirely different from that of Marxism-Leninism.

What are the fundamental contradictions in the contemporary world? Marxist-Leninists consistently hold that they are:

the contradiction between the socialist camp and the imperialist camp;

the contradiction between the proletariat and the bourgeoisie in the capitalist countries;

the contradiction between the oppressed nations and imperialism;

and

the contradictions among imperialist countries and among monopoly capitalist groups.

The contradiction between the socialist camp and the imperialist camp is a contradiction between two fundamentally different social systems: socialism and capitalism. It is undoubtedly very sharp. But Marxist-Leninists must not regard the contradictions in the world as consisting solely and simply of the contradiction between the socialist camp and the imperialist camp.

The international balance of forces has changed and has become increasingly favorable to socialism and to all the oppressed peoples and nations of the world, and most unfavorable to imperialism and the reactionaries of all countries. Nevertheless, the contradictions enumerated above still objectively exist.

These contradictions and the struggle to which they give rise are interrelated and influence each other. Nobody can obliterate any of these fundamental contradictions or subjectively substitute one for all the rest.

It is inevitable that these contradictions will give rise to popular revolutions, which alone can resolve them.

5. The following erroneous views should be repudiated on the question of the fundamental contradictions in the contemporary world:

(a) the view which blots out the class content of the contradiction between the socialist and the imperialist camps and fails to see this contradiction as one between states under the dictatorship of the proletariat and states under the dictatorship of the monopoly capitalists;

(b) the view which recognizes only the contradiction between the socialist and the imperialist camps, while neglecting or underestimating the contradictions between the proletariat and the bourgeoisie in the capitalist world, between the oppressed nations and imperialism, among the imperialist countries and among the monopoly capitalist groups, and the struggles to which these contradictions give rise;

(c) the view which maintains with regard to the capitalist world that the contradiction between the proletariat and the bourgeoisie can be resolved without a proletarian revolution in each country and that the contradiction between the oppressed nations and imperialism can be resolved without revolution by the oppressed nations;

(d) the view which denies that the development of the inherent contradictions in the contemporary capitalist world inevitably leads to a new situation in which the imperialist countries are locked in an intense struggle, and asserts that the contradictions among the imperialist countries can be reconciled, or even eliminated, by "international agreements among the big monopolies; and

(e) the view which maintains that the contradiction between the two world systems of socialism and capitalism will automatically disappear in the course of "economic competition," that the other fundamental world contradictions will automatically do so with the disappearance of the contradiction between the two systems, and that a "world without wars," a new world of "all-round cooperation," will appear.

It is obvious that these erroneous views inevitably lead to erroneous and harmful policies and hence to setbacks and losses of one kind or another to the cause of the people and socialism.

6. The balance of forces between imperialism and socialism has undergone a fundamental change since World War II. The main indication of this change is that the world now has not just one socialist country but a number of socialist countries forming the mighty socialist camp, and that the people who have taken the socalist road now number not two hundred million but a thousand million, or a third of the world's population.

The socialist camp is the outcome of the struggles of the international proletariat and working people. It belongs to the international proletariat and working people as well as to the people of the socialist countries.

The main common demands of the people of the countries in the socialist camp and the international proletariat and working people are that all the Communist and Workers' Parties in the socialist camp should:

Adhere to the Marxist-Leninist line and pursue correct Marxist-Leninist domestic and foreign policies;

Consolidate the dictatorship of the proletariat and the worker-peasant alliance led by the proletariat and carry the socialist revolution forward to the end on the economic, political, and ideological fronts;

Promote the initiative and creativeness of the broad masses, carry out socialist construction in a planned way, develop production, improve the people's livelihood, and strengthen national defense;

Strengthen the unity of the socialist camp on the basis of Marxism-Leninism, and support other socialist countries on the basis of proletarian internationalism;

Oppose the imperialist policies of aggression and war, and defend world peace;

Oppose the anti-Communist, antipopular, and counterrevolutionary policies of the reactionaries of all countries; and

Help the revolutionary struggles of the oppressed classes and nations of the world.

All Communist and Workers' Parties in the socialist camp owe it to their own people and to the international proletariat and working people to fulfill these demands.

By fulfilling these demands the socialist camp will exert a decisive influence on the course of human history.

For this very reason, the imperialists and reactionaries invariably try in a thousand and one ways to influence the domestic and foreign policies of the countries in the socialist camp, to undermine the camp and break up the unity of the socialist countries and particularly the unity of China and the Soviet Union. They invariably try to infiltrate and subvert the socialist countries and even entertain the extravagant hope of destroying the socialist camp.

The question of what is the correct attitude toward the socialist camp is a most important question of principle confronting all Communist and Workers' Parties.

It is under new historical conditions that the Communist and Workers' Parties are now carrying on the task of proletarian internationalist unity and struggle. When only one socialist country existed and when this country was faced with hostility and jeopardized by all the imperialists and reactionaries because it firmly pursued the correct Marxist-Leninist line and policies, the touchstone of proletarian internationalism for every Communist Party was whether or not it resolutely defended the only socialist country. Now there is a socialist camp consisting of thirteen countries, Albania, Bulgaria, China, Cuba, Czechoslovakia, the German Democratic Republic, Hungary, the Democratic People's Republic of Korea, Mongolia, Poland, Rumania, the Soviet Union, and the Democratic Republic of Viet Nam. In these circumstances, the touchstone of proletarian internationalism for every Communist Party is whether or not it resolutely defends the whole of the socialist camp, whether or not it defends the unity of all the countries in the camp on the basis of Marxism-Leninism, and whether or not it defends the Marxist-Leninist line and policies which the socialist countries ought to pursue.

If anybody does not pursue the correct Marxist-Leninist line and policies, does not defend the unity of the socialist camp but on the contrary creates tension and splits within it, or even follows the policies of the Yugoslav revisionists, tries to liquidate the socialist camp, or helps capitalist countries to attack fraternal socialist countries, then he is betraying the interests of the entire international proletariat and the people of the world.

If anybody, following in the footsteps of others, defends the erroneous opportunist line and policies pursued by a certain socialist country instead of upholding the correct Marxist-Leninist line and policies which the socialist countries ought to pursue, defends the policy of split instead of upholding the policy of unity, then he is departing from Marxism-Leninism and proletarian internationalism.

7. Taking advantage of the situation after World War II, the U. S. imperialists stepped into the shoes of the German, Italian, and Japanese fascists, and have been trying to erect a huge world empire such as has never been known before. The strategic objectives of U. S. imperialism have been to grab and dominate the intermediate zone lying between the United States and the socialist camp, put down the revolutions of the oppressed peoples and nations, proceed to destroy the socialist countries, and thus to subject all the peoples and countries of the world, including its allies, to domination and enslavement by U. S. monopoly capital.

Ever since World War II, the U. S. imperialists have been conducting propaganda for war against the Soviet Union and the socialist camp. There are two aspects to this propaganda. While the U. S. imperialists are actually preparing such a war, they also use this propaganda as a smokescreen for their oppression of the American people and for the extension of their aggression against the rest of the capitalist world.

The 1960 Statement points out:

> "U. S. imperialism has become the biggest international exploiter."
>
> "The United States is the mainstay of colonialism today."
>
> "U. S. imperialism is the main force of aggression and war."
>
> "International developments in recent years have furnished many new proofs of the fact that U. S. imperialism is the chief bulwark of world reaction and an international gendarme, that it has become an enemy of the peoples of the whole world."

U. S. imperialism is pressing its policies of aggression and war all over the world, but the outcome is bound to be the opposite of that intended—it will only be to hasten the awakening of the people in all countries and to hasten their revolutions.

The U. S. imperialists have thus placed themselves in opposition to the people of the whole world and have become encircled by them. The international proletariat must and can unite all the forces that can be united, make use of the internal contradictions in the enemy camp, and establish the broadest united front against the U. S. imperialists and their lackeys.

The realistic and correct course is to entrust the fate of the people and of mankind to the unity and struggle of the world proletariat and to the unity and struggle of the people in all countries.

Conversely, to make no distinction between enemies, friends, and ourselves and to entrust the fate of the people and of mankind to collaboration with U. S. imperialism are to lead people astray. The events of the last few years have exploded this illusion.

8. The various types of contradictions in the contemporary world are concentrated in the vast areas of Asia, Africa, and Latin America; these are the most vulnerable areas under imperialist rule and the storm centers of world revolution dealing direct blows at imperialism.

The national democratic revolutionary movement in these areas and the international socialist revolutionary movement are the two great historical currents of our time.

The national democratic revolution in these areas is an important component of the contemporary proletarian world revolution.

The anti-imperialist revolutionary struggles of the people in Asia, Africa, and Latin America are pounding and undermining the foundations of the rule of imperialism and colonialism, old and new, and are now a mighty force in defense of world peace.

In a sense, therefore, the whole cause of the international proletarian revolution hinges on the outcome of the revolutionary struggles of the people of these areas, who constitute the overwhelming majority of the world's population.

Therefore, the anti-imperialist revolutionary struggle of the people of Asia, Africa, and Latin America is definitely not merely a matter of regional significance but one of overall importance for the whole cause of proletarian world revolution.

Certain persons now go so far as to deny the great international significance of the anti-imperialist revolutionary struggles of the Asian, African, and Latin American peoples and, on the pretext of breaking down the barriers of nationality, color, and geographical location, are trying their best to efface the line of demarcation between oppressed and oppressor nations and between oppressed and oppressor countries and to hold down the revolutionary struggles of the peoples in these areas. In fact, they cater to the needs of imperialism and create a new "theory" to justify the rule of imperialism in these areas and the promotion of its policies of old and new colonialism. Actually, this "theory" seeks not to break down the barriers of nationality, color, and geographical location but to maintain the rule of the "superior nations" over the oppressed nations. It is only natural that this fraudulent "theory" is rejected by the people in these areas.

The working class in every socialist country and in every capitalist country must truly put into effect the fighting slogans, "Workers of all countries, unite!" and "Workers and oppressed nations of the world, unite!"; it must study the revolutionary experience of the peoples of Asia, Africa, and Latin America, firmly support their revolutionary actions, and regard the cause of their liberation as a most dependable support for itself and as directly in accord with its own interests. This is the only effective way to break down the barriers of nationality, color, and geographical location and this is the only genuine proletarian internationalism.

It is impossible for the working class in the European and American capitalist countries to liberate itself unless it unites with the oppressed nations and unless those nations are liberated. Lenin rightly said,

> The revolutionary movement in the advanced countries would actually be a sheer fraud if, in their struggle against capital, the workers of Europe and America were not closely and completely united with the hundreds upon hundreds of millions of "colonial" slaves who are oppressed by capital.

Certain persons in the international Communist movement are now taking a passive or scornful or negative attitude toward the struggles of the oppressed nations for liberation. They are, in fact, protecting the interest of monopoly capital, betraying those of the proletariat, and degenerating into social democrats.

The attitude taken toward the revolutionary struggles of the people in the Asian, African, and Latin American countries is an important criterion for differentiating those who want revolution from those who do not and those who are truly defending world peace from those who are abetting the forces of aggression and war.

9. The oppressed nations and peoples of Asia, Africa, and Latin America are faced with the urgent task of fighting imperialism and its lackeys.

History has entrusted to the proletarian parties in these areas the glorious mission of holding high the banner of struggle against imperialism, against old and new colonialism, and for national independence and people's democracy, of standing in the forefront of the national democratic revolutionary movement and striving for a socialist future.

In these areas, extremely broad sections of the population refuse to be slaves of imperialism. They include not only the workers, peasants, intellectuals, and petty bourgeoisie, but also the patriotic, national bourgeoisie, and even certain kings, princes, and aristocrats, who are patriotic.

The proletariat and its party must have confidence in the strength of the masses and, above all, must unite with the peasants and establish a solid worker-peasant alliance. It is of primary importance for advanced members of the proletariat to work in the rural areas, help the peasants to get organized, and raise their class consciousness and their national self-respect and self-confidence.

On the basis of the worker-peasant alliance, the proletariat and its party must unite all the strata that can be united and organize a broad united front against imperialism and its lackeys. In order to consolidate and expand this united front it is necessary that the proletarian party should maintain its ideological, political, and organizational independence and insist on the leadership of the revolution.

The proletarian party and the revolutionary people must learn to master all forms of struggle, including armed struggle. They must defeat counterrevolutionary armed force with revolutionary armed force whenever imperialism and its lackeys resort to armed suppression.

The nationalist countries which have recently won political independence are still confronted with the arduous tasks of consolidating it, liquidating the forces of imperialism and domestic reaction, carrying out agrarian and other social reforms, and developing their national economy and culture. It is of practical and vital importance for these countries to guard and fight against the neocolonialist policies which the old colonialists adopt to preserve their interests, and especially against the neocolonialism of U. S. imperialism.

In some of these countries, the patriotic national bourgeoisie continue to stand with the masses in the struggle against imperialism and colonialism and introduce certain measures of social progress. This requires the proletarian party to make a full appraisal of the progressive role of the patriotic national bourgeoisie and strengthen unity with them.

As the internal social contradictions and the international class struggle sharpen, the bourgeoisie, and particularly the big bourgeoisie, in some newly independent countries increasingly tend to become retainers of imperialism and to pursue antipopular, anti-Communist, and counterrevolutionary policies. It is necessary for the proletarian party resolutely to oppose these reactionary policies.

Generally speaking, the bourgeoisie in these countries have a dual character. When a united front is formed with the bourgeoisie, the policy of the proletarian party should be one of both unity and struggle. The policy should be to unite with the bourgeoisie, insofar as they tend to be progressive, anti-imperialist, and antifeudal, but to struggle against their reactionary tendencies to compromise and collaborate with imperialism and the forces of feudalism.

On the national question the world outlook of the proletarian party is internationalism, and not nationalism. In the revolutionary struggle it supports progressive nationalism and opposes reactionary nationalism. It must always draw a clear line of demarcation between itself and bourgeois nationalism, to which it must never fall captive.

The 1960 Statement says,

> Communists expose attempts by the reactionary section of the bourgeoisie to represent its selfish narrow class interests as those of the entire nation; they expose the demagogic use by bourgeois politicians of socialist slogans for the same purpose. . . .

If the proletariat becomes the tail of the landlords and bourgeoisie in the revolution, no real or thorough victory in the national democratic revolution is possible, and even if victory of a kind is gained, it will be impossible to consolidate it.

In the course of the revolutionary struggles of the oppressed nations and peoples, the proletarian party must put forward a program of its own which is thoroughly against imperialism and domestic reaction and for national independence and people's democracy, and it must work independently among the masses, constantly expand the progressive forces, win over the middle forces, and isolate the reactionary forces; only thus can it carry the national democratic revolution through to the end and guide the revolution on to the road of socialism.

10. In the imperialist and the capitalist countries, the proletarian revolution and the dictatorship of the proletariat are essential for the thorough resolution of the contradictions of capitalist society.

In striving to accomplish this task the proletarian party must in the present circumstances actively lead the working class and the working people in struggles to oppose monopoly capital, to defend democratic rights, to oppose the menace of fascism, to improve living conditions, to oppose imperialist arms expansion and war preparations, to defend world peace, and actively to support the revolutionary struggles of the oppressed nations.

In the capitalist countries which U. S. imperialism controls or is trying to control, the working class and the people should direct their attacks mainly against U. S. imperialism, but also against their own monopoly capitalists and other reactionary forces who are betraying the national interests.

Large-scale mass struggles in the capitalist countries in recent years have shown that the working class and working people are experiencing a new awakening. Their struggles, which are dealing blows at monopoly capital and reaction, have opened bright prospects for the revolutionary cause in their own countries and are also a powerful support for the revolutionary struggles of the Asian, African, and Latin American peoples and for the countries of the socialist camp.

The proletarian parties in imperialist or capitalist countries must maintain their own ideological, political, and organizational independence in leading revolutionary struggles. At the same time, they must unite all the forces that can be united and build a broad united front against monopoly capital and against the imperialist policies of aggression and war.

While actively leading immediate struggles, Communists in

the capitalist countries should link them with the struggle for long-range and general interests, educate the masses in a Marxist-Leninist revolutionary spirit, ceaselessly raise their political consciousness, and undertake the historical task of the proletarian revolution. If they fail to do so, if they regard the immediate movement as everything, determine their conduct from case to case, adapt themselves to the events of the day and sacrifice the basic interests of the proletariat, that is out-and-out social democracy.

Social democracy is a bourgeois ideological trend. Lenin pointed out long ago that the social democratic parties are political detachments of the bourgeoisie, its agents in the working-class movement and its principal social prop. Communists must at all times draw a clear line of demarcation between themselves and social democratic parties on the basic question of the proletarian revolution and the dictatorship of the proletariat and liquidate the ideological influence of social democracy in the international working-class movement and among the working people. Beyond any shadow of doubt, Communists must win over the masses under the influence of the social democratic parties and must win over those left and middle elements in the social democratic parties which are willing to oppose domestic monopoly capital and domination by foreign imperialism, and must unite with them in extensive joint action in the day-to-day struggle of the working-class movement and in the struggle to defend world peace.

In order to lead the proletariat and working people in revolution, Marxist-Leninist Parties must master all forms of struggle and be able to substitute one form for another quickly as the conditions of struggle change. The vanguard of the proletariat will remain unconquerable in all circumstances only if it masters all forms of struggle—peaceful and armed, open and secret, legal and illegal, parliamentary struggle and mass struggle, etc. It is wrong to refuse to use parliamentary and other legal forms of struggle when they can and should be used. However, if a Marxist-Leninist Party falls into legalism or parliamentary cretinism, confining the struggle within the limits permitted by the bourgeoisie, this will inevitably lead to renouncing the proletarian revolution and the dictatorship of the proletariat.

11. On the question of transition from capitalism to socialism, the proletarian party must proceed from the stand of class strug-

gle and revolution and base itself on the Marxist-Leninist teachings concerning the proletarian revolution and the dictatorship of the proletariat.

Communists would always prefer to bring about the transition to socialism by peaceful means. But can peaceful transition be made into a new worldwide strategic principle for the international Communist movement? Absolutely not.

Marxism-Leninism consistently holds that the fundamental question in all revolutions is that of state power. The 1957 Declaration and the 1960 Statement both clearly point out, "Leninism teaches, and experience confirms, that the ruling classes never relinquish power voluntarily." The old government never topples even in a period of crisis, unless it is pushed. This is a universal law of class struggle.

In specific historical conditions, Marx and Lenin did raise the possibility that revolution may develop peacefully. But, as Lenin pointed out, the peaceful development of revolution is an opportunity "very seldom to be met with in the history of revolutions."

As a matter of fact, there is no historical precedent for peaceful transition from capitalism to socialism.

Certain persons say there was no precedent when Marx foretold that socialism would inevitably replace capitalism. Then why can we not predict a peaceful transition from capitalism to socialism despite the absence of a precedent?

This parallel is absurd. Employing dialectical and historical materialism, Marx analyzed the contradictions of capitalism, discovered the objective laws of development of human society, and arrived at a scientific conclusion, whereas the prophets who pin all their hopes on "peaceful transition" proceed from historical idealism, ignore the most fundamental contradictions of capitalism, repudiate the Marxist-Leninist teachings on class struggle, and arrive at a subjective and groundless conclusion. How can people who repudiate Marxism get any help from Marx?

It is plain to everyone that the capitalist countries are strengthening their state machinery—and especially their military apparatus—the primary purpose of which is to suppress the people in their own countries.

The proletarian party must never base its thinking, its policies for revolution, and its entire work on the assumption that the imperialists and reactionaries will accept peaceful transformation.

The proletarian party must prepare itself for two eventualities —while preparing for a peaceful development of the revolution, it must also fully prepare for a nonpeaceful development. It should concentrate on the painstaking work of accumulating revolutionary strength, so that it will be ready to seize victory when the conditions for revolution are ripe or to strike powerful blows at the imperialists and the reactionaries when they launch surprise attacks and armed assaults.

If it fails to make such preparations, the proletarian party will paralyze the revolutionary will of the proletariat, disarm itself ideologically, and sink into a totally passive state of unpreparedness both politically and organizationally, and the result will be to bury the proletarian revolutionary cause.

12. All social revolutions in the various stages of the history of mankind are historically inevitable and are governed by objective laws independent of man's will. Moreover, history shows that there never was a revolution which was able to achieve victory without zigzags and sacrifices.

With Marxist-Leninist theory as the basis, the task of the proletarian party is to analyze the concrete historical conditions, put forward the correct strategy and tactics, and guide the masses in bypassing hidden reefs, avoiding unnecessary sacrifices and reaching the goal step by step. Is it possible to avoid sacrifices altogether? Such is not the case with the slave revolutions, the serf revolutions, the bourgeois revolutions, or the national revolutions; nor is it the case with proletarian revolutions. Even if the guiding line of the revolution is correct, it is impossible to have a sure guarantee against setbacks and sacrifices in the course of the revolution. So long as a correct line is adhered to, the revolution is bound to triumph in the end. To abandon revolution on the pretext of avoiding sacrifices is in reality to demand that the people should forever remain slaves and endure infinite pain and sacrifice.

Elementary knowledge of Marxism-Leninism tells us that the birthpangs of a revolution are far less painful than the chronic agony of the old society. Lenin rightly said that "even with the most peaceful course of events, the present [capitalist] system always and inevitably exacts countless sacrifices from the working class."

Whoever considers a revolution can be made only if everything is plain sailing, only if there is an advance guarantee against sacrifices and failure, is certainly no revolutionary.

However difficult the conditions and whatever sacrifices and defeats the revolution may suffer, proletarian revolutionaries should educate the masses in the spirit of revolution and hold aloft the banner of revolution and not abandon it.

It would be "left" adventurism if the proletarian party should rashly launch a revolution before the objective conditions are ripe. But it would be right opportunism if the proletarian party should not dare to lead a revolution and to seize state power when the objective conditions are ripe.

Even in ordinary times, when it is leading the masses in the day-to-day struggle, the proletarian party should ideologically, politically, and organizationally prepare its own ranks and the masses for revolution and promote revolutionary struggles, so that it will not miss the opportunity to overthrow the reactionary regime and establish a new state power when the conditions for revolution are ripe. Otherwise, when the objective conditions are ripe, the proletarian party will simply throw away the opportunity of seizing victory.

The proletarian party must be flexible as well as highly principled, and on occasion it must make such compromises as are necessary in the interests of the revolution. But it must never abandon principled policies and the goal of revolution on the pretext of flexibility and of necessary compromises.

The proletarian party must lead the masses in waging struggles against the enemies, and it must know how to utilize the contradictions among those enemies. But the purpose of using these contradictions is to make it easier to attain the goal of the people's revolutionary struggles and not to liquidate these struggles.

Countless facts have proved that, wherever the dark rule of imperialism and reaction exists, the people who form over 90 percent of the population will sooner or later rise in revolution.

If Communists isolate themselves from the revolutionary demands of the masses, they are bound to lose the confidence of the masses and will be tossed to the rear by the revolutionary current.

If the leading group in any Party adopt a nonrevolutionary line and convert it into a reformist party, then Marxist-Leninists inside and outside the Party will replace them and lead the people in making revolution. In another kind of situation, the bourgeois revolutionaries will come forward to lead the revolution and the party of the proletariat will forfeit its leadership of the revolution. When the reactionary bourgeoisie betray the revolution and suppress the people, an opportunist line will cause tragic and unnecessary losses to the Communists and the revolutionary masses.

If Communists slide down the path of opportunism, they will degenerate into bourgeois nationalists and become appendages of the imperialists and the reactionary bourgeoisie.

There are certain persons who assert that they have made the greatest creative contributions to revolutionary theory since Lenin and that they alone are correct. But it is very dubious whether they have ever really given consideration to the extensive experience of the entire world Communist movement, whether they have ever really considered the interests, the goal, and tasks of the international proletarian movement as a whole, and whether they really have a general line for the international Communist movement which conforms with Marxism-Leninism.

In the last few years the international Communist movement and the national liberation movement have had many experiences and many lessons. There are experiences which people should praise and there are experiences which make people grieve. Communists and revolutionaries in all countries should ponder and seriously study these experiences of success and failure, so as to draw correct conclusions and useful lessons from them.

13. The socialist countries and the revolutionary struggles of the oppressed peoples and nations support and assist each other.

The national liberation movements of Asia, Africa, and Latin America and the revolutionary movements of the people in the capitalist countries are a strong support to the socialist countries. It is completely wrong to deny this.

The only attitude for the socialist countries to adopt toward the revolutionary struggles of the oppressed peoples and nations is one of warm sympathy and active support; they must not adopt a perfunctory attitude, or one of national selfishness or of great-power chauvinism.

Lenin said, "Alliance with the revolutionaries of the advanced countries and with all the oppressed peoples against any and all the imperialists—such is the external policy of the proletariat." Whoever fails to understand this point and considers that the support and aid given by the socialist countries to the oppressed peoples and nations are a burden or charity is going counter to Marxism-Leninism and proletarian internationalism.

The superiority of the socialist system and the achievements of the socialist countries in construction play an exemplary role and are an inspiration to the oppressed peoples and the oppressed nations.

But this exemplary role and inspiration can never replace the revolutionary struggles of the oppressed peoples and nations. No oppressed people or nation can win liberation except through its own staunch revolutionary struggle.

Certain persons have one-sidedly exaggerated the role of peaceful competition between socialist and imperialist countries in their attempt to substitute peaceful competition for the revolutionary struggles of the oppressed peoples and nations. According to their preaching, it would seem that imperialism will automatically collapse in the course of this peaceful competition and that the only thing the oppressed peoples and nations have to do is to wait quietly for the advent of this day. What does this have in common with Marxist-Leninist views?

Moreover, certain persons have concocted the strange tale that China and some other socialist countries want "to unleash wars" and to spread socialism by "wars between states." As the Statement of 1960 points out, such tales are nothing but imperialist and reactionary slanders. To put it bluntly, the purpose of those who repeat these slanders is to hide the fact that they are opposed to revolutions by the oppressed peoples and nations of the world and opposed to others supporting such revolutions.

14. In the last few years much—in fact a great deal—has been said on the question of war and peace. Our views and policies on this question are known to the world, and no one can distort them.

It is a pity that, although certain persons in the international Communist movement talk about how much they love peace and hate war, they are unwilling to acquire even a faint understanding of the simple truth on war pointed out by Lenin.

Lenin said,

> It seems to me that the main thing that is usually forgotten on the question of war, which receives inadequate attention, the main reason why there is so much controversy, and, I would say, futile, hopeless, and aimless controversy, is that people forget the fundamental question of the class character of the war; why the war broke out; the classes that are waging it; the historical and historico-economic conditions that gave rise to it.

As Marxist-Leninists see it, war is the continuation of politics by other means, and every war is inseparable from the political system and the political struggles which give rise to it. If one departs from this scientific Marxist-Leninist proposition which has been confirmed by the entire history of class struggle, one will never be able to understand either the question of war or the question of peace.

There are different types of peace and different types of war. Marxist-Leninists must be clear about what type of peace or what type of war is in question. Lumping just wars and unjust wars together and opposing all of them undiscriminatingly is a bourgeois pacifist and not a Marxist-Leninist approach.

Certain persons say that revolutions are entirely possible without war. Now which type of war are they referring to—is it a war of national liberation or a revolutionary civil war, or is it a world war?

If they are referring to a war of national liberation or a revolutionary civil war, then this formulation is, in effect, opposed to revolutionary wars and to revolution.

If they are referring to a world war, then they are shooting at a nonexistent target. Although Marxist-Leninists have pointed out, on the basis of the history of the two world wars, that world wars inevitably lead to revolution, no Marxist-Leninist ever has held or ever will hold that revolution must be made through world war.

Marxist-Leninists take the abolition of war as their ideal and believe that war can be abolished.

But how can war be abolished?

This is how Lenin viewed it:

> . . . our object is to achieve the socialist system of society, which, by abolishing the division of mankind into classes, by abolishing all exploitation of man by man, and of one nation by other nations, will inevitably abolish all possibility of war.

The Statement of 1960 also puts it very clearly, "The victory of socialism all over the world will completely remove the social and national causes of all wars."

However, certain persons now actually hold that it is possible to bring about "a world without weapons, without armed forces, and without wars" through "general and complete disarmament" while the system of imperialism and of the exploitation of man by man still exists. This is sheer illusion.

An elementary knowledge of Marxism-Leninism tells us that the armed forces are the principal part of the state machine and that a so-called "world without weapons" and without armed forces can only be a world without states. Lenin said:

> Only *after* the proletariat has disarmed the bourgeoisie will it be able, without betraying its world-historical mission, to throw all armaments on the scrap heap; and the proletariat will undoubtedly do this, but *only when this condition has been fulfilled, certainly not before.*

What are the facts in the world today? Is there a shadow of evidence that the imperialist countries headed by the United States are ready to carry out general and complete disarmament? Are they not each and all engaged in general and complete arms expansion?

We have always maintained that, in order to expose and combat the imperialists' arms expansion and war preparations, it is necessary to put forward the proposal for general disarmament. Furthermore, it is possible to compel imperialism to accept some kind of agreement on disarmament, through the combined struggle of the socialist countries and the people of the whole world.

If one regards general and complete disarmament as the fundamental road to world peace, spreads the illusion that imperialism will automatically lay down its arms, and tries to liquidate the revolutionary struggles of the oppressed peoples and nations on the pretext of disarmament, then this is deliberately to deceive the people of the world and help the imperialists in their policies of aggression and war.

In order to overcome the present ideological confusion in the international working-class movement on the question of war and peace, we consider that Lenin's thesis, which has been discarded by the modern revisionists, must be restored in the interest of combating the imperialist policies of aggression and war and defending world peace.

The people of the world universally demand the prevention of a new world war. And it is possible to prevent a new world war.

The question then is, what is the way to secure world peace? According to the Leninist viewpoint, world peace can be won only by the struggles of the people in all countries and not by begging the imperialists for it. World peace can only be effectively defended by relying on the development of the forces of the socialist camp, on the revolutionary struggles of the proletariat and working people of all countries, on the liberation struggles of the oppressed nations, and on the struggles of all peace-loving people and countries.

Such is the Leninist policy. Any policy to the contrary definitely will not lead to world peace but will only encourage the ambitions of the imperialists and increase the danger of world war.

In recent years, certain persons have been spreading the argument that a single spark from a war of national liberation or from a revolutionary people's war will lead to a world conflagration destroying the whole of mankind. What are the facts? Contrary to what these persons say, the wars of national liberation and the revolutionary people's wars that have occurred since World War II have not led to world war. The victory of these revolutionary wars has directly weakened the forces of imperialism and greatly strengthened the forces which prevent the imperialists from launching a world war and which defend world peace. Do not the facts demonstrate the absurdity of this argument?

15. The complete banning and destruction of nuclear weapons is an important task in the struggle to defend world peace. We must do our utmost to this end.

Nuclear weapons are unprecedentedly destructive, which is why for more than a decade now the U. S. imperialists have been pursuing their policy of nuclear blackmail in order to realize their ambition of enslaving the people of all countries and dominating the world.

But when the imperialists threaten other countries with nuclear weapons, they subject the people in their own country to the same threat, thus arousing them against nuclear weapons and against the imperialist policies of aggression and war. At the same time, in their vain hope of destroying their opponents with nuclear weapons, the imperialists are in fact subjecting themselves to the danger of being destroyed.

The possibility of banning nuclear weapons does indeed exist. However, if the imperialists are forced to accept an agreement to ban nuclear weapons, it decidedly will not be because of their "love for humanity" but because of the pressure of the people of all countries and for the sake of their own vital interests.

In contrast to the imperialists, socialist countries rely upon the righteous strength of the people and on their own correct policies, and have no need whatever to gamble with nuclear weapons in the world arena. Socialist countries have nuclear weapons solely in order to defend themselves and to prevent imperialism from launching a nuclear war.

In the view of Marxist-Leninists, the people are the makers of history. In the present, as in the past, man is the decisive factor. Marxist-Leninists attach importance to the role of technological change, but it is wrong to belittle the role of man and exaggerate the role of technology.

The emergence of nuclear weapons can neither arrest the progress of human history nor save the imperialist system from its doom, any more than the emergence of new techniques could save the old systems from their doom in the past.

The emergence of nuclear weapons does not and cannot resolve the fundamental contradictions in the contemporary world, does not and cannot alter the law of class struggle, and does not and cannot change the nature of imperialism and reaction.

It cannot, therefore, be said that with the emergence of nuclear weapons the possibility and the necessity of social and national revolutions have disappeared, or the basic principles of Marxism-Leninism, and especially the theories of proletarian revolution and the dictatorship of the proletariat and of war and peace, have become outmoded and changed into stale "dogmas."

16. It was Lenin who advanced the thesis that it is possible for the socialist countries to practice peaceful coexistence with the capitalist countries. It is well known that after the great Soviet people had repulsed foreign armed intervention the Communist Party of the Soviet Union and the Soviet Government, led first by Lenin and then by Stalin, consistently pursued the policy of peaceful coexistence and that they were forced to wage a war of self-defence only when attacked by the German imperialists.

Since its founding, the People's Republic of China too has consistently pursued the policy of peaceful coexistence with countries having different social systems, and it is China which initiated the Five Principles of Peaceful Coexistence [in the 1954 Sino-Indian treaty on trade with Tibet].

However, a few years ago certain persons suddenly claimed Lenin's policy of peaceful coexistence as their own "great discovery." They maintain that they have a monopoly on the interpretation of this policy. They treat "peaceful coexistence" as if it were an all-inclusive, mystical book from heaven and attribute to it every success the people of the world achieve by struggle.

What is more, they label all who disagree with their distortions of Lenin's views as opponents of peaceful coexistence, as people completely ignorant of Lenin and Leninism, and as heretics deserving to be burnt at the stake.

How can the Chinese Communists agree with this view and practice? They cannot, it is impossible.

Lenin's principle of peaceful coexistence is very clear and readily comprehensible by ordinary people. Peaceful coexistence designates a relationship between countries with different social systems, and must not be interpreted as one pleases. It should never be extended to apply to the relations between oppressed and oppressor nations, between oppressed and oppressor countries, or between oppressed and oppressor classes, and never be described as the main content of the transition from capitalism to socialism, still less should it be asserted that peaceful coexistence is mankind's road to socialism. The reason is that it is one thing to practice peaceful coexistence between countries with different social systems. It is absolutely impermissible and impossible for countries practicing peaceful coexistence to touch even a hair of each other's social system. The class struggle, the struggle for national liberation, and the transition from capitalism to socialism in various countries are quite another thing. They are all bitter, life-and-death revolutionary struggles which aim at changing the social system. Peaceful coexistence cannot replace the revolutionary struggles of the people. The transition from capitalism to socialism in any country can only be brought about through the proletarian revolution and the dictatorship of the proletariat in that country.

In the application of the policy of peaceful coexistence, struggles between the socialist and imperialist countries are unavoidable in the political, economic, and ideological spheres, and it is absolutely impossible to have "all-round cooperation."

It is necessary for the socialist countries to engage in negotiations of one kind or another with the imperialist countries. It is possible to reach certain agreements through negotiation by relying on the correct policies of the socialist countries and on the pressure of the people of all countries. But necessary compromises between the socialist countries and the imperialist countries do not require the oppressed peoples and nations to follow suit and compromise with imperialism and its lackeys. No one should ever demand in the name of peaceful coexistence that the oppressed peoples and nations should give up their revolutionary struggles.

The application of the policy of peaceful coexistence by the socialist countries is advantageous for achieving a peaceful international environment for socialist construction, for exposing the imperialist policies of aggression and war, and for isolating the imperialist forces of aggression and war. But if the general line of the foreign policy of the socialist countries is confined to peaceful coexistence, then it is impossible to handle correctly either the relations among socialist countries or those between the socialist countries and the oppressed peoples and nations. Therefore it is wrong to make peaceful coexistence the general line of the foreign policy of the socialist countries.

In our view, the general line of the foreign policy of the socialist countries should have the following content: to develop relations of friendship, mutual assistance, and cooperation among the countries in the socialist camp in accordance with the principle of proletarian internationalism; to strive for peaceful coexistence on the basis of the Five Principles with countries having different social systems and oppose the imperialist policies of aggression and war; and to support and assist the revolutionary struggles of all the oppressed peoples and nations. These three aspects are interrelated and indivisible, and not a single one can be omitted.

17. For a very long historical period after the proletariat takes power, class struggle continues as an objective law independent of man's will, differing only in form from what it was before the taking of power.

After the October Revolution, Lenin pointed out a number of times that:

(a) The overthrown exploiters always try in a thousand and one ways to recover the "paradise" they have been deprived of.

(b) New elements of capitalism are constantly and spontaneously generated in the petty-bourgeois atmosphere.

(c) Political degenerates and new bourgeois elements may emerge in the ranks of the working class and among government functionaries as a result of bourgeois influence and the pervasive, corrupting atmosphere of the petty bourgeoisie.

(d) The external conditions for the continuance of class struggle within a socialist country are encirclement by international capitalism, the imperialists' threat of armed intervention, and their subversive activities to accomplish peaceful disintegration.

Life has confirmed these conclusions of Lenin's.

For decades or even longer periods after socialist industrialization and agricultural collectivization, it will be impossible to say that any socialist country will be free from those elements which Lenin repeatedly denounced, such as bourgeois hangers-on, parasites, speculators, swindlers, idlers, hooligans, and embezzlers of state funds; or to say that a socialist country will no longer need to perform or be able to relinquish the task laid down by Lenin of conquering "this contagion, this plague, this ulcer that socialism has inherited from capitalism."

In a socialist country, it takes a very long historical period gradually to settle the question of who will win—socialism or capitalism. The struggle between the road of socialism and the road of capitalism runs through this whole historical period. This struggle rises and falls in a wavelike manner, at times becoming very fierce, and the forms of the struggle are many and varied.

The 1957 Declaration rightly states that "the conquest of power by the working class is only the beginning of the revolution, not its conclusion."

To deny the existence of class struggle in the period of the dictatorship of the proletariat and the necessity of thoroughly completing the socialist revolution on the economic, political, and ideological fronts is wrong, does not correspond to objective reality, and violates Marxism-Leninism.

18. Both Marx and Lenin maintained that the entire period before the advent of the higher stage of Communist society is the period of transition from capitalism to communism, the period of the dictatorship of the proletariat. In this transition period, the dictatorship of the proletariat, that is to say, the proletarian state, goes through the dialectical process of establishment, consolidation, strengthening, and withering away.

In the *Critique of the Gotha Programme,* Marx posed the question as follows:

> Between capitalist and Communist society lies the period of the revolutionary transformation of the one into the other. There corresponds to this also a political transition period in which the state can be nothing but *the revolutionary dictatorship of the proletariat.*

Lenin frequently emphasized Marx's great theory of the dictatorship of the proletariat and analyzed the development of this theory, particularly in his outstanding work, *The State and Revolution,* where he wrote:

> . . . the transition from capitalist society—which is developing toward communism—to a Communist society is impossible without a "political transition period," and the state in this period can only be the revolutionary dictatorship of the proletariat.

He further said:

> The essence of Marx's teaching on the state has been mastered only by those who understand that the dictatorship of a *single* class is necessary not only for every class society in general, not only for the *proletariat* which has overthrown the bourgeoisie, but also for the entire *historical period* which separates capitalism from "classless society," from communism.

As stated above, the fundamental thesis of Marx and Lenin is that the dictatorship of the proletariat will inevitably continue for the entire historical period of the transition from capitalism to communism—that is, for the entire period up to the abolition of all class differences and the entry into a classless society, the higher stage of Communist society.

What will happen if it is announced, halfway through, that the dictatorship of the proletariat is no longer necessary? [In this section the Chinese are condemning specific points in the new Party Program adopted by the 22d Congress of the C.P.S.U. in 1961.]

Does this not fundamentally conflict with the teachings of Marx and Lenin on the state of the dictatorship of the proletariat?

Does this not license the development of "this contagion, this plague, this ulcer that socialism has inherited from capitalism"?

In other words, this would lead to extremely grave consequences and make any transition to communism out of the question.

Can there be a "state of the whole people"? Is it possible to replace the state of the dictatorship of the proletariat by a "state of the whole people"?

This is not a question about the internal affairs of any particular country but a fundamental problem involving the universal truth of Marxism-Leninism.

In the view of Marxist-Leninists, there is no such thing as a nonclass or supraclass state. So long as the state remains a state, it must bear a class character; so long as the state exists, it cannot be a state of the "whole people." As soon as society becomes class-less, there will no longer be a state.

Then what sort of thing would a "state of the whole people" be?

Anyone with an elementary knowledge of Marxism-Leninism can understand that the so-called "state of the whole people" is nothing new. Representative bourgeois figures have always called the bourgeois state a "state of all the people," or a "state in which power belongs to all the people."

Certain persons may say that their society is already one without classes. We answer: No, there are classes and class struggles in all socialist countries without exception.

Since remnants of the old exploiting classes who are trying to stage a comeback still exist there, since new capitalist elements are constantly being generated there, and since there are still parasites, speculators, idlers, hooligans, embezzlers of state funds, etc., how can it be said that classes or class struggles no longer exist? How can it be said that the dictatorship of the proletariat is no longer necessary?

Marxism-Leninism tells us that, in addition to the suppression of the hostile classes, the historical tasks of the dictatorship of the proletariat in the course of building socialism necessarily include the correct handling of relations between the working class and peasantry, the consolidation of their political and economic alliance, and the creation of conditions for the gradual elimination of the class difference between worker and peasant.

When we look at the economic base of any socialist society, we find that the difference between ownership by the whole people and collective ownership exists in all socialist countries without exception, and that there is individual ownership too. Ownership by the whole people and collective ownership are two kinds of ownership and two kinds of relations of production in socialist society. The workers in enterprises owned by the whole people and the peasants on farms owned collectively belong to two different categories of laborers in socialist society. Therefore, the class difference between worker and peasant exists in all socialist countries without exception. This difference will not disappear until the transition to the higher stage of communism is achieved. In their present level of economic development all socialist countries are still far, far removed from the higher stage of communism in which "from each according to his ability, to each according to his needs" is put into practice. Therefore, it will take a long, long time to eliminate the class difference between worker and peasant. And until this difference is eliminated, it is impossible to say that society is classless or that there is no longer any need for the dictatorship of the proletariat.

In calling a socialist state the "state of the whole people," is one trying to replace the Marxist-Leninist theory of the state by the bourgeois theory of the state? Is one trying to replace the state of the dictatorship of the proletariat by a state of a different character?

If that is the case, it is nothing but a great historical retrogression. The degeneration of the social system in Yugoslavia is a grave lesson.

19. Leninism holds that the proletarian party must exist together with the dictatorship of the proletariat in socialist countries. The party of the proletariat is indispensable for the entire historical period of the dictatorship of the proletariat. The reason is that the dictatorship of the proletariat has to struggle against the enemies of the proletariat and of the people, remold the peasants and other small producers, constantly consolidate the proletarian ranks, build socialism, and effect the transition to communism; none of these things can be done without the leadership of the party of the proletariat.

Can there be a "party of the entire people"? Is it possible to replace the party which is the vanguard of the proletariat by a "party of the entire people"?

This, too, is not a question about the internal affairs of any particular party, but a fundamental problem involving the universal truth of Marxism-Leninism.

In the view of Marxist-Leninists, there is no such thing as a nonclass or supraclass political party. All political parties have a class character. Party spirit is the concentrated expression of class character.

The party of the proletariat is the only party able to represent the interests of the whole people. It can do so precisely because it represents the interests of the proletariat, whose ideas and will it concentrates. It can lead the whole people because the proletariat can finally emancipate itself only with the emancipation of all mankind, because the very nature of the proletariat enables its party to approach problems in terms of its present and future interests, because the party is boundlessly loyal to the people and has the spirit of self-sacrifice; hence its democratic centralism and iron discipline. Without such a party, it is impossible to maintain the dictatorship of the proletariat and to represent the interests of the whole people.

What will happen if it is announced halfway before entering the higher stage of Communist society that the party of the proletariat has become a "party of the entire people" and if its proletarian class character is repudiated?

Does this not fundamentally conflict with the teachings of Marx and Lenin on the party of the proletariat?

Does this not disarm the proletariat and all the working people, organizationally and ideologically, and is it not tantamount to helping restore capitalism?

Is it not "going south by driving the chariot north" to talk about any transition to Communist society in such circumstances?

20. Over the past few years, certain persons have violated Lenin's integral teachings about the interrelationship of leaders, party, class, and masses, and raised the issue of "combating the cult of the individual"; this is erroneous and harmful. [In essence, the Chinese are giving their view of Stalin in this section.]

The theory propounded by Lenin is as follows:

(a) the masses are divided into classes;

(b) classes are usually led by political parties;

(c) political parties, as a general rule, are directed by more or less stable groups composed of the most authoritative, influential, and experienced members, who are elected to the most responsible positions and are called leaders.

Lenin said, "All this is elementary."

The party of the proletariat is the headquarters of the proletariat in revolution and struggle. Every proletarian party must practice centralism based on democracy and establish a strong Marxist-Leninist leadership before it can become an organized and battle-worthy vanguard. To raise the question of "combating the cult of the individual" is actually to counterpose the leaders to the masses, undermine the party's unified leadership which is based on democratic centralism, dissipate its fighting strength, and disintegrate its ranks.

Lenin criticized the erroneous views which counterpose the leaders to the masses. He called them "ridiculously absurd and stupid."

The Communist Party of China has always disapproved of

exaggerating the role of the individual, has advocated and persistently practiced democratic centralism within the Party, and advocated the linking of the leadership with the masses, maintaining that correct leadership must know how to concentrate the views of the masses.

While loudly combating the so-called "cult of the individual," certain persons are in reality doing their best to defame the proletarian party and the dictatorship of the proletariat. At the same time, they are enormously exaggerating the role of certain individuals, shifting all errors onto others, and claiming all credit for themselves.

What is more serious is that, under the pretext of "combating the cult of the individual," certain persons are crudely interfering in the internal affairs of other fraternal Parties and fraternal countries and forcing other fraternal Parties to change their leadership in order to impose their own wrong line on these Parties. What is all this if not great-power chauvinism, sectarianism, and splittism? What is all this if not subversion?

It is high time to propagate seriously and comprehensively Lenin's integral teachings on the interrelationship of leaders, party, class, and masses.

21. Relations between socialist countries are international relations of a new type. Relations between socialist countries, whether large or small, and whether more developed or less developed economically, must be based on the principles of complete equality, respect for territorial integrity, sovereignty, and independence, and noninterference in each other's internal affairs, and must also be based on the principles of mutual support and mutual assistance in accordance with proletarian internationalism.

Every socialist country must rely mainly on itself for its construction.

In accordance with its own concrete conditions, every socialist country must rely first of all on the diligent labor and talents of its own people, utilize all its available resources fully and in a planned way, and bring all its potential into play in socialist construction. Only thus can it build socialism effectively and develop its economy speedily.

This is the only way for each socialist country to strengthen the might of the entire socialist camp and enhance its capacity to assist the revolutionary cause of the international proletariat. Therefore, to observe the principle of mainly relying on oneself in construction is to apply proletarian internationalism concretely.

If, proceeding only from its own partial interests, any socialist country unilaterally demands that other fraternal countries submit to its needs, and uses the pretext of opposing what they call "going it alone" and "nationalism" to prevent other fraternal countries from applying the principle of relying mainly on their own efforts in their construction and from developing their economies on the basis of independence, or even goes to the length of putting economic pressure on other fraternal countries—then these are pure manifestations of national egoism.

It is absolutely necessary for socialist countries to practice mutual economic assistance and cooperation and exchange. Such economic cooperation must be based on the principles of complete equality, mutual benefit, and comradely mutual assistance.

It would be great-power chauvinism to deny these basic principles and, in the name of "international division of labor" or "specialization," to impose one's own will on others, infringe on the independence and sovereignty of fraternal countries, or harm the interests of their people. [Here the Chinese are denouncing the Soviet-sponsored Council for Mutual Economic Assistance for coordination of economic plans in the bloc. China is not a member of the Council.]

In relations among socialist countries it would be preposterous to follow the practice of gaining profit for oneself at the expense of others, a practice characteristic of relations among capitalist countries, or go so far as to take the "economic integration" and the "common market," which monopoly capitalist groups have instituted for the purpose of seizing markets and grabbing profits, as examples which socialist countries ought to follow in their economic cooperation and mutual assistance.

22. The 1957 Declaration and the 1960 Statement lay down the principles guiding relations among fraternal Parties. These are the principle of solidarity, the principle of mutual support and mutual assistance, the principle of independence and equality, and the principle of reaching unanimity through consultation— all on the basis of Marxism-Leninism and proletarian internationalism.

We note that in its letter of March 30 the Central Committee of the C.P.S.U. says that there are no "superior" and "subordinate" Parties in the Communist movement, that all Communist Parties are independent and equal, and that they should all build their relations on the basis of proletarian internationalism and mutual assistance.

It is a fine quality of Communists that their deeds are consistent with their words. The only correct way to safeguard and strengthen unity among the fraternal Parties is genuinely to adhere to, and not to violate, the principle of proletarian internationalism and genuinely to observe, and not to undermine, the principles guiding relations among fraternal Parties—and to do so not only in words but, much more important, in deeds.

If the principle of independence and equality is accepted in relations among fraternal Parties, then it is impermissible for any Party to place itself above others, to interfere in their internal affairs, and to adopt patriarchal ways in relations with them.

If it is accepted that there are no "superiors" and "subordinates" in relations among fraternal Parties, then it is impermissible to impose the program, resolutions, and line of one's own Party on other fraternal Parties as the "common program" of the international Communist movement.

If the principle of reaching unanimity through consultation is accepted in relations among fraternal Parties, then one should not emphasize "who is in the majority" or "who is in the minority" and bank on a so-called "majority" in order to force through one's own erroneous line and carry out sectarian and splitting policies.

If it is agreed that differences between fraternal Parties should be settled through inter-Party consultation, then other fraternal Parties should not be attacked publicly and by name at one's own congress or at other Party congresses, in speeches by Party leaders, resolutions, statements, etc.; and still less should the ideological differences among fraternal Parties be extended into the sphere of state relations.

We hold that in the present circumstances, when there are differences in the international Communist movement, it is particularly important to stress strict adherence to the principles guiding relations among fraternal Parties as laid down in the Declaration and the Statement.

In the sphere of relations among fraternal Parties and countries, the question of Soviet-Albanian relations is an outstanding one at present. Here the questions are, what is the correct way to treat a fraternal Party and country, and whether the principles guiding relations among fraternal Parties and countries stipulated in the Declaration and the Statement are to be adhered to. The correct solution of this question is an important matter of principle in safeguarding the unity of the socialist camp and the international Communist movement.

How to treat the Marxist-Leninist fraternal Albanian Party of Labor is one question. How to treat the Yugoslav revisionist clique of traitors to Marxism-Leninism is quite another question. These two essentially different questions must on no account be placed on a par.

Your letter says that you "do not relinquish hope that the relations between the C.P.S.U. and the Albanian Party of Labor may be improved," but at the same time you continue to attack the Albanian comrades for what you call "splitting activities." Clearly this is self-contradictory and in no way contributes to resolving the problem of Soviet-Albanian relations.

Who is it that has taken splitting actions in Soviet-Albanian relations?

Who is it that has extended the ideological differences between the Soviet and Albanian Parties to state relations?

Who is it that has brought the divergences between the Soviet and Albanian Parties and between the two countries into the open before the enemy?

Who is it that has openly called for a change in the Albanian Party and state leadership?

All this is plain and clear to the whole world.

Is it possible that the leading comrades of the C.P.S.U. do not really feel their responsibility for the fact that Soviet-Albanian relations have so seriously deteriorated?

We once again express our sincere hope that the leading comrades of the C.P.S.U. will observe the principles guiding relations among fraternal Parties and countries and take the initiative in seeking an effective way to improve Soviet-Albanian relations.

In short, the question of how to handle relations with fraternal Parties and countries must be taken seriously. Strict adherence to the principles guiding relations among fraternal Parties and countries is the only way forcefully to rebuff slanders such as those spread by the imperialists and reactionaries about the "hand of Moscow."

Proletarian internationalism is demanded of all Parties without exception, whether large or small, and whether in power or not. However, the larger Parties and the Parties in power bear a particularly heavy responsibility in this respect. The series of distressing developments which have occurred in the socialist camp in the past period have harmed the interests not only of the fraternal Parties concerned but also of the masses of the people in their countries. This convincingly demonstrates that the larger countries and Parties need to keep in mind Lenin's behest never to commit the error of great-power chauvinism.

The comrades of the C.P.S.U. state in their letter that "the Communist Party of the Soviet Union has never taken and will never take a single step that could sow hostility among the peoples of our country toward the fraternal Chinese people or other peoples." Here we do not desire to go back and enumerate the many unpleasant events that have occurred in the past, and we only wish that the comrades of the C.P.S.U. will strictly abide by this statement in their future actions.

During the past few years, our Party members and our people have exercised the greatest restraint in the face of a series of grave incidents which were in violation of the principles guiding relations among fraternal Parties and countries and despite the many difficulties and losses which have been imposed on us. The spirit of proletarian internationalism of the Chinese Communists and the Chinese people has stood a severe test.

The Communist Party of China is unswervingly loyal to proletarian internationalism, upholds and defends the principles of the 1957 Declaration and the 1960 Statement guiding relations among fraternal Parties and countries, and safeguards and strengthens the unity of the socialist camp and the international Communist movement.

23. In order to carry out the common program of the international Communist movement unanimously agreed upon by the fraternal Parties, an uncompromising struggle must be waged against all forms of opportunism, which is a deviation from Marxism-Leninism.

The Declaration and the Statement point out that revisionism, or, in other words, right opportunism, is the main danger in the international Communist movement. Yugoslav revisionism typifies modern revisionism.

The Statement points out particularly:

> The Communist Parties have unanimously condemned the Yugoslav variety of international opportunism, a variety of modern revisionist "theories" in concentrated form.

It goes on to say:

> After betraying Marxism-Leninism, which they termed obsolete, the leaders of the League of Communists of Yugoslavia opposed their anti-Leninist revisionist program to the Declaration of 1957; they set the League of Communists of Yugoslavia against the international Communist movement as a whole, severed their country from the socialist camp, made it dependent on so-called "aid" from U. S. and other imperialists. . . .

The Statement says further:

> The Yugoslav revisionists carry on subversive work against the socialist camp and the world Communist movement. Under the pretext of an extra-bloc policy, they engage in activities which prejudice the unity of all the peace-loving forces and countries.

Therefore, it draws the following conclusion:

> Further exposure of the leaders of Yugoslav revisionists and active struggle to safeguard the Communist movement and the working-class movement from the anti-Leninist ideas of the Yugoslav revisionists remains an essential task of the Marxist-Leninist Parties.

The question raised here is an important one of principle for the international Communist movement.

Only recently the Tito clique has publicly stated that it is persisting in its revisionist program and anti-Marxist-Leninist stand in opposition to the Declaration and the Statement.

U. S. imperialism and its NATO partners have spent several thousand millions of U. S. dollars nursing the Tito clique for a long time. Cloaked as "Marxist-Leninists" and flaunting the banner of a "socialist country," the Tito clique has been undermining the international Communist movement and the revolutionary cause of the people of the world, serving as a special detachment of U. S. imperialism.

It is completely groundless and out of keeping with the facts to assert that Yugoslavia is showing "definite positive tendencies," that it is a "socialist country," and that the Tito clique is an "anti-imperialist force."

Certain persons are now attempting to introduce the Yugoslav revisionist clique into the socialist community and the international Communist ranks. This is openly to tear up the agreement unanimously reached at the 1960 meeting of the fraternal Parties and is absolutely impermissible.

Over the past few years, the revisionist trend flooding the

international working-class movement and the many experiences and lessons of the international Communist movement have fully confirmed the correctness of the conclusion in the Declaration and the Statement that revisionism is the main danger in the international Communist movement at present.

However, certain persons are openly saying that dogmatism and not revisionism is the main danger, or that dogmatism is no less dangerous than revisionism, etc. What sort of principle underlies all this?

Firm Marxist-Leninists and genuine Marxist-Leninist Parties must put principles first. They must not barter away principles, approving one thing today and another tomorrow, advocating one thing today and another tomorrow.

Together with all Marxist-Leninists, the Chinese Communists will continue to wage an uncompromising struggle against modern revisionism in order to defend the purity of Marxism-Leninism and the principled stand of the Declaration and the Statement.

While combating revisionism, which is the main danger in the international Communist movement, Communists must also combat dogmatism.

As stated in the 1957 Declaration, proletarian parties "should firmly adhere to the principle of combining . . . universal Marxist-Leninist truth with the specific practice of revolution and construction in their countries."

That is to say:

On the one hand, it is necessary at all times to adhere to the universal truth of Marxism-Leninism. Failure to do so will lead to right opportunist or revisionist errors.

On the other hand, it is always necessary to proceed from reality, maintain close contact with the masses, constantly sum up the experience of mass struggles, and independently work out and apply policies and tactics suited to the conditions of one's own country. Errors of dogmatism will be committed if one fails to do so, if one mechanically copies the policies and tactics of another Communist Party, submits blindly to the will of others, or accepts without analysis the program and resolutions of another Communist Party as one's own line.

Some people are now violating this basic principle, which was long ago affirmed in the Declaration. On the pretext of "creatively developing Marxism-Leninism," they cast aside the universal truth of Marxism-Leninism. Moreover, they describe as "universal

Marxist-Leninist truths" their own prescriptions which are based on nothing but subjective conjecture and are divorced from reality and from the masses, and they force others to accept these prescriptions unconditionally.

That is why many grave phenomena have come to pass in the international Communist movement.

24. A most important lesson from the experience of the international Communist movement is that the development and victory of a revolution depend on the existence of a revolutionary proletarian party.

There must be a revolutionary party.

There must be a revolutionary party built according to the revolutionary theory and revolutionary style of Marxism-Leninism.

There must be a revolutionary party able to integrate the universal truth of Marxism-Leninism with the concrete practice of the revolution in its own country.

There must be a revolutionary party able to link the leadership closely with the broad masses of the people.

There must be a revolutionary party that perseveres in the truth, corrects its errors, and knows how to conduct criticism and self-criticism.

Only such a revolutionary party can lead the proletariat and the broad masses of the people in defeating imperialism and its lackeys, winning a thorough victory in the national democratic revolution, and winning the socialist revolution.

If a party is not a proletarian revolutionary party but a bourgeois reformist party;

If it is not a Marxist-Leninist party but a revisionist party;

If it is not a vanguard party of the proletariat but a party tailing after the bourgeoisie;

If it is not a party representing the interests of the proletariat and all the working people but a party representing the interests of the labor aristocracy;

If it is not an internationalist party but a nationalist party;

If it is not a party that can use its brains to think for itself and acquire an accurate knowledge of the trends of the different classes in its own country through serious investigation and study, and knows how to apply the universal truth of Marxism-Leninism and integrate it with the concrete practice of its own country, but instead is a party that parrots the words of others, copies foreign experience without analysis, runs hither and thither in response to the baton of certain persons abroad, and has become a hodge-podge of revisionism, dogmatism, and everything but Marxist-Leninist principle;

Then such a party is absolutely incapable of leading the proletariat and the masses in revolutionary struggle, absolutely incapable of winning the revolution, and absolutely incapable of fulfilling the great historical mission of the proletariat.

This is a question all Marxist-Leninists, all class-conscious workers, and all progressive people everywhere need to ponder deeply.

25. It is the duty of Marxist-Leninists to distinguish between truth and falsehood with respect to the differences that have arisen in the international Communist movement. In the common interest of the unity for struggle against the enemy, we have always advocated solving problems through inter-Party consultations and opposed bringing differences into the open before the enemy.

As the comrades of the C.P.S.U. know, the public polemics in the international Communist movement have been provoked by certain fraternal Party leaders and forced on us.

Since a public debate has been provoked, it ought to be conducted on the basis of equality among fraternal Parties and of Democracy, and by presenting the facts and reasoning things out.

Since certain Party leaders have publicly attacked other fraternal Parties and provoked a public debate, it is our opinion that they have no reason or right to forbid the fraternal Parties attacked to make public replies.

Since certain Party leaders have published innumerable articles attacking other fraternal Parties, why do they not publish in their own press the articles those Parties have written in reply?

Latterly, the Communist Party of China has been subjected to preposterous attacks. The attackers have raised a great hue and cry and, disregarding the facts, have fabricated many charges against us. We have published these articles and speeches attacking us in our own press.

We have also published in full in our press the Soviet leader's report at the meeting of the Supreme Soviet on December 12, 1962, the *Pravda* Editorial Board's article of January 7, 1963, the speech of the head of the C.P.S.U. delegation at the Sixth Congress of the Socialist Unity Party of Germany on January 16,

1963, and the *Pravda* Editorial Board's article of February 10, 1963.

We have also published the full text of the two letters from the Central Committee of the C.P.S.U. dated February 21 and March 30, 1963.

We have replied to some of the articles and speeches in which fraternal Parties have attacked us, but have not yet replied to others. For example, we have not directly replied to the many articles and speeches of the comrades of the C.P.S.U.

Between December 15, 1962, and March 8, 1963, we wrote seven articles in reply to our attackers. These articles are entitled:

"Workers of All Countries, Unite, Oppose Our Common Enemy!,"

"The Differences Between Comrade Togliatti and Us,"

"Leninism and Modern Revisionism,"

"Let Us Unite on the Basis of the Moscow Declaration and the Moscow Statement,"

"Whence the Differences?—A Reply to Thorez and Other Comrades,"

"More on the Differences Between Comrade Togliatti and Us—Some Important Problems of Leninism in the Contemporary World,"

"A Comment on the Statement of the Communist Party of the U.S.A."

Presumably, you are referring to these articles when toward the end of your letter of March 30 you accuse the Chinese press of making "groundless attacks" on the C.P.S.U. It is turning things upside down to describe articles replying to our attackers as "attacks."

Since you describe our articles as "groundless" and as so very bad, why do you not publish all seven of these "groundless attacks," in the same way as we have published your articles, and let all the Soviet comrades and Soviet people think for themselves and judge who is right and who wrong? You are of course entitled to make a point-by-point refutation of these articles you consider "groundless attacks."

Although you call our articles "groundless" and our arguments wrong, you do not tell the Soviet people what our arguments actually are. This practice can hardly be described as showing a serious attitude toward the discussion of problems by fraternal Parties, toward the truth, or toward the masses.

We hope that the public debate among fraternal Parties can be stopped. This is a problem that has to be dealt with in accordance with the principles of independence, of equality, and of reaching unanimity through consultation among fraternal Parties. In the international Communist movement, no one has the right to launch attacks whenever he wants, or to order the "ending of open polemics" whenever he wants to prevent the other side from replying.

It is known to the comrades of the C.P.S.U. that, in order to create a favorable atmosphere for convening the meeting of the fraternal Parties, we have decided temporarily to suspend, as from March 9, 1963, public replies to the public attacks directed by name against us by comrades of fraternal Parties. We reserve the right of public reply.

In our letter of March 9, we said that on the question of suspending public debate "it is necessary that our two Parties and the fraternal Parties concerned should have some discussion and reach an agreement that is fair and acceptable to all."

The foregoing are our views regarding the general line of the international Communist movement and some related questions of principle. We hope, as we indicated at the beginning of this letter, that the frank presentation of our views will be conducive to mutual understanding. Of course, comrades may agree or disagree with these views. But in our opinion, the questions we discuss here are the crucial questions calling for attention and solution by the international Communist movement. We hope that all these questions and also those raised in your letter will be fully discussed in the talks between our two Parties and at the meeting of representatives of all the fraternal Parties.

In addition, there are other questions of common concern, such as the criticism of Stalin and some important matters of principle regarding the international Communist movement which were raised at the 20th [1956] and 22nd [1961] Congresses of the C.P.S.U., and we hope that on these questions, too, there will be a frank exchange of opinion in the talks.

With regard to the talks between our two Parties, in our letter of March 9 we proposed that Comrade Khrushchev come to Peking; if this was not convenient, we proposed that another responsible comrade of the Central Committee of the C.P.S.U. lead a delegation to Peking or that we send a delegation to Moscow.

Since you have stated in your letter of March 30 that Comrade Khrushchev cannot come to China, and since you have not expressed a desire to send a delegation to China, the Central Committee of the Communist Party of China has decided to send a delegation to Moscow.

In your letter of March 30, you invited Comrade Mao Tse-tung to visit the Soviet Union. As early as February 23, Comrade Mao Tse-tung in his conversation with the Soviet Ambassador to China clearly stated the reason why he was not prepared to visit the Soviet Union at the present time. You were well aware of this.

When a responsible comrade of the Central Committee of the Communist Party of China received the Soviet Ambassador to China on May 9, he informed you that we would send a delegation to Moscow in the middle of June. Later, in compliance with the request of the Central Committee of the C.P.S.U., we agreed to postpone the talks between our two Parties to July 5.

We sincerely hope that the talks between the Chinese and Soviet Parties will yield positive results and contribute to the preparations for convening the meeting of all Communist and Workers' Parties.

It is now more than ever necessary for all Communists to unite on the basis of Marxism-Leninism and proletarian internationalism and of the Declaration and the Statement unanimously agreed upon by the fraternal Parties.

Together with Marxist-Leninist Parties and revolutionary people the world over, the Communist Party of China will continue its unremitting efforts to uphold the interests of the socialist camp and the international Communist movement, the cause of the emancipation of the oppressed peoples and nations, and the struggle against imperialism and for world peace.

We hope that events which grieve those near and dear to us and only gladden the enemy will not recur in the international Communist movement in the future.

The Chinese Communists firmly believe that the Marxist-Leninists, the proletariat, and the revolutionary people everywhere will unite more closely, overcome all difficulties and obstacles, and win still greater victories in the struggle against imperialism and for world peace and in the fight for the revolutionary cause of the people of the world and the cause of international communism.

Workers of all countries, unite! Workers and oppressed peoples and nations of the world, unite! Oppose our common enemy! With Communist greetings,

THE CENTRAL COMMITTEE OF
THE COMMUNIST PARTY OF CHINA

Chapter 9

The Economy

"**B**RIMMING OVER with happiness, the Chinese people have entered a new year, the year 1963, after striding through 1962, a year woven of struggles and victories." With this introduction, *People's Daily,* on January 1, 1963, summarized the mood of Chinese Communist planners and the tasks they had set for the Chinese nation in the coming year. The mood was one of relief. The agricultural situation apparently had stabilized after "three successive hard years." The mood was one of martyrdom. The Chinese had struggled in isolation against overwhelming odds and foreign criticism and had won. And, the mood was defiant. The Communists said: Now that we have survived this extraordinary crisis, we shall step by step build the mightiest nation in the world. In the words of *People's Daily:* "Our country has become more and more powerful. We are facing boundlessly bright prospects. Ours is a great cause without precedent: to build a new society and a new world."

The mood of emergency and blame that pervaded the Chinese press from 1959 to 1962 has not disappeared, but it was changed markedly at the September 1962 plenum of the Central Committee, meeting for the first time since January 1961. At this 1962 Tenth Plenum, the Party leaders set the tasks in order to begin once again the advance toward industrialization and economic development. Unlike that of the first three years of the "great leap forward," the emphasis now was focused on gradual, balanced development and on the production of raw materials (particularly coal) and agricultural goods (particularly cotton and timber as well as basic food staples) and on technical and communications work. The new general policy continued the ambivalent line of "developing the national economy with agriculture as the foundation and industry as the leading factor." The Communist leaders insisted on "the guiding leadership of the Party" and demanded that "the whole Party and the whole people put overall interests and the interests of the whole country in first place." Centralized planning superseded the extreme decentralization of the 1958 commune system. Treatment of the "whole nation as a chess game" would lay the basis for the inauguration of the Third Five-Year Plan—which should have been launched on January 1, 1963.

The current state of Chinese economic development is only partially known. Since 1959 Peking has banned the export of many publications and since 1960 the Chinese Communists have failed to release figures on the economy. We cannot even be certain that reliable figures on the economy were available to the Chinese themselves. Foreign guesses vary widely about the impact on industrialization of the 1959–1962 agricultural failures, although data on emergency policies (including the shift of urban workers back to the villages) and scattered reports on modified factory production targets suggest that the impact was serious and widely ramified. The convocation in secret of the 1962 session of the National People's Congress and the modification of political qualifications for rural and technical cadres would seem to have been further indications of the magnitude of the concern with economic problems.

The selections in this chapter have been drawn from the great variety and quantity of available material on economic questions and deal largely with economic problems since the launching of the Second Five-Year Plan in 1958 and the "great leap forward." Instead of presenting a flood of facts and figures that may not be reliable, the selections sample Party doctrine on economic policy, rural organization, and industrial management, balancing official pronouncements with statements of affected individual peasants or articles relating to daily factory life. Communist doctrine most frequently touches the Chinese citizen within the framework of his economic tasks, for whatever his occupation he labors in a work group under the direction of a Party cadre. The Party attempts to penetrate and control all phases of the economic life of the villages and cities, and on their success in the economic area Communist leaders have staked the future of revolutionary doctrine and the fate of the mass-line method of leadership. Under

Communist policies and programs the faces of villages and cities have changed dramatically, yet some of these changes have run counter to planned objectives and predictions. Information published in the Chinese press in 1962 indicates that the Party encountered substantial resistance from village peasants and had to accommodate some of its doctrines to village parochialism and that in the cities Party cadres in industrial plants had to bow to the non-Party trained technicians.

Economic Tasks in Transition

Chou En-lai • The Central Committee of the Party considers that in drawing up the Second Five-Year Plan for Development of the National Economy we should start from the anticipated achievements of the First Five-Year Plan [1953–1957], bear in mind the basic requirement that by about the end of the Third Five-Year Plan period we must fulfill the fundamental task of the state in the transition period [see above, pp. 212–213], and make a practical appraisal of the various conditions inside and outside the country during the Second Five-Year Plan period [1958–1962], so that the planning may be all-embracing. Only in this way can the plan be both forward-looking and sound.

The Central Committee of the Party suggests that the fundamental tasks of the Second Five-Year Plan for Development of the National Economy should be: (1) to continue industrial construction with heavy industry as its core and promote technical reconstruction of the national economy, and build a solid foundation for socialist industrialization; (2) to carry through socialist transformation, and consolidate and expand the system of collective ownership and the system of ownership by the whole people; (3) to increase further the production of industry, agriculture, and handicrafts and correspondingly develop transport and commerce on the basis of developing capital construction and carrying through socialist transformation; (4) to make vigorous efforts to train personnel for construction work and strengthen scientific research to meet the needs of the development of social-

From Chou En-lai, "Report on the Proposals for the Second Five-Year Plan for Development of the National Economy" [September 16, 1956], Eighth National Congress of the Communist Party of China, Vol. I (Peking: Foreign Languages Press, 1956).

ist economy and culture; and (5) to reinforce the national defenses and raise the level of the people's material and cultural life on the basis of increased industrial and agricultural production.

The main purpose of the socialist industrialization of our country is to build up, in the main, a comprehensive industrial system approximately within a period of three Five-Year Plans. Such an industrial system will be able to produce the principal machinery, equipment, and materials to meet, in the main, the needs of our expanded reproduction and of the technical reconstruction of our national economy. It will also be able to produce various types of consumer goods to satisfy suitably the needs born of the ever-rising living standards of the people.

Liu Shao-ch'i • The current mighty leap forward in socialist construction is the product not only of the successful development of the antirightist struggle and the rectification campaign but also of a correct implementation of the Party's general line—to build socialism by exerting our utmost efforts, and pressing ahead consistently to achieve greater, faster, better, and more economical results.

Comrade Mao Tse-tung has often said that there are two methods of carrying on socialist transformation and construction: One will result in doing the work faster and better; the other slowly and not so well. Which method shall we adopt? This has been an issue. In his work *On the Question of Agricultural Co-operation* published in 1955, Comrade Mao Tse-tung provided a theoretical solution to the struggle between these two methods regarding the socialist revolution in the ownership of the means of production. Furthermore, this struggle was decided in practice by the upsurge in socialist transformation which took place between the autumn of 1955 and the spring of 1956. There was also a conflict between the two methods in connection with the socialist revolution on the political and ideological fronts, and this too was worked out theoretically by Comrade Mao Tse-tung in his article *On the Correct Handling of Contradictions Among the People* published last year [1957], and was resolved in practice by the rectification campaign and antirightist struggle which began last year. In connection with socialist construction

From Liu Shao-ch'i, "Report on the Work of the Central Committee" [May 5, 1958], Second Session of the Eighth National Congress of the Communist Party of China *(Peking: Foreign Languages Press, 1958).*

too, the Central Committee of the Party and Comrade Mao Tse-tung have always taken a clear-cut stand, insisting that the method of working faster and better be adopted and the other method, of working slowly and not so well, be rejected. However, on this question some comrades still clung to such outmoded ideas as "keeping to the right is better than keeping to the left," "it's better to go slower than faster," or "it's better to take small steps than to go striding forward." The struggle between the two methods in dealing with this question was not fully decided until the launching of the rectification campaign and the antirightist struggle.

Ninth Plenum Communiqué • The ninth plenary session of the Eighth Central Committee . . . heard and discussed a report on the fulfillment of the 1960 national economic plan and the main targets for the 1961 national economic plan by Comrade Li Fu-ch'un, member of the Political Bureau of the Central Committee, Vice Premier of the State Council, and Chairman of the State Planning Commission. The plenary session pointed out that during 1960 the people of the whole country continued to hold aloft the three red banners of the Party's general line, the big leap forward, and the people's communes and won victory in the continued leap forward of the national economy on the basis of the great leap forward of 1958 and 1959. China's level of industrial production has been greatly raised as a result of the big leap forward in three consecutive years. In steel output, China's place in the world has risen from ninth in 1957 to sixth, and in coal output from fifth to second. The material and technical base of industry has been enormously strengthened. The stock of machine tools is more than double that of 1957; and the number of engineers and technicians has also more than doubled. In the past three years, the gross value of industrial output increased at an average annual rate of over 40 per cent, or more than double the average annual rate of increase during the First Five-Year Plan. In agriculture, the production plan was not fulfilled in 1960 because the country suffered the most severe natural calamities in a century following upon the serious natural calamities of 1959. In the past three years, however, the organization of the people's communes has steadily improved and become more firmly

From Communiqué of the Ninth Plenary Session of the Eighth Central Committee [meeting in Peking, January 14–18, 1961], January 20, 1961.

consolidated. Rural water conservancy work has made tremendous progress with an increase of more than 300 million *mou* [one *mou* equals about one sixth of an acre] in the effectively irrigated area in three years. . . .

The ninth plenary session of the Eighth Central Committee held that, in view of the serious natural calamities that affected agricultural production for two successive years, the whole nation in 1961 must concentrate on strengthening the agricultural front. It must thoroughly carry out the policies of taking agriculture as the foundation of the national economy and the whole Party and the entire people going in for agriculture and grain production in a big way. All trades and professions must step up support for agriculture, and we must exert our utmost effort to win a better harvest in agricultural production.

National People's Congress Communiqué • Premier Chou En-lai . . . dealt with the situation at home and the present tasks. In an analysis of the current domestic situation, he pointed out, first of all, that under the leadership of the Chinese Communist Party and Chairman Mao Tse-tung and on the basis of the successful completion of the First Five-Year Plan, the people of various nationalities of the country had embarked in 1958 on the Second Five-Year Plan for Development of the National Economy. In the past few years, the general line of going all out, aiming high and achieving greater, faster, better, and more economical results in building socialism had demonstrated its great might and had been developed still further. People's communes, which were of great historic significance, had been set up in China's vast rural areas and had gradually embarked on the road of sound development. A big leap forward had taken place in the economic and cultural construction of the country, which had brought tremendous achievements and laid the preliminary foundation for the building of a system of an independent, complete, and modern national economy. At the same time, China had suffered from serious natural calamities for three consecutive years from 1959 to 1961, and considerable difficulties had occurred in the national economy. The people of various nationalities throughout the country had made tremendous efforts and achieved out-

From Communiqué of the Third Session of the Second National People's Congress of China [meeting in Peking, March 27–April 16, 1962, in secret session], April 16, 1962.

standing results in overcoming the natural calamities and economic difficulties. Many new questions which had emerged during the great socialist development had been tackled step by step. At present, the economic situation of the country has already begun to take a turn for the better.

In his report, Premier Chou En-lai described in detail the successes and shortcomings in the past few years in socialist construction and summed up the experience in work. He stressed: The present tasks were to continue to hold aloft the three red banners of the general line, the big leap forward, and the people's communes, unite the people of various nationalities of the country still more, conscientiously and effectively do the work of adjusting the national economy, consolidate the successes already won, do more in overcoming the present difficulties, and strive for new victories.

Referring to the work of adjusting the national economy and the present tasks, Premier Chou En-lai stated that the policy of adjusting, consolidating, filling out, and raising standards must continue to be carried out in the national economy, centered on adjustment. He put forward the ten tasks for the adjustment of the national economy in 1962:

(1) To strive to increase agricultural production, first of all the production of grain-, cotton-, and oil-bearing crops; (2) to make a rational arrangement for the production of light and heavy industry and increase the output of daily necessities as much as possible; (3) to continue to cut back capital construction and to use material, equipment, and manpower where they are most urgently needed; (4) to reduce the urban population and the number of workers and functionaries to an appropriate extent by persuading, first of all, those workers and functionaries who had come from the rural areas to return to rural productive work and strengthen the agricultural front; (5) to make stock inventories and to examine and fix the amount of funds for each enterprise so that the unused material and funds could be used where they are most needed during the present adjustment; (6) to insure that the purchase and supply of commodities are well done and that market supply conditions are improved; (7) to work energetically to fulfill foreign trade tasks; (8) to adjust cultural, educational, scientific research, and public health undertakings and improve the quality of their work; (9) to carry out, firmly and thoroughly, the policy of building the country with diligence and

thrift to reduce expenditures and increase revenues; and (10) to continue to improve the work of planning to insure an all-round balance between the branches of the national economy in the order of agriculture, light industry, and heavy industry.

To Communes and Back

Central Committee Resolution • 1. The people's communes are the logical result of the march of events. Large, comprehensive people's communes have made their appearance, and in several places they are already widespread. They have developed very rapidly in some areas. It is highly probable that there will soon be an upsurge in setting up people's communes throughout the country and the development is irresistible. The basis for the development of the people's communes is mainly the all-round, continuous leap forward in China's agricultural production and the ever-rising political consciousness of the 500 million peasants. An unprecedented advance has been made in agricultural capital construction since the advocates of the capitalist road were fundamentally defeated economically, politically, and ideologically. This has created a new basis for practically eliminating flood and drought, and for insuring the comparatively stable advance of agricultural production. Agriculture has leaped forward since right conservatism has been overcome and the old technical norms in agriculture have been broken down. The output of agricultural products has doubled or increased severalfold, in some cases more than ten times or scores of times. This has further stimulated emancipation of thought among the people. Large-scale agricultural capital construction and the application of more advanced agricultural technique are making their demands on labor power. The growth of rural industry also demands the transfer of some manpower from agriculture. The demand for mechanization and electrification has become increasingly urgent in China's rural areas. Capital construction in agriculture and the struggle for bumper harvests involve large-scale cooperation which cuts across the boundaries between cooperatives, townships, and counties. The people have taken to organizing themselves along mili-

---

Full text of Resolution of the Central Committee of the Chinese Communist Party on the Establishment of People's Communes in the Rural Areas, August 29, 1958.

tary lines, working with militancy, and leading a collective life, and this has raised the political consciousness of the 500 million peasants still further. Community dining rooms, kindergartens, nurseries, sewing groups, barber shops, public baths, happy homes for the aged, agricultural middle schools, "red and expert" schools, are leading the peasants toward a happier collective life and further fostering ideas of collectivism among the peasant masses. What all these things illustrate is that the agricultural cooperative [the form of collective organization that preceded the commune] with scores of families or several hundred families can no longer meet the needs of the changing situation. In the present circumstances, the establishment of people's communes with all-round management of agriculture, forestry, animal husbandry, side-occupations, and fishery, where industry (the worker), agriculture (the peasant), exchange (the trader), culture and education (the student), and military affairs (the militiaman) merge into one, is the fundamental policy to guide the peasants to accelerate socialist construction, complete the building of socialism ahead of time, and carry out the gradual transition to communism.

2. Concerning the organization and size of communes. Generally speaking, it is at present better to establish one commune to a township with the commune comprising about 2,000 peasant households. [The official figures state that China has 24,000 rural communes with an average of 5,000 households in each.] Where a township embraces a vast area and is sparsely populated, more than one commune may be established, each with less than 2,000 households. In some places, several townships may merge and form a single commune comprising about 6,000 or 7,000 households, according to topographical conditions and the needs for the development of production. As to the establishment of communes of more than 10,000 or even more than 20,000 households, we need not oppose them, but for the present we should not take the initiative to encourage them.

As the people's communes grow there may be a tendency to form federations with the county as a unit. Plans should be drawn up right now on a county basis to insure the rational distribution of people's communes.

The size of the communes and the all-round development of agriculture, forestry, animal husbandry, subsidiary production, and fishery as well as of industry (the worker), agriculture (the peasant), exchange (the trader), culture and education (the student), and military affairs (the militiaman), demand an appropriate division of labor within the administrative organs of the communes; a number of departments, each responsible for a particular kind of work, should be set up, following the principle of compactness and efficiency in organization and of cadres taking direct part in production. The township governments and the communes should become one, with the township committee of the Party becoming the Party committee of the commune and the township people's council becoming the administrative committee of the commune.

3. Concerning the methods and steps to be adopted to merge small cooperatives into bigger ones and transform them into people's communes. The merger of small cooperatives into bigger ones and their transformation into people's communes is now a common mass demand. The poor and lower-middle peasants firmly support it; most upper-middle peasants also favor it. We must rely on the poor and the lower-middle peasants and fully encourage the masses to air their views and argue it out, unite the majority of the upper-middle peasants who favor it, overcome vacillation among the remainder, and expose and foil rumor-mongering and sabotage by landlord and rich-peasant elements, so that the mass of the peasants merge the smaller cooperatives into bigger ones and transform them into communes through ideological emancipation and on a voluntary basis, without any compulsion. As to the steps to be taken, it is of course better to complete the merger into bigger co-ops and their transformation into communes at once; but where this is not feasible, it can be done in two stages, with no compulsory or rash steps. In all counties, experiments should first be made in some selected areas and the experience gained should then be popularized gradually.

The merger of smaller cooperatives into bigger ones and their transformation into communes must be carried out in close coordination with current production to insure that it not only has no adverse effect on current production, but becomes a tremendous force stimulating an even greater leap forward in production. Therefore, in the early period of the merger, the method of "changing the upper structure while keeping the lower structure unchanged" may be adopted. The original, smaller cooperatives may at first jointly elect an administrative committee for the merged co-ops to unify planning and the arrangement of work, and transform themselves into farming zones or production brigades. The original organization of production and system of administration may, for the time being, remain unchanged and continue as before; and then later, step by step, merge, readjust, and settle whatever needs merging or readjusting and whatever specific questions demand solution during the merger, so as to make sure there is no adverse effect on production.

The size of the communes, the speed of carrying out the merger of small cooperatives into bigger ones and their transformation into communes, and the methods and steps to be taken in this connection will be decided in accordance with the local conditions by the various provinces, autonomous regions, and municipalities directly under the central authorities. But no matter when the merger takes place, whether before or after autumn, in the coming winter, or next spring, the small cooperatives which are prepared to merge should be brought together from now on to discuss and jointly work out unified plans for postautumn capital construction in agriculture and to make unified arrangements of all kinds for preparatory work for an even bigger harvest next year.

4. Concerning some questions of the economic policy involved in the merger of cooperatives. In the course of the merger, education should be strengthened to prevent the growth of departmentalism among a few cooperatives, which might otherwise share out too much or all of their income and leave little or no common funds before the merger. On the other hand, it must be understood that with various agricultural cooperatives established on different foundations, the amount of their public property, their indebtedness inside and outside the cooperatives, and so on will not be completely equal when they merge into bigger cooperatives. In the course of the merger, the cadres and the masses should be educated in the spirit of communism so as to recognize these differences and not resort to minute squaring of accounts, insisting on equal shares, and bothering with trifles.

When a people's commune is established, it is not necessary to deal with the questions of reserved private plots of land, scattered fruit trees, share funds, and so on in a great hurry; nor is it necessary to adopt clear-cut stipulations on these questions. Generally speaking, reserved private plots of land may perhaps be turned over to collective management in the course of the merger of cooperatives; scattered fruit trees, for the time being, may remain privately owned and be dealt with some time later. Share funds and so on can be handled after a year or two, since the funds will automatically become publicly owned with the development of production, the increase of income, and the advance in the people's consciousness.

5. Concerning the name, ownership, and system of distribution of the communes. All the big merged cooperatives will be called people's communes. There is no need to change them into state-owned farms, for it is not proper for farms to embrace industry, agriculture, exchange, culture and education, and military affairs at the same time.

After the establishment of people's communes, there is no need immediately to transform collective ownership into ownership by the people as a whole [*i.e.*, state ownership]. It is better at present to maintain collective ownership to avoid unnecessary complications arising in the course of the transformation of ownership. In fact, collective ownership in people's communes already contains some elements of ownership by the people as a whole. These elements will grow constantly in the course of the continuous development of people's communes and will gradually replace collective ownership. The transition from collective ownership to ownership by the people as a whole is a process, the completion of which may take less time—three or four years—in some places, and longer—five or six years or even longer—elsewhere. Even with the completion of this transition, people's communes, like state-owned industry, are still socialist in character, where the principle of "from each according to his ability and to each according to his work" prevails. After a number of years, as the social product increases greatly, the Communist consciousness and morality of the entire people are raised to a much higher degree, and universal education is instituted and developed, the differences between workers and peasants, town and country, and mental and manual labor—legacies of the old society that have inevitably been carried over into the socialist period—and the remnants of unequal bourgeois rights which are the reflection of these differences will gradually vanish, and the function of the state will be limited to protecting the country from external aggression, but it will play no role internally. At that time Chinese society will enter the era of communism where the principle of "from each according to his ability and to each according to his needs" will be practiced.

After the establishment of people's communes it is not necessary to hurry the change from the original system of distribution, in order to avoid any unfavorable effect on production. The system of distribution should be determined according to specific conditions. Where conditions permit, the shift to a wage system may be made. But where conditions are not yet ripe, the original system of payment according to workdays may be temporarily retained (such as the system of fixed targets for output, workdays, and costs, with a part of the extra output as reward; or the system of calculating workdays on the basis of output). This can be changed when conditions permit.

Although ownership in the people's communes is still collective ownership and the system of distribution, either the wage system or payment according to workdays, is "to each according to his work" and not "to each according to his needs," the people's communes are the best form of organization for the attainment of socialism and gradual transition to communism. They will develop into the basic social units in Communist society.

6. At the present stage our task is to build socialism. The primary purpose of establishing people's communes is to accelerate the speed of socialist construction and the purpose of building socialism is to prepare actively for the transition to communism. It seems that the attainment of communism in China is no longer a remote future event. We should actively use the form of the people's communes to explore the practical road of transition to communism.

Central Committee Resolution · The organizational principle of the people's commune is democratic centralism. This principle must be thoroughly applied in the management of production, in the distribution of income, in the work concerning the life and welfare of commune members, and in all other aspects of work.

Unified leadership as well as management at different levels should be put into effect in the people's commune. The administrative set-up of the commune may in general be divided into three levels, namely: the commune administrative committee, the administrative district (or production brigade), and the production team. The administrative district (or production brigade) is in general the unit which manages industry, agricul-

From Resolution of the Central Committee of the Chinese Communist Party on Some Questions Concerning the People's Communes, December 10, 1958.

ture, trade, education, and military affairs in a given area and forms a business accounting unit, with its gains and losses pooled in the commune as a whole. The production team is the basic unit of labor organization. Under the unified leadership of the commune administrative committee, necessary powers should be given to the administrative district (or production brigade) and the production team over such matters as the organization of production work and capital construction, finances and welfare, in order to bring their initiative into full play. . . .

In running a people's commune well the fundamental question is to strengthen the leading role of the Party. It is only by strengthening the Party's leading role that the principle of "politics in command" can be realized, that socialist and Communist ideological education among the cadres and commune members and the struggle against all kinds of erroneous tendencies can be conducted in a thoroughgoing way, and that the Party's line and policy can be implemented correctly. There are some people who think that with the emergence of the commune the Party can be dispensed with, and that they can practice what they call "merging the Party and the commune in one." This kind of thinking is wrong.

In its work in the people's commune, the Party, besides its task of insuring that the correct line and policy are put into effect, should also pay attention to educating the commune staffs to develop good styles of work—first of all the mass line and a practical style of work.

People's Daily • The first reason that the rural people's communes adopt a system of ownership at three levels with the production brigades as the foundation at the present stage is that the adoption of the production brigades—which correspond in the main to the higher-level agricultural producers' cooperatives [the predominant collective form from 1956–1958] of former days—as the fundamental accounting units enable the people's commune to overcome certain limitations inherent in the higher-level cooperatives and to develop fully the positive aspects of some good systems and methods of proved effectiveness of the higher-level cooperatives of former days. On the one hand, it enables the principal means of production such as draft animals,

From Jen-min jih-pao [People's Daily], *December 3, 1960.*

farm implements, and tools for subsidiary production—and which are of relative importance to the commune as a whole—to remain basically under the production brigade . . . and to be put at the permanent disposal of the production team. This makes it possible to develop the operation of these means of production. On the other hand, large-scale agricultural machines which are beyond the means of individual production brigades are placed under the control of the commune for the joint use of the brigades within the confines of the commune. This also benefits the advancement of the rate of labor productivity of the whole commune.

The enforcement of the system of ownership at three levels with the production brigades as the foundation provides the communes, the production brigades, and the production teams with the responsibilities and power befitting the needs of the current level of production and is extremely beneficial to the development of production. At the present stage, the production brigades of the people's communes are the basic accounting units. In the case of the agricultural produce and side-products of the production brigades, with the exception of a small part which is handed to the commune for accumulation purposes and for the payment of taxes to the state, they are distributed centrally within the confines of the production brigades. The arrangements for crops, the output targets, and technical measures are jointly discussed by commune members and jointly mapped out by the production brigades and production teams.

The output, work, and production costs of the production brigade are underwritten by the production teams which constitute the production organizations at the basic level. On the assumption that the fulfillment of the task of underwriting production is insured, the production teams may take up small-scale subsidiary production which is inconvenient for the production brigade to take up, and make full use of the marginal and corner land by the side of fields and other land which lies idle. The whole of the output underwritten by the teams is surrendered to the production brigade for central distribution. The part in excess of the production task underwritten and the income from business not falling within the production task underwritten, with the exception of that part which must be surrendered to the production brigade, go to the production teams themselves. The teams may make use of a fixed quantity of manpower, land, draft animals, and farm implements. They have the right to plant according to the conditions of the land. They have the right to formulate technical measures and to arrange all kinds of farm work.

The production plan of a commune is founded on the production plans of the production brigades and the production-underwriting plans of the production teams. The commune has also the right to make suggestions to the production brigades and to balance and adjust the plans put forward by the production brigades whenever necessary to adjust to the provisions of the state plans.

Southern Daily * •

Comrade Editor:

I am a production brigade cadre in a people's commune. I have been a basic-level cadre for seven or eight years. To be honest, I now feel that it is very difficult to be a production brigade cadre. I am perplexed.

My perplexity began with the proposition that all the powers of production teams should be respected. I remember hearing a commune cadre say that production teams had seven powers, such as the power of suiting the crop to the field and the time of the year, the power of planning farm jobs, and the power of deciding on measures for increasing production. I began to feel perplexed then. Since production teams are not only [basic] units of production, but also the [basic] units of distribution, their power is greater than it has been. It appears that we should not interfere with their operations, for if we do people will say, "Don't encroach on the production teams' power of making decisions on their own. If you do, you will be responsible for their failure to deliver the required quantities of products [to the production brigade]." In this way, people have imposed one restriction after another on us. For instance, when late-crop rice

---

* This published letter and the reply that appeared in the same newspaper provide some insight into the 1961 policy change that made the production team the basic level of ownership, production, distribution, and accounting instead of the production brigade. The production team corresponds to a small village, averaging 20 to 30 households, and hence to a lower-level agricultural producers' cooperative, which had been the major form of collective organization from 1952 to 1954.

From Nan-fang jih-pao [Southern Daily], *April 8, 1962 and June 20, 1962.*

seedlings were transplanted last year, the administrative committee of our production brigade appointed me to inspect the quality of such transplantings in the production teams. I found that late-crop seedlings were transplanted at too great distances from one another in one production team. At first, I thought that this was due to the fault of a few commune members who were sacrificing quality to quantity and speed. But, when I saw that one of the members of the administrative committee of the production team was doing the same, I became angry. Thereupon, I criticized him severely. However, instead of accepting my view, he said, "What do you want, that I complete my task in respect to requisition and purchase or that I transplant seedlings in accordance with your instructions? If you want grain, then don't interfere with my way of transplanting seedlings so long as I can complete my task with respect to requisition and purchase. If you want me to transplant seedlings in accordance with your instructions, then you will have to insure that we can top our output target, and you will be responsible for our lack of food and our failure to complete our task." What could I say in reply? So I turned around and walked away. Eventually, because of this technical retrogression, production in this production team suffered. However, if the same should happen again, I still shall not be able to do anything about it. In short, nowadays what jobs are there for us production brigade cadres to do apart from transmitting instructions from the higher levels to production team cadres and urging production teams to deliver and sell required quantities of farm products and agricultural by-products? No wonder some production brigade cadres say that nowadays production brigade cadres are mere propagandists and collectors and that production brigades are mere "transportation stations."

In our production brigade, I am not the only one who says that nowadays it is difficult to be a production brigade cadre. The other cadres here say the same. "When there is no rice in your hands, even the chickens will not come to you." This common saying is quite true. Now that production brigades have been deprived even of their authority over production and over distribution, on what basis are we to carry out our work? What should we do if a production team does not listen to us? I am not sure of the answers to these questions. As a result, I am not working as actively as I used to. When the higher levels send people over to inspect work, I will refer them to the lower levels and say that production plans are drawn up by production teams which are free to do what they like, and we may not and cannot interfere.

In the production teams in our production brigade, the strength of the cadres is weak, and many of the cadres are new ones. They are as a rule inexperienced in administering the affairs of production teams. . . . We production brigade cadres are aware of this. Although I want to help them, when I think of the things mentioned above I feel discouraged.

Comrade editor, I have been a cadre for many years, and I am also a Communist Party member. So, I should not be disheartened by all these things. But, I really do not know what I should do. I hope that you will help me solve my troubles.   WANG KUAN-HSIANG
                                      P'anyü *hsien*

Here let us begin with Comrade Wang's agony. . . . When the power of distribution and the power of production were all put in the hands of the production team and the production team was taken as the basic accounting unit [in 1961], he felt that there was nothing on which he could lay his hand and practically nothing for him to do. This is the background to the view formed by Wang regarding the problem of duties and responsibilities of brigade cadres. We believe that all brigade cadres should conduct concrete analysis of this background so that they can correctly comprehend their own duties and avoid unnecessary agonies.

In the first place, it should be confirmed that since the production team was taken as the basic accounting unit, the important thing was that the means of production belonged to the production team which also has the right to plan production and distribution. The management authority of the production team in other fields also increased. In these circumstances, the duties of the production brigades have necessarily been changed. Also the scope of work on the part of brigade cadres will also have to be reduced. Experience proves that giving a free hand to the production team to exercise its own powers—for instance, letting it arrange its own farm work, to decide what kind of land on which particular types of crops should be grown, to manage its own financial affairs, and to distribute its own products in its own way after selling the required quantities to the state—will be favorable to the operation of the commune democratically and along industrious and economical lines, while in production it will help to facilitate the taking of actual local conditions into account. The result of all this will favor the development of production and an increase in income. This being the case, if the brigade cadres arbitrarily demand that the production brigade directly arrange the production work for its production teams even to the extent of assigning the teams work on a daily basis, or that the production brigade manage the financial affairs of the production teams, or even that the production teams must deliver their products to the production brigade for distribution, they would violate the Party's policy. The production teams would then have the power to refuse such "leadership" in accordance with the policy set. It can thus be seen that after the production team was taken as the basic accounting unit, the brigade cadres should have seen the changes that have taken place in brigade duties and in the scope of their work, so that their thinking might be consistent with the new objective conditions and that they might be able to respect the right of ownership and other powers of the production teams without interfering with them. Otherwise, the important policy of taking the production team as the basic accounting unit would not be truly enforced, and everything would become empty. The enthusiasm of the production team cadres and commune members would thus be repressed, and the teams would not be consolidated. As a consequence, the work of the production brigade would be worse and not better. This our brigade cadres must clearly understand.

However, when we said that the duties of production brigades have changed and the scope of their work has also been reduced, we did not mean that the brigade cadres were left with nothing to do. With the production team taken as the basic accounting unit, the brigade cadres still have a series of tasks to perform. In the light of the requirements of the state for farm products and the concrete conditions of the production teams, they should help the teams draw up good production plans. In the brigade as a whole, they should see to it that the state's tasks of requisitioning and quota purchasing are fulfilled. They should give correct guidance to the production teams in productive work, in distribution work, and in financial management work, in addition to examining, supervising, and helping them improve their business management. They should direct the construction of rural capital-construction projects and water conservancy works to be undertaken within the framework of the whole production brigade or to be undertaken jointly by several production teams. They should operate those enterprises which really need to be operated by the production brigade and take care of the large-sized farm machinery and transportation vehicles owned by the production brigade. They should sponsor collective welfare institutions for the whole brigade, and together with the production teams hold themselves responsible for working out favorable arrangements for the livelihood of those households which have run into financial difficulties. They should lead the work of civil administration, militia and social security, cultural, educational, and health work in the entire brigade, besides conducting ideological and political work. What is especially important is that the Party organization of the brigade looks after the Party members in such a good way as to give full scope to their initiative and enthusiasm and to strengthen Party leadership within the framework of the brigade. Thus it can be seen that the brigade absolutely does not become a so-called "transmission station" but exercises unified leadership in all areas under its control.

Proletarian Workers and Industrial Management

Li Hsüeh-feng • With regard to the strengthening of the Party leadership in the state industrial enterprises, the Central Committee of the Party has decided to put into effect the system whereby the director (or the manager) takes the responsibility of the enterprise under the leadership of the Party committee—that is, a system of leadership which combines the collective leadership of the Party with individual responsibility. This system has been confirmed only after summarizing the Party's experiences and lessons in the various aspects of the work in the past few years. In the period of our economic restoration [1949–1952], the work of getting the enterprises back into normal operation and effecting the democratic reform in the state industrial enterprises

From "Speech by Comrade Li Hsüeh-feng," Eighth National Congress of the Communist Party of China, *Vol. II (Peking: Foreign Languages Press, 1956).*

was generally carried out under the unified leadership of the local Party committee. The system adopted in enterprises at the time was mainly that of the collective leadership of the Party combined with individual responsibility. But in carrying out this system there was a tendency on the part of the Party committee to take over all the work of the management, and this caused some confusion. Nevertheless, viewed as a whole, it gave full play to the Party's leading role in the enterprises and insured the successful fulfillment of the various tasks at the time. Beginning with the implementation of the First Five-Year Plan in 1953, the various localities and industrial departments introduced in the enterprises a system of unified leadership under a single head [an adaptation by the Chinese of the Soviet system of industrial management], for the better ordering of production and the improvement of management. Insofar as it redressed the lack of well-defined responsibility for production and established a system of responsibility, the adoption of this measure proved effective up to a point. However, it was wrongly emphasized that the man responsible for the management of the enterprise had full authority, that the duties of the Party organization were only to guarantee production and give general supervision, and that the director or manager need not carry out the resolutions of the Party organization regarding the management of production if he disagreed with them. In effect, this wrong emphasis placed the leadership of the management of the enterprise in opposition to that of the Party and rejected the leadership given by the Party organization to the management of production, thereby reducing the Party organization to a subordinate position. As a result, in those enterprises which adopted this "single-head" system the understanding of the Party members and the masses about the leading role of the Party was obscured in varying degrees, and the Party spirit of the cadres, especially of certain cadres responsible for management, was corroded. Bureaucracy and commandism became rife, bourgeois ideas of management throve accordingly, arrogant and self-complacent feelings and arbitrary behavior were common. And, among the leading personnel themselves, between the cadres and the masses, and between the various enterprises, instances of bickering, misunderstanding, and disunity increased. In such conditions, the work of these enterprises naturally suffered. However, even in the period when this so-called "single-head" system was in operation, the leading personnel of many enterprises maintained the fine tradition which our Party had fostered in the long revolutionary struggle and adhered to the Party's principle of combining collective leadership with individual responsibility in their work. As a result, they did somewhat better in the management of their enterprises and gained some valuable experience as to how the Party should exercise its leadership. The way of management which has been proved by experience to be effective is that all the major questions of the enterprises, including management, should be discussed exhaustively by the Party committee, and decisions should be reached by pooling the experience and wisdom of the collective. Then, the comrades in charge of management should, in accordance with the principle of personal responsibility, be entrusted with the task of making arrangements to carry out the decisions. These comrades also have the sole responsibility of dealing with routine administrative and technical work. The Party organization should not interfere with them, but should support them in every possible way. Urgent questions that press for an immediate decision should also be dealt with by the leading comrades of the enterprises, with the support of the Party committees. In those enterprises where the Party organization exercises its leadership correctly, the experience and wisdom of the individual and that of the collective are combined to insure that the leaders of these enterprises, in making important decisions, will commit few if any mistakes; and even when mistakes have been made, they are comparatively easy to rectify. At the same time, thanks to its political work among the masses, the Party's decisions are translated into action by the masses of their own accord. Consequently, the orders issued by the administrative chiefs are carried out quite smoothly, and they enjoy a comparatively high prestige among the masses. Thus, centralized command is achieved, and management is efficient.

Bright Daily • In the management of our state-operated industrial enterprises, two great systems are practiced—the system of responsibility of factory managers under the leadership of the Party and the system of conferences of workers' representatives under the leadership of the Party. The workers' representatives

From an article by the Office of the General Trade Union of the Sinkiang Uighur Autonomous Region in Kuang-ming jih-pao [Bright Daily], *February 27, 1962.*

conference is called at least four times a year. It aims to meet the enterprise's demand for stronger democratic management. How can we properly call such a general meeting and steer it away from formalism and toward the solution of practical problems so as to insure the desired results? This is a problem which calls for immediate attention and solution. Here are some of our views for our readers' reference.

Choose the Right Representative

Choosing the right representative is a prerequisite for a successful conference of workers' representatives. A representative of workers undertakes to brief the leadership on the opinions of the worker masses and to convey the leadership's intentions to the latter. He also exercises various rights of the workers at the conference of workers' representatives on their behalf. The basis of the conference should therefore be broadened so as to become representative. Representatives must be chosen from among both old workers and new workers, male and female. Representatives should also include people of different nationalities and workers' wives and dependents. Workers constitute the majority, and their representatives should be proportionately more numerous. Generally, they should make up more than 50 per cent of the total number of representatives. Only in this way can we make the opinions from all sides heard in an overall and thorough manner.

Propaganda combined with education conducted along various lines provides the key to the proper choice of representatives. It enables the worker masses to see the importance of choosing the right representatives and choosing the representatives who have won their support and trust.

Make Every Conference a Success

The main object of a workers' representatives conference is to pool the opinions of the masses and mold them into resolutions for implementation among the masses. Such a conference counts on the workers' representatives to make it successful. We must organize the representatives to solicit widely the views of the worker masses by such methods as making observations, holding forums, calling on individuals, and so on. We strongly object to the practice of subjectively confining the canvassing of opinion to a certain segment of the people. What all the people say should be reported factually. We must take note of the positive as well as the negative opinions and listen to the views of both the minority and the majority. We should make analyses in a down-to-earth spirit. The opinions of the minority may not always be wrong. . . .

Execution of Resolutions

Giving effect to the resolutions of a workers' representatives conference is the last but most important step toward the fulfillment of the conference's tasks. . . . Such processes as election of representatives, making preparations for a successful conference, and implementation of resolutions should be regarded as an integrated whole. A conference cannot indulge in discussion without reaching a decision and much less can it leave a resolution without providing for effective action.

Constitution of the Trade Unions • The trade unions of China are the voluntary, broad, mass organizations of the working class. Regardless of nationalist, sex, or religious belief, all workers by hand or by brain, who depend entirely or mainly upon their wages for the means of life, may join the trade unions.

The modern working-class movement of China has all along developed under the leadership of the Communist Party. The trade unions of China are the mass organizations of the working class led by the Chinese Communist Party and are the transmission lines between the Party and the masses. Under the people's democratic dictatorship, the trade unions are a school of administration, a school of management, and a school of communism for the workers.

In building socialism in a country like China which has an enormous population and backward economy, the fundamental question is to increase industrial and agricultural production and steadily raise social labor productivity. To achieve that aim, the trade unions must, under the leadership of the Communist Party, educate the workers better in the spirit of Communist principles and carry out the policy of building the country, operating enterprises, and running all undertakings with diligence and thrift. The trade unions should organize socialist emulation and bring the energy and creative ability of all the workers into full play, so that they will voluntarily observe work discipline and insure fulfillment of the national construction plan and endeavor to overfulfill it. On the basis of developing

From the General Program of the Constitution of the Trade Unions of the People's Republic of China, December 12, 1957.

social production, the trade unions should gradually improve the material and cultural well-being of the workers.

The trade unions are the strongest social support of our people's democratic dictatorship. The trade unions should participate actively in the drawing up of state policies, laws, and decrees concerning production, labor, and the material and cultural life of the workers; organize mass supervision over implementation of these policies, laws, and decrees; and fight against all acts which violate state laws and decrees and social and work discipline, or damage the interests of the state and the people. At the same time, the trade unions should educate the workers to set a good example in observing the laws and the Constitution of the People's Republic of China and giving firm support to all state policies and decrees.

Under the leadership of the working class, the interests of the state are identical with the common interests of the entire people and also with the fundamental interests of our working class. The trade unions should educate the workers to recognize the unity of interests between the state and the individual and, when these two conflict, realize that individual interests should be subordinated to state interests. At the same time, the trade unions, proceeding from the overall interests of the state, should support the just demands of the masses and protect their proper material interests and democratic rights. The trade unions should combat bureaucratic practices which contravene the vital interests of the workers.

Daily Worker • In order to lead the trade unions to implement the guiding principles and policies of the Party, the Party committee itself must first do a good job in studying and comprehending the basic spirit of the policies (including directives having a bearing on trade-union work) and heighten the Party cadres' knowledge of policies. This will enable Party organizations to point out a better direction for and to examine trade-union work.

In the beginning, however, not all Party cadres were able to comprehend clearly the importance of this problem. Some comrades made an insufficient effort to learn and study the directives of the Party and the problems involving important principles related to trade-union work, because they thought that this was

---

From an article by the Chinese Communist Party Committee of the "May 3" Factory in Kung-jen jih-pao [Daily Worker], *September 19, 1961.*

the business of the trade-union cadres. The Party committee pointed out that the implementation of the directives and decisions of the Party relating to trade-union work was not only the task of the trade unions but also of the Party organizations. Because of this, all important directives of the Party relating to trade-union work were transmitted to the Party committee. Study was organized to increase understanding and attain unity of thought. After these directives were studied by the Party committee in session, a meeting was then convened for the Party members and leadership cadres of the whole factory. In this meeting, the Party committee secretary transmitted the report, arranged work, and set out specific demands for the Party branches. In this way, an ideological foundation was established for the implementation of the guiding principles and policies of the Party on trade-union work.

Shih K'e-chien • All technical personnel who are willing to work for socialism should be treated on the basis of equality in our country. They should be given work according to their qualifications. At their jobs they should be given authority and responsibility. Industrial enterprises owned by the whole people [*i.e.,* state owned] are engaged in mass production on the basis of modern technology, and therefore it is required that production be organized and directed scientifically and elaborately. This is the reason that in enterprises and in other technical departments leading posts of a technical nature should generally be filled by technical personnel, and technical problems must be decided on mainly by the technicians.* For instance, in an enterprise the chief engineer is a technical authority. Under the leadership of the factory director (manager) or the vice factory director (assistant manager) in charge of production, he assumes overall responsibility for the technical operations of the enterprise. Specialized organs placed in technical control at various levels must be subordinated to the command of the chief engineer in technical matters. Experience proves that only thus will it be possible to run socialist enterprises well and promote the development of production.

* This reverses the 1957–1961 "red and expert" line under which Party cadres filled technical posts and made key technical decisions. See above, Chapter 2, pages 75–77.

From Hung-ch'i [Red Flag], *No. 8–9, April 25, 1962.*

So that the strength of technical personnel is brought into full play, administrative leadership personnel in various units should develop democracy, be good at canvassing the opinions of technicians, and carry out comradely discussion with them whenever problems arise. As far as technical problems are concerned, nobody is permitted to adopt an arbitrary attitude. Divergent technical opinions should not be regarded as political opinions. Different opinions on scientific and technical problems should be freely and earnestly discussed in accordance with the policy of "letting all flowers blossom and all schools of thought contend." In this way, different sorts of opinions may be fully expressed and the best solution found after discussions. Meanwhile, technical personnel should, in the spirit of being responsible to the state and the people, dare to adhere to the truth and persist in their opinions if they are correct.

All departments concerned should create favorable conditions in various respects under which technical personnel can engage in their professional research. For instance, they should reasonably arrange for the time of their work and study so that they can devote a greater part of time to and concentrate their main energy on technical work. In the light of various possibilities, they should provide the technicians with the necessary data, reference books, and equipment and give them facilities for participating in academic activities. If necessary, assistants should be assigned to certain senior technicians so as to release them from auxiliary technical work and enable them to concentrate on the technical work, and so on. As for technical personnel in general, they should be given the opportunity for advanced study. And, with respect to technical personnel promoted from among the workers, special attention should be given to their training and to helping them master technical theories and raise their technical standards without interruption.

Chapter 10

Intellectuals, the Arts, and Education

THE CHINESE COMMUNIST PARTY requires the services and the prestige of intellectuals to carry forward its programs, yet all the while it suspects the intelligentsia of harboring latent anti-Communist tendencies. This ambivalence has been reflected in a carrot-and-stick approach that until 1957 obtained calculated responses from a great majority of the intellectuals. But since the disastrous betrayal of these so-called "bourgeois elements" in 1957 —when Communist leaders encouraged intellectuals to criticize the Party and government and then turned on their critics as "rightists" and counterrevolutionaries—no thinking Chinese is likely to accept a Communist-dangled carrot at face value again.

Behind the dramatic events of 1957 lay a tortuous policy toward the intellectuals in China. In the years just after 1949, and particularly during the first part of the Korean War, the Communist Party launched a major campaign to reeducate teachers and scientists and discredit Western-trained scholars. In 1951, emphasis shifted from a general campaign to self-reform and in 1955, to intensive rectification with attacks on Hu Feng, the Party's erstwhile tsar of art and literature, and on a scholarly study of *Dream of the Red Chamber*, the eighteenth-century novel of tragic love and declining fortunes in a Chinese family. Social novels without a clear class moral received blistering criticism as did any hint that the Party should not command art and literature, while "reactionary Hu Feng elements" were exposed among intellectuals in schools, factories, and cooperatives.

The intensity of the attacks slackened in early 1956, when

Party leaders met to discuss the role of intellectuals in the new tasks of socialist construction and shortly thereafter adopted the line of "letting a hundred flowers blossom, a hundred schools of thought contend." Prescribed for a broad group of technical and cultural intellectuals—who are defined simply as middle-school graduates ("intellectuals") and those who have received college or advanced professional training ("higher intellectuals") —this line explicitly encouraged "free-ranging" discussion and inquiry in order to prove the superiority of Marxism-Leninism and to remold and mobilize the intelligentsia. Cautiously and gradually the intellectuals responded to the Party's invitation to discuss and criticize openly. Instead of embracing Marxism, however, many used the opportunity to translate and discuss Western works and blithely debated "reactionary" doctrines at the very moment Hungarian intellectuals were triggering the wave of anti-Communist sentiment in Budapest. What followed is subject to dispute. Either the Communist leaders had set out deliberately to trap the intellectuals by encouraging criticism of the Party and government and now sprang the trap, or they used the metaphor of the trap to rationalize their violent reaction to the unanticipated criticism. Whatever the explanation, the Communist leaders turned on their critics as "rightists" and "counter-revolutionaries," and in June 1957 non-Communists who had thrown caution to the winds reaped the full fury of the "hundred-flowers" retaliation.

In addition to a general consideration of the policies toward the intellectuals since 1956, the selections in this chapter pinpoint Party doctrine on the arts and education. Both the arts and education relate to the intelligentsia and are conceived as propaganda and training instruments of the Party. Their missions are functionally specific but interrelated. With more than 300 million Chinese engaged in formal study in 1960, education—as is the case with the arts—applies to the entire population, not just to children. The difference between education and the arts in Chinese Communist theory is that the former directly molds the mind and personality, while the latter reshapes the individual's intellectual products. By a Machiavellian combination of policies on the arts and education, the Party manipulates the mind by controlling its inputs and outputs.

Maoist principles of art combine Soviet-style "socialist realism" with the more delicate and sophisticated forms of traditional Chinese painting and writing. Although the emphasis has shifted from form to content, Chinese art, unlike Soviet art, seeks to preserve an element of imagination, myth, and fancy. This element, however, must further socialist aims and, thus conceived, has been labeled "revolutionary romanticism." Mao is credited with the synthesis of "revolutionary realism" and "revolutionary romanticism" or with integrating "realistic reproduction of the class struggle" and "revolutionary enthusiasm, vigor, and hope." Nevertheless, the synthesis has remained as meaningless as the term "revolutionary romanticism." Contrary to support for creativity and vigor, press campaigns have glorified the writing of canned articles and stories and have sponsored general movements to rid the "socialist flower beds" of "poisonous weeds." Most writing and other art forms, now dutifully reproducing Mao's own style and tastes, lack originality, and many publishing houses and operatic companies have begun to reissue newly revised classics as a supplement to the dreary parade of heroic tales of the revolutionary struggle and socialist construction. The once-active pens of important Chinese novelists and essayists are now largely laid aside or put to trivial tasks dictated by the Party.

Education in China mirrors some of the precut patterns evident in the arts, but recent programs stressing scientific and technical achievement outside oppressive Party domination have permitted the application of rigorous professional standards in the training of the youth. Nonetheless, by early 1963, the Chinese schools had not yet recovered from the dramatic intrusion of political study and the excessive demands for physical work so evident in the post-1958 policy of making all students "red and expert," though the Party since 1960 has sought to enhance the quality of training at all levels from kindergarten through university. The attempt has been made to preserve some of the features of the "red-and-expert" education, notably speed and quantity of output, while raising the level of classroom instruction. The selections on education summarize the major proposals made in 1960 for a general ten-year curriculum based on languages, mathematics, and technical-scientific subjects, under which all youth would attain first-year college competency. When the proposals are realized, a small number of the most gifted students will be allowed to undertake advanced professional and university study, but most will have to accept state-assigned careers with prospects for additional training on the job.

The Party expects a long period of transition to occur before the ten-year "universal" system replaces the present twelve-year course of study. In the interim, the Chinese utilize part-time and limited-purpose schools and classes to impart specific techniques and have launched an ambitious program for the elimination of illiteracy. These *ad hoc* arrangements supplement the regular school system. The table below summarizes the growth in full-time school enrollments between 1949 and 1959 and suggests the general scope of the full-time educational enterprise in

GROWTH OF STUDENT ENROLLMENT FOR SELECTED YEARS, 1949–1959

School Enrollment (in thousands)

	Higher	Middle	Primary	Kindergarten	Totals
1949	117	1,268	24,391	—	25,776+
1952	191	3,126	51,100	424	54,841
1958	660	9,990	86,400	29,501	126,451
1959	810	12,900	90,000	67,700	171,410

the overall Chinese society. As of 1959, about one Chinese in four reportedly attended school on a full-time basis. The final selection in this chapter on the spectacular "learn from Lei Feng" campaign, which began to dominate the educational processes in early 1963, indicates that "full-time" education in China is much more than simply reading, writing, and arithmetic.

Intellectual Flowering in Marxist Soil

Chou En-lai • Our basic reason for building up a socialist economy is to provide the greatest possible satisfaction for the constantly increasing material and cultural demands of society as a whole. To reach this goal, we must never cease to develop the

From *Chou En-lai*, Report on the Question of Intellectuals [*January 14, 1956*] (*Peking: Foreign Languages Press, 1956*).

productive forces of society, raise the productivity of labor, and expand and improve socialist production on the basis of advanced technique. Hence the age of socialism, more than any previous age, requires a comprehensive raising of productive technique, as well as a comprehensive development of science and utilization of scientific knowledge. It follows from this that if we want to go ahead with our socialist construction on the largest possible scale, quickly, effectively, and economically, we must rely on the energetic labor not only of the working class and the broad masses of the peasants, but also of the intellectuals. In other words, we must rely on close cooperation between manual work and brain work, on the fraternal alliance of workers, peasants, and intellectuals. The different construction projects on which we are now engaged require the participation of intellectuals in ever-growing numbers. . . . Thus intellectuals have become an important factor in every aspect of our national life. To find a correct solution for the question of intellectuals, to mobilize them more effectively and make fuller use of their abilities in our gigantic work of building socialism, has therefore become essential if we are to fulfill the fundamental tasks of the transition period. Every department of our Party and Party organizations at all levels should pay serious attention to this question.

What is the question of intellectuals at present? The fundamental question at present is that the forces of our intelligentsia are insufficient in number, professional skill, and political consciousness to meet the requirements of our ever-expanding socialist construction. Certain irrational features in our present employment and treatment of intellectuals and, in particular, certain sectarian attitudes on the part of some of our comrades toward intellectuals outside the Party have to some extent handicapped us in bringing the existing strength of the intelligentsia into full play. It is imperative that we give firmer leadership, overcome our shortcomings, and take a series of effective measures to mobilize the intellectuals to the fullest possible extent and bring into full play their strength by ceaselessly raising their political consciousness, training new recruits on a large scale to add to their ranks, and raising their professional skill as far as possible to meet the ever-growing demands made on them by the state. This is now the fundamental task for our Party on the question of intellectuals.

Mao Tse-tung • Since the social system of our country has changed and the economic basis of bourgeois ideology has in the main been destroyed, it is not only necessary but also possible for large numbers of our intellectuals to change their world outlook. But a thorough change in world outlook takes quite a long time, and we should go about it patiently and not be impetuous. Actually there are bound to be some who are all along reluctant, ideologically, to accept Marxism-Leninism and communism. We should not be too exacting in what we expect of them; as long as they comply with the requirements of the state and engage in legitimate pursuits, we should give them opportunities for suitable work.

There has been a falling off recently in ideological and political work among students and intellectuals, and some unhealthy tendencies have appeared. Some people apparently think that there is no longer any need to concern themselves about politics, the future of their motherland, and the ideals of mankind. It seems as if Marxism that was once all the rage is not so much in fashion now. This being the case, we must improve our ideological and political work. Both students and intellectuals should study hard. In addition to specialized subjects, they should study Marxism-Leninism, current events, and political affairs in order to progress both ideologically and politically.* Not to have a correct political point of view is like having no soul. Ideological remolding in the past was necessary and has yielded positive results. But it was carried on in a somewhat rough-and-ready way and the feelings of some people were hurt—this was not good. We must avoid such shortcomings in future. All departments and organizations concerned should take up their responsibilities with regard to ideological and political work. . . .

"Let a hundred flowers blossom," and "let a hundred schools of thought contend," "long-term coexistence and mutual supervision"—how did these slogans come to be put forward [in 1956]?

They were put forward in the light of the specific conditions existing in China, on the basis of the recognition that various kinds of contradictions still exist in a socialist society, and in

---

* For a shift in emphasis, however, see pages 75–77.

From Mao Tse-tung, On the Correct Handling of Contradictions Among the People [*February 27, 1957*] (*Peking: Foreign Languages Press, 1957*).

response to the country's urgent need to speed up its economic and cultural development. . . .

On the surface, these two slogans—let a hundred flowers blossom and a hundred schools of thought contend—have no class character; the proletariat can turn them to account, so can the bourgeoisie and other people. But, different classes, strata, and social groups each have their own views on what are fragrant flowers and what are poisonous weeds. So what, from the point of view of the broad masses of the people, should be the criteria to-day for distinguishing between fragrant flowers and poisonous weeds?

In the political life of our country, how are our people to determine what is right and what is wrong in our words and actions? Basing ourselves on the principles of our Constitution, the will of the overwhelming majority of our people, and the political programs jointly proclaimed on various occasions by our political parties and groups, we believe that, broadly speaking, words and actions can be judged right if they:

1. Help to unite the people of our various nationalities, and do not divide them;

2. Are beneficial, not harmful, to socialist transformation and socialist construction;

3. Help to consolidate, not undermine or weaken, the people's democratic dictatorship;

4. Help to consolidate, not undermine or weaken, democratic centralism;

5. Tend to strengthen, not to cast off or weaken, the leadership of the Communist Party;

6. Are beneficial, not harmful, to international socialist solidarity and the solidarity of the peace-loving peoples of the world.

Of these six criteria, the most important are the socialist path and the leadership of the Party. These criteria are put forward in order to foster, and not hinder, the free discussion of various questions among the people. Those who do not approve of these criteria can still put forward their own views and argue their case. When the majority of the people have clear-cut criteria to go by, criticism and self-criticism can be conducted along proper lines, and these criteria can be applied to people's words and actions to determine whether they are fragrant flowers or poison-ous weeds. These are political criteria. Naturally, in judging the truthfulness of scientific theories or assessing the aesthetic value of works of art, other pertinent criteria are needed, but these six political criteria are also applicable to all activities in the arts and sciences. In a socialist country like ours, can there possibly be any useful scientific or artistic activity which runs counter to these political criteria?

Teng Hsiao-p'ing • The present struggle against the rightists is primarily being carried out among the bourgeoisie and intellectuals. Among them are industrialists and businessmen, members of the democratic parties, and those in educational, journalistic, publishing, literary and art, scientific and technological, and medical circles, as well as many employees in government offices and university students. Intellectuals do not constitute a class, but individually belong to different classes. However, in the present situation of our country most of the intellectuals come from bourgeois or petty-bourgeois families, and their education has been bourgeois in nature. So, for the sake of convenience, they are mentioned together with the bourgeoisie.

The elimination of the bourgeoisie as a class is a fundamental question for the socialist revolution. The bourgeoisie, and especially its intellectuals, now constitute the main force that can set itself out to oppose the proletariat. Politically they have the qualifications which still can be used to their advantage. They still have political status and influence, and the proletariat needs their knowledge. But unless they firmly undertake socialist remolding, conflict between them and the proletariat is inevitable. . . .

Apart from a small number of people who hold rightist views, bourgeois intellectuals in general have other seriously erroneous points of view, particularly of individualism, liberalism, anarchism, equalitarianism, and nationalism. In the stage of ideological education, criticism and self-criticism, we must concentrate our efforts on making a systematic criticism of such erroneous viewpoints. This is one of the most important tasks that has to be fulfilled during the current rectification campaign.

The ideological remolding of the intellectuals is a long-term task, likely to take another ten years or more to complete. In the current campaign, however, efforts should be made to give widespread socialist education to bourgeois intellectuals and mem-

From *Teng Hsiao-p'ing*, Report on the Rectification Campaign [*September 23, 1957*] (*Peking: Foreign Languages Press, 1957*).

bers of industrial and commercial circles in general; to demolish the strongholds of bourgeois ideology; to change fundamentally the political situation in many cultural and educational departments and the democratic parties; and to establish and consolidate, as soon as possible, firm Party leadership over the middle elements.

Social Purpose and Creative Art

Mao Tse-tung • The purpose of our meeting today is precisely to fit art and literature properly into the whole revolutionary machine as one of its component parts, to make them a powerful weapon for uniting and educating the people and for attacking and annihilating the enemy, and to help the people to fight the enemy with one heart and one mind. What are the problems to be solved in order to achieve this objective? I think they are the problems of the standpoint, the attitude, and the audience of the artists and writers and of how they should work and how they should study.

Standpoint: Our standpoint is that of the proletariat and the broad masses of the people. For members of the Communist Party this means that they must adopt the standpoint of the Party and adhere to Party spirit and Party policies. Are there any of our artists and writers who still lack a correct or clear understanding on this point? I think there are. Quite a number of our comrades have often departed from the correct standpoint.

Attitude: Our specific attitudes toward specific things arise from our standpoint. For example: Should we praise or should we expose? This is a question of attitude. Which of these two attitudes should we adopt? I should say both and it all depends on whom you are dealing with. There are three kinds of people: the enemy, the allies in the united front, and our own people, namely, the masses and their vanguard. Three different attitudes must be adopted toward these three kinds of people. . . .

Audience, *i.e.,* for whom are the artistic and literary works produced? . . . Since the audience for our art and literature is made up of workers, peasants, soldiers, and their cadres, the problem arises of how to understand these people and to know

From *Mao Tse-tung,* Talks at the Yenan Forum on Art and Literature [*May 23, 1942*] (*Peking: Foreign Languages Press, 1956*).

them well. . . . Having become a revolutionary I found myself in the same ranks as the workers, peasants, and soldiers of the revolutionary army, and gradually I became familiar with them and they with me too. It was then and only then that a fundamental change occurred in the bourgeois and petty-bourgeois feelings implanted in me by the bourgeois schools. I came to feel that it was those unremolded intellectuals who were unclean as compared with the workers and peasants, while the workers and peasants are after all the cleanest persons, cleaner than both the bourgeois and the petty-bourgeois intellectuals even though their hands are soiled and their feet smeared with cow dung. This is what is meant by having one's feelings transformed, changed from those of one class into those of another. If our artists and writers from the intelligentsia want their works to be welcomed by the masses, they must transform and remold their thoughts and feelings. Without such transformation and remolding they can do nothing well and will be ill adapted to any kind of work.

Lin Mo-han • Mao Tse-tung's thought on art and literature creatively develops Lenin's views in these fields. This finds concentrated expression in Comrade Mao Tse-tung's *Talks at the Yenan Forum on Art and Literature.* . . . Mao Tse-tung's thought on art and literature is so rich that each time we read his *Talks,* or other articles by him on these subjects, we obtain new enlightenment and education. Therefore I cannot hope to encompass all his views here. I believe the most important of all is his solution of the following basic problems.

First: Comrade Mao Tse-tung completely settles the question of the relation between art and literature and the revolution. . . . The relation between artistic and literary activities and Party activities in general is that revolutionary art and literature are a part of the overall revolutionary cause, they are cogs and screws in the whole machine; their task should be to serve the revolution. . . .

Second: Comrade Mao Tse-tung solves the problem of the relation between art and literature and the masses. In this connection also, Comrade Mao Tse-tung develops Lenin's thought. . . . The manner in which art and literature should serve the workers, peasants, and soldiers is mainly as follows: A writer

From Lin Mo-han, Raise Higher the Banner of Mao Tse-tung's Thought on Art and Literature (*Peking: Foreign Languages Press, 1961*).

should observe and depict things from the standpoint of the proletariat; he should strive to portray workers, peasants, and soldiers; he should seek to strengthen their unity of heart and mind, not to weaken it; he should try to bring the readers closer to, not farther away from, the workers, peasants, and soldiers. To serve successfully, the writer must correctly integrate popularization with elevation. . . .

Third: Comrade Mao Tse-tung settles the question of the relation between art and life; he settles it excellently in conformity with dialectical materialism. First of all, man's social life is the sole source of art and literature, and all artistic and literary works are reflections of life. . . . This same life of the people, reflected through the brains of reactionary artists and writers, cannot become revolutionary art and literature; it becomes counterrevolutionary. . . . Life is the source of art and literature; art and literature come from life. At the same time because they are on a much higher level than real life, they can influence it and urge it on. This is Comrade Mao Tse-tung's fundamental view on the relation between life and art and literature.

Fourth: Comrade Mao Tse-tung excellently solves the problem of the relation between the artist or writer and the masses. The key to art and literature serving the revolution and the workers, peasants, and soldiers and correctly reflecting the life of the people lies in artists and writers going into the midst of the masses, and in the course of so doing, remolding their own ideology while tapping the source of creative works. . . .

Fifth: Comrade Mao Tse-tung settles the question of the relation between art and literature and national cultural traditions. Proletarian art and literature have not dropped on us from the sky; they are of necessity built on the foundation of traditions. Developing Lenin's "two-national-cultures" thesis, Comrade Mao Tse-tung asks that we first subject our national cultural traditions to scientific analysis. In our cultural legacy are both democratic revolutionary qualities and feudal reactionary qualities. We should "throw away their feudal dross and absorb their democratic essence." Traditions should be analyzed from the standpoint of historical materialism and be given their proper place in history.

The Practice of Art

Ho Ch'i-fang • There are no ghosts such as are described in the old stories, but there are actually many things in this world which are like ghosts. Some are big, such as international imperialism and its henchmen in various countries, modern revisionism represented by the Tito clique of Yugoslavia, serious natural calamities, and certain not-yet-reformed members of the landlord and bourgeois classes who have usurped leadership in some organizations at the primary level and staged a comeback there. Some are small, such as difficulties and setbacks in ordinary work, etc. All these can be said to be ghostlike things. Imperialism, reaction, revisionism, and so on differ from ghosts in that they really exist while ghosts do not. But they have something in common with the ghosts in the tales: They are always up to deviltry, they always create disturbance and make trouble. Sometimes they are ferociously vicious, with hideous features; at other times they take on enchanting guises to bewitch people; they all know how to mask themselves, how to fascinate or terrify people, and their ability to transform and metamorphose themselves puts the ghosts in the old stories completely in the shade. But the most important thing is that, like the ghosts in the tales, they appear frightful but actually are not. Some people fear them and this, just as with fear of ghosts, is due to their backward thinking, to their failure to emancipate their minds and to do away with superstition, and to their cowardice stemming from the fact that their subjective understanding does not conform to objective reality. To make a clean sweep of such backward "ghost-fearing" ideas is a serious fighting task for every revolutionary. There are people of another kind who are "half-man-half-ghost." If they are not remolded into complete human beings, they are likely to turn into complete "ghosts." While they are still "half-man-half-ghost," their reactionary aspect will play the devil and stir up trouble like all the rest of the "ghost" species. It will do a lot of good for people to read the old stories about not being afraid of ghosts and for everyone to promote the spirit of not being afraid of ghosts. . . .

From Preface to Stories About Not Being Afraid of Ghosts, *compiled by the Chinese Academy of Sciences, Institute of Literature (Peking: Foreign Languages Press, 1961).*

The Institute of Literature of the Chinese Academy of Sciences started compiling this book in the spring of 1959, when, all over the world, imperialism, the reactionaries in various countries, and the revisionists organized a big anti-China chorus; by the summer of that year the compilation was basically completed. That was the time when revisionists inside the country rose in response to international revisionism and launched their frenzied attack against the leadership of the Party. We decided then to make a further careful selection from the first manuscript and enrich its content; it was also decided that I should write a preface. At the end of 1960, a great change took place in the international situation; 81 Communist and Workers' Parties held a meeting in Moscow of their representatives and issued a statement against imperialism, reaction, and revisionism. This "ghost-defying" statement has greatly augmented the power and influence of the revolutionary people all over the world, plunged the devils and goblins into dejection, and in the main broken up the big anti-China chorus. But readers should understand that there are still plenty of devils, ghosts, and goblins in the world, and it will take some time to wipe them out. Within the country, too, there are still great difficulties; the remnants of the devils in Chinese shape are still making trouble; and there are still many obstacles to overcome in the path of our great socialist construction. It seems very necessary, therefore, to publish this book. After the ninth plenary session of the Eighth Central Committee of the Communist Party of China adopted its resolution of January 1961 in support of the statement of the Moscow meeting and formulated the policies to be followed in the domestic political, economic, and ideological fields, and since more people have come to understand the strategy and tactics of revolutionary struggle under present conditions, publication of this book of *Stories About Not Being Afraid of Ghosts* may not come as such a big surprise to the public.

Mao Tse-tung •

Changsha

Alone I stand in the autumn cold
And watch the river northward flowing

From *Mao Tse-tung*, Nineteen Poems *(Peking: Foreign Languages Press, 1958)*.

Past the Orange Island shore,
And I see a myriad hills all tinged with red,
Tier upon tier of crimsoned woods.
On the broad stream, intensely blue,
A hundred jostling barges float;
Eagles strike at the lofty air,
Fish hover among the shallows;
A million creatures under this freezing sky are striving
    for freedom.
In this immensity, deeply pondering,
I ask the great earth and the boundless blue
Who are the masters of all nature?

I have been here in days past with a throng of companions;
During those crowded months and years of endeavor,
All of us students together and all of us young,
Our bearing was proud, our bodies strong,
Our ideals true to a scholar's spirit;
Just and upright, fearless and frank,
We pointed the finger at our land,
We praised and condemned through our writings,
And those in high positions we counted no more than dust.
But don't you remember
How, when we reached midstream, we struck the waters,
How the waves dashed against the speeding boats?

Swimming

I have just drunk the waters of Changsha,
And eaten the fish of Wuchang;
Now I am crossing the thousand-mile-long river,
Looking afar to the open sky of Chu.
I care not that the wind blows and the waves beat;
It is better than idly strolling in a courtyard.
Today I am free!
It was on a river that the Master said:
"Thus is the whole of Nature flowing!"

Masts move in the swell;
Tortoise and Snake are still.
Great plans are being made;

A bridge will fly to join the north and south,
A deep chasm become a thoroughfare;
Walls of stone will stand upstream to the west
To hold back Wushan's clouds and rain,
And the narrow gorges will rise to a level lake.
The mountain goddess, if she still is there,
Will be startled to find her world so changed.

Kuo Han-cheng • China's classical drama is a composite art combining singing and dancing, both highly developed. In the early theater, one or two simple tunes were used to depict straightforward episodes or unsophisticated stories. But by the thirteenth century a more developed form with four scenes had appeared, known as *tsa chu,* and from this many different schools of drama evolved, each with its own distinctive characteristics. There are nearly 400 different types of local drama in China and more than 50,000 operas. Since liberation much has been done to bring to light old scripts and to edit them. A just appreciation of this precious cultural heritage can contribute much to the growth and development of Chinese drama, but this does not mean simply taking over the old operas and restaging them without any changes. . . .

When we revise traditional operas, we must see to it that the spirit of the age is reflected. Operas produced in feudal society must on the whole reflect life in feudal times, the outlook and emotions of feudal people. The heroes of old could at most have fairly democratic ideas and patriotic feelings—they could not think like modern people. Although there is historical continuity between the life and thought of our forebears and ourselves, a fundamental difference remains. For instance, a number of the old operas adapted present a love story which ends with an elopement; yet this conclusion depends on the characters and the plot. We cannot say that eloping is impossible, nor that it is the only solution. In the Han dynasty, a young widow named Tso Wen-chun fell in love with a scholar whom she heard playing music and finally eloped with him. Evidently such a thing was possible in ancient times, although the motivation must have differed from age to age. So when we describe an elopement we must make sure that it corresponds to the specific historical conditions of the characters, otherwise the result will be a travesty of history. A popular Chinese folk tale is that about Wang Pao-chuan who waited in a wretched hut for her husband's return; for although the daughter of a minister, she had married poor Hsueh Ping-kuei against her father's wish. Her husband went to the war, but she waited for him for eighteen years and the story has a happy ending. Pao-chuan's resolution was admired by all. If we try to improve on this by revising the plot so that she sees her husband off with no sign of sadness, like a modern woman revolutionary who gladly sends her man to join the army, this simply would not be true to life in those days. So when adapting a traditional opera, we must reflect the spirit of its age, seeing life in the correct historical perspective. . . .

Admittedly, the limitations of a subject make a considerable difference to its adaptation. If we recognize its limitations we can dispose of the dregs and preserve the essence of the original as regards theme, character, and style; whereas if we fail to recognize it we jettison the original to start afresh, throwing out the baby with the bath water. It frequently happens that operas can be kept unchanged except for certain minor revisions, yet our new interpretation of the action and characters in it improves both its message and artistic quality. An example is the *Drunken Beauty* played by Mei Lan-fang. This opera had its vulgar, frivolous side, but Mei Lan-fang improved on it and greatly enriched it, bringing out the loneliness of a court lady in feudal society through this episode. In cases where good and bad are intermingled, more revision is necessary; while when the original suffers from many shortcomings and a weak central theme, yet is still worth reviving, radical changes are needed. The Fukien opera *Reunion* is a case in point. In the original, when a young bride discovers that her mother-in-law has a lover, the older woman kills herself for shame; but the bride will not tell the truth for fear of spoiling her mother-in-law's good name. In the end the court finds out the truth and the lover is put to death; the good daughter-in-law is praised while the mother-in-law and her lover are condemned in accordance with the feudal code of morality. This opera has been revised as follows: The mother-in-law falls in love with her cousin and becomes pregnant, but is then forced to marry another man. Afterward she gives birth to a son who grows up to pass the palace examination, so that honors are bestowed on his mother. When her secret is discovered by her

daughter-in-law, she commits suicide; but the new bride to preserve her husband's good name claims to have killed her. The
magistrate insists on getting to the bottom of this case, till finally
the whole family is forced to commit suicide. This tragedy pre-
serves the best of the original while adding something new, and
this new version has received a warm welcome.

Another important point to bear in mind in adapting old
operas is the attention that must be paid to acting. A play must
reach the audience by means of stagecraft and the actors' performance. And stagecraft in the classical theater has particular
importance owing to the composite character of traditional opera:
complex stage conventions, the dominant role of music, the strict
physical and technical requirements made of the actors. In some
old dramas in which the main emphasis is on acting, the scripts
were never written out in full but scope was given to the actors
to show initiative. When, therefore, we revise old plays like these,
we must study the stage performance as well as the script, regarding such operas as stage productions as well as literature. Often
we may find that brilliant acting, of which no indication is
found in the written script, brings out a character most vividly.
. . . This happens when an actor knows his audience well and
has mastered his art. And the more we understand about acting,
the better we shall understand the plays themselves and the
easier we shall find it to adapt them.

Concept and Practice in Chinese Education

Lu Ting-yi • Our country's present school system is inherited
from the days of Kuomintang rule. It was copied from the United
States and is a backward system. With primary and secondary
education taking up too long a time, it is difficult to popularize
education and raise its quality. If the term of study is too long
and level of the education too low, this is naturally disadvantageous to our work of national construction, to our students and
our progeny. We have carried out reforms in educational work
and scored considerable achievements, but we have not yet had
time to reform the primary and secondary school systems.

From Lu Ting-yi, "Our Educational Work Must Be Reformed" [April 9,
1960], Second Session of the Second National People's Congress of the People's
Republic of China (Documents) (Peking: Foreign Languages Press, 1960).

Bourgeois education is of course progressive compared with the education of the feudal landlord class. Otherwise our country would not have abolished the old "examination system" and established the "modern school system." But the aim of bourgeois education, compared with that of working-class education, is not only extremely trivial but also has its reactionary aspect. The aim of bourgeois education is to carry out so-called "compulsory education." But what is "compulsory education"? On the one hand, it compels the laboring people to get an education but only allows them a low level of education and not higher learning, only teaches them enough so that they will not get the capitalists' machines out of order but does not allow them equality of learning with the bourgeois intellectuals. On the other hand, "compulsory education" means that only the wealthy, who do not have to work for their living, have the opportunity for higher learning, so that a batch of bourgeois intellectuals can be turned out to serve the bourgeois class and rule over the laboring people. Our educational aim is diametrically opposed to the bourgeois one. We want to universalize and elevate education among the whole people, greatly raise the Communist consciousness and morality of the whole people, so as to eliminate the difference between mental and manual labor. This is, of course, far superior and greater than "compulsory education."

Different classes have different aims, and therefore their policy lines and methods are different too. We advocate education serving working-class politics, while the bourgeoisie stands for "education for education's sake," which actually means education serving bourgeois class politics. We advocate that education must be combined with productive labor, while the bourgeoisie maintains that education should be divorced from productive labor. We advocate that educational work must be led by the Party and follow the mass line, whereas the bourgeoisie holds that only experts can run education and they follow a line of relying on only experts. We advocate a rapid development of education by "walking on two legs," which is also different from the bourgeois stand of restricting the advance of education.

As regards teaching, there are also two different views. We advocate that teaching should be done in the spirit of achieving more, faster, better, and more economical results, while the bourgeois educationalists are contented with getting few, slow, poor, and expensive results. Greatly prolonging the terms of primary and secondary education and lowering the educational level benefits only the bourgeoisie and not the working class.

There is a principle of bourgeois pedagogy known as the "capacity principle." It has its correct side, in that it holds that students must not be overburdened, but should be taught in accordance with their specific talents. Our pedagogy should include this aspect. But this principle of bourgeois pedagogy has its wrong and reactionary side. It treats students not as conscious human beings with initiative but as abstract biological human beings or other animals, plants, or "bottles." It stands for the "prenatal theory," which holds that "God (or Nature) decides everything" and regards the children of the laboring people as inferiors. Bourgeois pedagogy also holds that "a teacher is the servant of nature, not its master." Thus, bourgeois pedagogy is full of idealist concepts and ideas hostile to the working people, [ideas] which we resolutely oppose. The "capacity principle" of bourgeois pedagogy is actually an apology for achieving few, slow, poor, and expensive results in education, and makes it hardly possible for the working people to obtain higher education. A few examples from our own history make this abundantly clear. When the Kuomintang prolonged the primary and secondary school terms from elevel to twelve years, the bourgeois pedagogues did not regard it as violating the "capacity principle." Since liberation, although primary and secondary school education has on the whole made great progress, still in some subjects the standards have been lowered. For example, in mathematics, analytical geometry was removed from the upper secondary school curriculum. Another example is the teaching of foreign languages, which has been weakened. But this did not meet with any opposition from the bourgeois pedagogues. No one said it was against the "capacity principle." Now, when we propose that education should be carried on with more, faster, better, and more economical results, the "capacity principle" is trotted out as a theoretical weapon to oppose educational reform. However, the signs of fewer, slower, poorer, and more expensive results in primary and secondary education are really so clear that there is no apologizing for them. We are entirely confident that the overwhelming bulk, *i.e.*, over 90 per cent, of society and educational circles, are in favor of educational reform, and only a tiny minority are against it. It is impossible to overawe us with bourgeois pedagogy.

Since 1958 our educationalists who advocate reforms in education have been carrying out experiments in reforming the school system, the primary and secondary school curricula, and teaching methods. Although the period of experimentation is still not a long one, it can be seen already that educational reform is practicable and no idle fancy. . . .

It takes a relatively long time to carry out experiments in the educational system. We should not prematurely draw an all-round conclusion. But it can be affirmed that if a good job is done of reforming teaching methods, textbooks are reedited, plus the strengthening of the leadership of the Communist Party committee in the schools, and the organization of an all-round collaboration among teachers so as to change the practice of each teacher sticking to his own business without mutual collaboration, then it is possible appropriately to shorten the schooling period, appropriately raise the educational level, appropriately control the study hours, and appropriately increase participation in physical labor. Organizing all-round collaboration among the teachers under the leadership of the Party committees is extremely important. The most important subjects in full-time primary and secondary schools are languages (including Chinese and foreign languages) and mathematics. These are the most fundamental tools for the pupils to master. If they have learned languages and mathematics well, it is easier for them to learn physics, chemistry, biology, history, and geography. Joint efforts are required on the part of all teachers for pupils to learn languages and mathematics well, and in their turn, teachers of languages and mathematics have the same responsibility to help the pupils learn their physics, chemistry, biology, history, and geography well. Collaboration under the leadership of the Communist Party committees will yield twofold results with half the effort, whereas the practice of each sticking to his own business without collaboration like a heap of loose sand, only gets half the results with double the effort. . . .

Our preliminary conception of a new educational system is a full-time primary and secondary education with the time reduced to about ten years and the standard raised to approximate the first year of the present universities. Why do we stand for "about ten years"? Because it takes about ten years for children who go to school at the age of six or seven to become sixteen or seventeen years old, when they become able-bodied persons as to labor power. It will be comparatively easy to introduce about ten years of universal education after capital construction on the farm land has been more or less completed and mechanization of agriculture realized, because it will draw very little on the able-bodied labor power. The introduction of an integrated education of about ten years and the raising of the students' standard to approximate the first year in the present universities [are] . . . also feasible. If this preliminary conception of ours can be materialized and an education of about ten years universally introduced, then all our youth who become able-bodied labor power at the age of sixteen or seventeen will in the future have already received about ten years of education and attained a level of knowledge approximating that of the present first-year university student. At present, the students in our full-time upper secondary schools are full labor power [which means sufficiently mature to accept an adult-level position], and therefore we cannot enroll an excessive number of them. At present only several hundred thousand graduate from upper secondary school each year. However hard we may try, we can only hope to increase the number to over one million annually. A further increase would draw too much on the full labor power. With the new educational system which we conceive tentatively materialized, however, we can have well over 10 million upper secondary school graduates a year while drawing very little on the full labor power. That is because well over 10 million people reach the age of sixteen or seventeen in our country each year. When we have so many upper secondary school graduates with high standards and young in age, it will be possible for us to carry out the following: in addition to the institutes of higher learning run by the central, provincial, municipal, and special region authorities, each of China's 1,700-odd counties will be running one or more full-time or half-day institutes of higher learning and all industrial and mining enterprises, government organizations, and people's communes will also be running spare-time higher education. In this way, it will be easy for us, by using the method of "walking on two legs," to enable all who are above the age of sixteen or seventeen to receive higher education. This will certainly be the bright and glorious future of education in our country. In this way, our requirements for technical and theoretical cadres will certainly be further met, technical innovations and technical revolution will further develop at an accelerated pace, and the difference between mental and manual labor will be greatly reduced.

This will be in the interest of the state as well as of the individual. The advantages are obvious and can be secured by making an effort. In the interest of the majority of people and of society as a whole, we must take this road.

Naturally, experimentation alone is not enough for the reform of educational work. The material and ideological conditions must be provided.

First, the level of the teachers must be raised. This requires a corresponding reform of teachers' education, and care must be taken to organize the present teachers for advanced studies. Second, the existing schools with two half-time shifts must gradually go over, step by step and group by group, to the full-time system, and then become boarding schools, which requires capital construction work. Third, kindergartens should be improved, and in this connection the nurseries should also be improved, which requires a great growth of schools training teachers and nurses for young children. Fourth, new teaching media, such as gramophone records, tape recordings, lantern slides, films, broadcasting, and television, must be used and the necessary modern facilities, such as laboratory equipment and models, should be adequately provided. Fifth, there should be ample supplies of paper. The above are the material conditions.

The ideological conditions are mainly a thorough critique of bourgeois pedagogy and the development of the Communist theory of education. We must oppose slavish adulation of bourgeois pedagogy and propagate the Communist spirit of breaking down superstitions and fetishes, emancipating the mind, thinking, speaking, and acting with courage and daring, and fully mobilizing the masses and doing everything only after experimentation. Our research institutes in pedagogy and psychology and our normal colleges must take up this work as their unshirkable responsibility. . . .

We are fully confident that through experimentation a new educational system, new teaching methods, and new textbooks will take shape in the course of practice and will gradually crystallize into a new system, creating new theories of pedagogy and psychology. For the present we are in no hurry to establish the new educational system throughout the country by laws and decrees. Later, when the new educational system is promulgated, we should still let people conduct further new experiments. Education and teaching, like other things, should go through uninterrupted revolution. It can be taken for granted that certain scientific knowledge which seems over our heads now may become just plain common sense several decades or a hundred years from now. Therefore, the content of education will certainly change. Just as the growth of the social productive forces and the development of science have no limits, so, too, the advance of educational thought has no limits. Therefore, in the future we must continue to conduct new experiments and carry out educational reforms to meet the needs of the growth of the social productive forces and eliminate the difference between mental and manual labor.

People's Daily • Although Comrade Lei Feng * lived for only 22 years, he wrote in his diary: "The life of man is limited, but rendering service to the people is unlimited. I want to devote my limited life to the unlimited cause of 'rendering service to the people.'" Comrade Lei Feng made good his pledge throughout his lifetime. Although he died a martyr in an unfortunate occurrence while performing his duties [Lei was crushed by a truck in 1962], his life becomes immortal in the unlimited undertaking of rendering service to the people. . . . Comrade Lei Feng will live forever in our minds.

The life of Comrade Lei Feng was a militant one. He never forgot the class hatred in the old society where people perished and families fell apart. He constantly remained alert, "never forgetting the pain when the scars are healed." His eyes were

---

* Lei Feng was the squad leader of an engineering unit of the People's Liberation Army until his death in August 1962. Born in 1940, Lei suffered from maltreatment at the hands of the Japanese and the "landlord" in his native village in Liaoning Province. Filled with hatred, Lei watched gleefully when the landlord was executed by the Communists and thereupon vowed to serve the Party as his life's goal. He faithfully studied the works of Party leaders and sought to model his life according to the dictates of Mao and along the patterns set by Communist martyrs. In his own writings, he dutifully recorded his boyish dreams to become an active tool of the Chinese Communist Party, and in his daily life he reportedly practiced his personal desire to "become a 'rust-free screw' in the great revolutionary cause." When Lei died, Party leaders directed the youth of China to study his writings and to learn from his life those lessons that would make them "rust-free screws" in the revolutionary movement.

From Jen-min jih-pao [People's Daily], *February 7, 1963.*

constantly fixed on the whole world in which he noted that "two thirds of the poor people of the world have not yet been emancipated." This proletarian revolutionary spirit of "taking up the responsibility of the world as one's own" pervaded the life of Comrade Lei Feng. He lived his life with strong class feelings and a burning fighting will. He consciously responded to every appeal made by the Party. In the high tide of agricultural co-operativization [in 1956], he left the classroom of a middle school and headed for the agricultural production front. During the period of the Second Five-Year Plan [1958–1962], he went to Anshan Iron and Steel Works from his home on the Hsiang River. In the struggle for the defense of the motherland, he became an excellent people's warrior. At any work post, he would apply himself industriously to work. In T'uanshanhu Farm, he was a fine tractor driver and an activist in socialist construction. By his operation of an earth-mover at Anshan Iron and Steel Works, he was thrice rated an advanced producer of the plant, a standard bearer 18 times, and a red-banner hand five times. He also attended the Representative Congress of Young Activists of Socialist Construction held at Anshan municipality. As he had established meritorious records in the armed forces on numerous occasions, he was rated a "five-good" warrior and a standard bearer of frugality and was conferred the title of "Model Youth League Member." Accordingly, he was elected a people's deputy for Fushun municipality. Not only would he wholeheartedly do a good job of any work which was not within his duty, but he would also try in every possible way to do a little more that was of benefit to the people and to his comrades around him. In the sphere of social work, he was a Young Pioneer instructor of a primary school in the neighborhood of the area in which his unit was stationed. Even on board a train, he was restless, his heart burning with eagerness to render service to the people. Wearing the arm band of a "train representative," he helped women to carry their babies or found seats for old people. Comrade Lei Feng was exactly this kind of person: "Doing everything for others' benefit and nothing for his own." These words are taken from Comrade Mao Tse-tung's article, "In Memory of Norman Bethune" [Mao, *Selected Works*, III, 104], in praise of the spirit of a revolutionary. This article was read and reread by Comrade Lei Feng when he was alive to spur himself to devote all his efforts and dedicate his whole life, like Comrade Bethune had done, to the emancipation of mankind and to the cause of building communism. As Comrade Lei Feng's words were consistent with his deeds, he eventually became a great revolutionary warrior.

Youths living in the era of Mao Tse-tung are indeed fortunate. Like Comrade Lei Feng, tens of thousands of young workers, peasants, warriors, and students have understood their own youth and their own happiness through the proletarian world outlook. Comrade Lei Feng wrote in his diary: "I feel that the purpose of keeping myself alive is to make other people live better." This is the heroic attitude of a great proletarian warrior. What is youth? How should one make the best use of one's youth? He wrote: "Youth is forever beautiful, but real youth belongs only to those people who forever strive to forge ahead and to those who toil and are forever humble." What is happiness? He wrote: "My happiest moment is when I can make the broad masses of people cherish warmer love for the Party, for Chairman Mao, and for the Liberation Army. . . . Toiling a little more myself and helping others to do some good deeds are my greatest joy and happiness." Some egoists might think it too foolish of him. He also wrote: "If it is said that this is foolish, I would rather be a fool, for the revolution needs such a fool and the building of the motherland also needs such a fool. I have only one purpose and one mind; that is, my heart goes to the Party, to socialism, and to communism." What a strong will and how noble his character was!

That the Communist spirit gleamed with such brilliance in the person of Comrade Lei Feng stemmed from a deep-rooted cause. As Comrade Lei Feng had suffered deeply in his childhood from class oppression and class exploitation, he later quickly accepted the Party's education. Another important factor was that Comrade Lei Feng was able to remold and transform himself continuously and consciously. As an avid and earnest reader of the works of Comrade Mao Tse-tung, he studied these writings for the purpose of remolding his own thought and guiding his own action. He said: "As far as I am concerned, the works of Chairman Mao are like food and weapons and the steering wheel of an automobile. Man must eat, and in fighting a war we must have weapons. Without the steering wheel, one cannot drive a car and without studying the works of Chairman Mao one cannot take up revolution as a career!" He left four volumes of Mao

Tse-tung's *Selected Works* with many passages underlined by him as well as his diaries which contain over 200,000 characters. These are the records of the way he applied the thought of Mao Tse-tung to his own practical action. It was in the course of studying the works of Comrade Mao Tse-tung and arming himself with Marxist-Leninist ideas that this unfortunate child of the old society grew up rapidly. He wrote: "The more I have studied penetratingly the works of Chairman Mao, the more I am enlightened, the more open-minded I become, the firmer will be my stand, and the more far-reaching ideals I will cherish!" From the growth of Comrade Lei Feng, we have noted that studying the works of Comrade Mao Tse-tung is of vital significance to the fostering of the younger generation into tough warriors of the proletarian revolution!

Bibliography

FOR CONVENIENCE, the bibliography is divided into three major sections: (1) sources used for the selections in this volume; (2) major compilations of translated materials; and (3) a selected bibliography of secondary works and serials.

1. Sources Used for the Selections in this Volume

a. Books, Essays, and Documents

All-China Federation of Trade Unions. Constitution of the Trade Unions of the People's Republic of China, December 12, 1957.

Ch'en Chang-feng. On the Long March with Chairman Mao. Peking: Foreign Languages Press, 1959.

Ch'en Po-ta. Mao Tse-tung on the Chinese Revolution. Peking: Foreign Languages Press, 1953.

Chinese Academy of Sciences, Institute of Literature, comp. Stories About Not Being Afraid of Ghosts. Peking: Foreign Languages Press, 1961.

Chinese Communist Party. Constitution of the Communist Party of China, September 26, 1956.

Chinese Communist Party, Central Committee. Communique of the Ninth Plenary Session of the Eighth Central Committee, January 20, 1961.

—— Communique of the Tenth Plenary Session of the Eighth Central Committee, September 28, 1962.

—— Directive Concerning the Campaign to Rectify Working Style, April 27, 1957.

—— Directive on Leading Personnel at All Levels Taking Part in Physical Labor, May 14, 1957.

—— A Proposal Concerning the General Line of the International Communist Movement. Peking: Foreign Languages Press, 1963.

—— Resolution on Some Questions Concerning the People's Communes, December 10, 1958.

—— Resolution on the Establishment of People's Communes in the Rural Areas, August 29, 1958.

Chinese People's Republic. Constitution of the People's Republic of China, September 20, 1954.

Chinese People's Republic, National People's Congress. Communique of the Third Session of the Second National People's Congress of China, April 16, 1962.

Chou En-lai. Report on the Question of Intellectuals. Peking: Foreign Languages Press, 1956.

Documents of the First Session of the First National People's Congress of the People's Republic of China. Peking: Foreign Languages Press, 1955.

Documents of the National Conference of the Communist Party of China, March 1955. Peking: Foreign Languages Press, 1955.

Eighth National Congress of the Communist Party of China. 3 vols. Peking: Foreign Languages Press, 1956.

Lin Mo-han. Raise Higher the Banner of Mao Tse-tung's Thought on Art and Literature. Peking: Foreign Languages Press, 1961.

Liu Shao-ch'i. Address at the Meeting in Celebration of the 40th Anniversary of the Founding of the Communist Party of China. Peking: Foreign Languages Press, 1961.

—— How to Be a Good Communist. Peking: Foreign Languages Press, 1951 [as revised in 1962].

—— Internationalism and Nationalism. Peking: Foreign Languages Press, 1951.

—— On Inner-Party Struggle. Peking: Foreign Languages Press, n.d.

—— On the Party. Peking: Foreign Languages Press, 1950.

Mao Tse-tung. Combat Liberalism. Peking: Foreign Languages Press, 1954.

—— Nineteen Poems. Peking: Foreign Languages Press, 1958.

—— On Contradiction. Peking: Foreign Languages Press, 1958.

—— On Methods of Leadership. Peking: Foreign Languages Press, 1955.

—— On New Democracy. Peking: Foreign Languages Press, 1954.

—— On People's Democratic Dictatorship. Peking: Foreign Languages Press, 1959.

—— On Practice. Peking: Foreign Languages Press, 1958.

—— On the Correct Handling of Contradictions Among the People. Peking: Foreign Languages Press, 1957.

—— Rectify the Party's Style in Work. Peking: Foreign Languages Press, 1955.

—— The Role of the Chinese Communist Party in the National War. Peking: Foreign Languages Press, 1956.

—— Selected Works. Peking: Foreign Languages Press, 1961. Vol. IV.

—— Talks at the Yenan Forum on Art and Literature. Peking: Foreign Languages Press, 1956.

Second Session of the Eighth National Congress of the Communist Party of China. Peking: Foreign Languages Press, 1958.

Second Session of the Second National People's Congress of the People's Republic of China (Documents). Peking: Foreign Languages Press, 1960.

Ten Glorious Years. Peking: Foreign Languages Press, 1960.

Teng Hsiao-p'ing. Report on the Rectification Campaign. Peking: Foreign Languages Press, 1957.

U.S. Department of State. United States Relations with China; With Special Reference to the Period 1944–1949. Washington: U.S. Government Printing Office, 1949.

b. Serials

Chinese Literature. Monthly. Peking.
Chung-kuo ch'ing-nien [China Youth]. Monthly. Peking.
Chung-kuo ch'ing-nien pao [China Youth News]. Daily. Peking.
Hung-ch'i [Red Flag]. Semimonthly. Peking.
Jen-min jih-pao [People's Daily]. Daily. Peking.
Jen-min shou-ts'e [People's Handbook]. Annual. Peking.
Kuang-ming jih-pao [Bright Daily]. Daily. Peking.
Kung-jen jih-pao [Daily Worker]. Daily. Peking.
Li-shih yen-chiu [Historical Research]. Bi-monthly. Peking.
Nan-fang jih-pao [Southern Daily]. Daily. Canton.
Peking Review. Weekly. Peking.
People's China. Semimonthly. Peking.
Wen-hui pao [Cultural Exchange News]. Daily. Hong Kong.

2. Major Compilations of Translated Materials

U.S. Consulate General in Hong Kong. *Current Background.* No. 1—(1950—).
——— *Extracts from China Mainland Magazines.* Nos. 1–212 (1955–1960).
——— *Selections from China Mainland Magazines.* No. 213—(1960—).
——— *Survey of China Mainland Press.* No. 1—(1950—).
U.S. Joint Publications Research Service. *JPRS Reports.* [Various series with regular and irregular issue.] 1958—.

3. A Selected Bibliography of Secondary Works and Serials

a. Books

Aird, John S. *The Size, Composition and Growth of the Population of Mainland China.* Washington: U.S. Government Printing Office, 1961.
Barnett, A. Doak. *China on the Eve of Communist Takeover.* New York: Praeger, 1963.
——— *Communist China and Asia: Challenge to American Policy.* New York: Vintage Books, 1960.
Boorman, Howard L., ed. "Contemporary China and the Chinese," *The Annals of the American Academy of Political and Social Science,* no. 321 (January 1959).
———, Alexander Eckstein, Philip Mosely, and Benjamin Schwartz. *Moscow-Peking Axis; Strengths and Strains.* New York: Harper and Bros., 1957.
Boyd, R. G. *Communist China's Foreign Policy.* New York: Praeger, 1962.
Brandt, Conrad. *Stalin's Failure in China, 1924–1927.* Cambridge: Harvard University Press, 1958.

———, Benjamin Schwartz, and John K. Fairbank. *A Documentary History of Chinese Communism.* Cambridge: Harvard University Press, 1952.

Chao, Kuo-chün. *Agrarian Policy of the Chinese Communist Party, 1921–1959.* Bombay: Asia Publishing House, 1960.

Chen, Theodore H. E. *Thought Reform of the Chinese Intellectuals.* Hong Kong: Hong Kong University Press, 1960.

Chiang Kai-shek. *Soviet Russia in China: A Summing-up at Seventy.* New York: Farrar, Straus and Cudahy, 1957.

Chow, Tse-tsung. *The May Fourth Movement.* Cambridge: Harvard University Press, 1960.

Communist China 1955–1959: Policy Documents with Analysis. Cambridge: Harvard University Press, 1962.

Compton, Boyd, trans. *Mao's China: Party Reform Documents, 1942–1944.* Seattle: University of Washington Press, 1952.

Eckstein, Alexander. *The National Income of Communist China.* New York: Free Press, 1961.

Fairbank, John K. *The United States and China.* Rev. ed. Cambridge: Harvard University Press, 1958.

Fitzgerald, C. P. *Flood Tide in China.* London: Cresset Press, 1958.

Gould, Sidney H., ed. *Sciences in Communist China.* Washington: American Association for the Advancement of Science, 1961.

Houn, Franklin W. *To Change a Nation: Propaganda and Indoctrination in Communist China.* New York: Free Press, 1961.

Hsia, C. T. *A History of Modern Chinese Fiction, 1917–1957.* New Haven: Yale University Press, 1961.

Hsiao, Tso-liang. *Power Relations within the Chinese Communist Movement, 1930–1934.* Seattle: University of Washington Press, 1961.

Hudson, G. F. and others. *The Sino-Soviet Dispute.* New York: Praeger, 1961.

——— and others. *The Chinese Communes.* London: Oxford University Press, 1960.

Hughes, T. J. and D. E. T. Luard. *The Economic Development of Communist China, 1949–1958.* London: Oxford University Press, 1959.

Isaacs, Harold R. *The Tragedy of the Chinese Revolution.* 2nd rev. ed. Stanford: Stanford University Press, 1961.

Johnson, Chalmers A. *Peasant Nationalism and Communist Power: The Emergence of Revolutionary China, 1937–1945.* Stanford: Stanford University Press, 1962.

Leng, Shao-chuan and Norman D. Palmer. *Sun Yat-sen and Communism.* New York: Praeger, 1960.

Lewis, John W. *Leadership in Communist China.* Ithaca: Cornell University Press, 1963.

Li, Choh-ming. *Economic Development of Communist China: An Appraisal of the First Five Years of Industrialization.* Berkeley and Los Angeles: University of California Press, 1959.

Lifton, Robert J. *Thought Reform and the Psychology of Totalism: A Study of "Brainwashing" in China.* New York: W. W. Norton, 1961.

Liu, Ta-chung and Kung-chia Yeh. *The Economy of the Chinese Mainland: National Income and Economic Development, 1933–1959.* 2 vols. Santa Monica: The Rand Corporation, 1963.

London, Kurt, ed. *Unity and Contradiction: Major Aspects of Sino-Soviet Relations.* New York: Praeger, 1962.

MacFarquhar, Roderick. *Hundred Flowers Campaign and the Chinese Intellectuals.* New York: Praeger, 1960.

McLane, Charles B. *Soviet Policy and the Chinese Communists, 1931–1946.* New York: Columbia University Press, 1958.

Mu, Fu-sheng. *The Wilting of the Hundred Flowers: The Chinese Intelligentsia Under Mao.* New York: Praeger, 1963.

North, Robert C. *Kuomintang and Chinese Communist Elites.* Stanford: Stanford University Press, 1952.

—— and Xenia J. Eudin. *M. N. Roy's Mission to China: The Communist-Kuomintang Split of 1927.* Berkeley and Los Angeles: University of California Press, 1963.

—— *Moscow and Chinese Communists.* 2nd ed. Stanford: Stanford University Press, 1963

Orleans, Leo A. *Professional Manpower and Education in Communist China.* Washington: National Science Foundation, 1961.

Payne, Robert. *Portrait of a Revolutionary: Mao Tse-tung.* New rev. ed. London: Abelard-Schuman, 1961.

Schein, Edgar and others. *Coercive Persuasion: A Socio-psychological Analysis of the "Brainwashing" of American Civilian Prisoners by the Chinese Communists.* New York: W. W. Norton, 1961.

Schram, Stuart R. *The Political Thought of Mao Tse-tung.* New York: Praeger, 1963.

Schwartz, Benjamin I. *Chinese Communism and the Rise of Mao.* Cambridge: Harvard University Press, 1951.

Scott, A. C. *Literature and the Arts in Twentieth Century China.* Garden City: Doubleday, 1963.

Snow, Edgar. *The Other Side of the River: Red China Today.* New York: Random House, 1962.

—— *Red Star Over China.* New York: Random House, 1944.

Tang, Peter S. H. *Communist China Today: Domestic and Foreign Policies.* New York: Praeger, 1957.

Union Research Institute. *Communist China, 1949–1959.* Hong Kong: Union Research Institute, 1961.

Walker, Richard L. *China Under Communism: The First Five Years.* New Haven: Yale University Press, 1955.

Whiting, Allen S. *China Crosses the Yalu: The Decision to Enter the Korean War.* New York: Macmillan, 1960.

—— *Soviet Policies in China, 1917–1924.* New York: Columbia University Press, 1954.

Wilbur, C. Martin and Julie Lien-ying How, ed. *Documents on Communism, Nationalism, and Soviet Advisers in China, 1918–1927.* New York: Columbia University Press, 1956.

Yang, C. K. *The Chinese Family in the Communist Revolution.* Cambridge: Technology Press, 1959.

—— *A Chinese Village in Early Communist Transition.* Cambridge: Technology Press, 1959.

Zagoria, Donald S. *The Sino-Soviet Conflict, 1956–1961.* Princeton: Princeton University Press, 1962.

b. Periodicals

Asian Survey. Monthly. Berkeley. 1961—.

China Quarterly. London. 1960—.

Journal of Asian Studies. Quarterly. Ann Arbor. 1941—.

Pacific Affairs. Quarterly. Vancouver. 1928—.

Index

Activists, 172, 189

Administration, 62–63, 102–103, 137, 180, 185, 195, 207–208, 217, 221, 290, 293–294; assignment of tasks, 175–176; *see also* Bureaucratism; Collective leadership; Organization of CCP; State organization

Agricultural producers' cooperative, 16, 17, 19, 45, 46, 134, 200, 288–291, 294, 296, 308

Agriculture, 16, 17, 35, 45–46, 48, 72–73, 116, 117, 154–157, 160, 184, 186, 187, 194, 198, 213, 263, 281–287, 288–300, 328; "foundation of national economy," 51, 282, 286; *see also* Agricultural producers' cooperative; Commune; Economic crisis; Production brigade; Production team

Albania, 244, 270–271

Antagonism, 97–98, 99, 146, 187, 192–194; *see also* Contradiction

Anyüan strike, 68–70

Army, 23–30, 34, 37, 43, 49, 53, 54, 60, 63–65, 70–71, 74, 106, 130–131, 134, 137, 171, 173, 182–183, 192, 202, 207, 218, 224, 252, 323, 330, 333; *see also* War

Arts and literature, 56, 309–310, 316–324

Bandung, 16, 196

Bourgeoisie, 8, 16, 21–34, 44, 46, 49, 50, 90, 93, 95, 99, 101–102, 106, 108, 109, 144, 192, 218, 230, 248–251, 254–255, 263, 264, 265, 275, 301, 308, 313, 315, 317, 319, 325–330; *see also* United front

Branches; *see* Organization of CCP

Bureaucratism, 40–42, 119, 137, 139, 163, 174, 176, 181, 301, 305; *see also* Ideology; Physical labor; Rectification

Cadres, 6, 14, 15, 18, 39, 41–42, 49, 52–77, 111–117, 130, 132, 134, 139, 141, 150, 155, 159, 161–163, 166, 167, 168, 173, 175, 178, 180, 186, 193, 195, 217, 219, 282–283, 291, 294, 296–300, 301, 305–306, 316; numbers of, 61; *see also* Committees; Leaders; Organization of CCP

Central Committee of Chinese Communist Party, 13, 14, 24, 25–27, 36, 37–38, 47–53, 61, 77, 105, 106, 122, 125–127, 129–130, 132, 134, 138, 160, 166, 167, 171, 177, 178, 179, 186, 187, 195, 226, 279, 283, 285, 300; bureaus of, 129; factionalism in, 13; meetings of, 24, 25, 27, 36, 38, 41, 48–51, 52, 56, 281, 285–286, 320; organization of, 52–53, 130–131; writings of, 41, 42, 73, 238, 285, 288, 293; *see also* Cadres; Committees; Leaders; Organization of CCP; Political Bureau; Secretariat

Central Control Commission; *see* Control commissions

Centralism; *see* Democratic centralism; Discipline; Leadership

Chairman of Central Committee and Political Bureau, 131; *see also* Mao Tse-tung

Chairman of People's Republic of China, 54, 195, 203, 204, 206–207, 219; *see also* Liu Shao-ch'i

Chang Kuo-t'ao, 22

Ch'en T'an-ch'iu, 20

Ch'en Tu-hsiu, 13, 21–25

Ch'en Yi, writings of, 75

Ch'en Yün, 53

Chiang Kai-shek, 5, 13, 15, 23–27, 49, 226, 229

Chinese Communist Party (CCP): anniversary of, 20, 34, 44, 81; *see individual topics*

Chinese people, 4; *see also* "People"; Population

Chinese People's Political Consultative Conference, 192–193; Common Program of, 193, 198, 213; *see also* United front

Chinese People's Republic (CPR): founding of, 16, 28, 192; *see individual topics*

Chinese society, 142

Chinese Soviet Republic, 13, 14, 26

Chingkang Mountains, 24, 63–64

Chou En-lai, 24, 53, 195, 286, 287; writings of, 22, 283, 311; *see also* State Council

Ch'ü Ch'iu-pai, 24, 25

Chu Teh, 13, 24, 25, 26, 28, 53, 65, 66, 195

Citizenship, 33; *see also* Rights

Collective leadership, 120, 127, 166–167, 177–182, 300–302

Colonialism, 25, 31, 32, 118, 232–233, 246, 247, 248, 249